A People's History of the Second World War

A PEOPLE'S HISTORY OF THE SECOND WORLD WAR

Resistance versus Empire

Donny Gluckstein

 **PLUTO PRESS**

First published 2012 by Pluto Press
345 Archway Road, London N6 5AA

www.plutobooks.com

British Library Cataloguing in Publication Data
A catalogue record for this book is available from the British Library

ISBN   978 0 7453 2803 4   Hardback
ISBN   978 0 7453 2802 7   Paperback
ISBN   978 1 84964 719 9   PDF
ISBN   978 1 84964 721 2   Kindle
ISBN   978 1 84964 720 5   ePub

Library of Congress Cataloging in Publication Data applied for

10   9   8   7   6   5   4   3   2   1

Designed and produced for Pluto Press by Chase Publishing Services Ltd
Typeset from disk by Stanford DTP Services, Northampton, England

To Penny

Contents

Acknowledgements

I am indebted to many people who helped so generously with this book. Special thanks are due to Nick Howard, Neil Davidson, Manfred Ecker, Owen Gower, Gordon Davie, Gajendra Singh, Nelly and David Bouttier, and Charlotte Bence.

Preface

There is an official version of the Second World War that is relatively easy to unearth. Alongside the paper record, the Allied establishment happily proclaims its triumph in public monuments like the Cenotaph in London. Public parades, films, books and TV series like *Band of Brothers*, also testify to Allied victory. Others are calmer. Westerplatte, where the Second World War began outside Gdansk, Poland has a sombre atmosphere, as does the ruined Kaiser Wilhelm church, which still bears witness to the power of aerial bombardment in the centre of Berlin.

By contrast, the other war, the people's war, is largely hidden. So unearthing it proved a challenge in time and space. It took as long as the Second World War itself to write this book and involved travel to the countries listed in the contents (as well as several excluded due to limitations of space). Sometimes concealment is deliberate, such as the resistance radio transmitter secreted in the roof of a warehouse in Bergen, Norway. Sometimes the motivation is more pernicious. At the Military Museum, Athens, there is absolutely no mention of the resistance movement that liberated Greece, because its politics was too radical.

When it fits the official narrative there are resistance museums, ranging from the spectacular Warsaw Uprising Museum, the futuristic Slovak National Uprising Museum in Banska Bystrica, to the Danish Resistance Museum in Copenhagen and the Vredeburg Museum's diorama in Yogyakarta, Indonesia. Most resistance museums are tiny, however, sometimes in one or two rooms in obscure towns and villages. More often simple plaques tell the story – from the one dedicated to the Indian National Army in a quiet park in Singapore, to the bustling main square in Bologna. Other evidence can range from cemeteries, to the direct memory of participants, or even workshops for the disabled descendants of those genetically damaged by Agent Orange during the long Vietnamese war. Anywhere that fighting occurred, and that is almost everywhere, there is something to be found if it is looked for.

The difference between the two wars – the imperialist war and the people's war – is well symbolised in my home town, Edinburgh. Towering above the streets on the Castle Rock stands Scotland's

National War Memorial. Hundreds of metres below, down a dark staircase, in a corner under a tree near the railway line, is a metal plate, hardly larger in size than this book. It is dedicated to those who died fighting fascism in the Spanish Civil War. Hopefully this work will put both aspects into a more balanced perspective.

Introduction

THE IMAGE OF THE SECOND WORLD WAR – A PARADOX

The Second World War is unique among twentieth-century conflicts. Other wars, such as the First World War, Vietnam, Iraq, or Afghanistan, began with public support whipped up by a supine media, but lost it once the deadly reality and the true motivations of governments broke through the propaganda smokescreen. The Second World War escapes this paradigm. Its reputation was positive from start to finish and it remains untarnished even now.

There was understandable joy at the defeat of the Germany, Italy and Japan in countries under the Axis heel. But pollsters in the United States found that the war's popularity only increased as the death toll mounted. While approval for President Roosevelt never fell below 70 per cent, support for peace initiatives declined.[1]

A similar situation prevailed in Britain, where Mass Observation volunteers measured public opinion. They assiduously recorded overheard conversations, and gauged attitudes. A 'typical' remark of the early 'phoney war' period (when hostilities had been declared but virtually no military action taken) was: 'I cannot see why we are not doing something … Why don't we go and attack Italy, or start something in Abyssinia.' One Observer noted the 'overwhelming acclamation with which the news of any offensive action is received'.[2] Today's imperialists do not shake cans in the streets to finance their bombing operations, but in 1940 a 'Fighter Plane Fund' was established whose 'most striking feature was the way in which everyone joined in the collection …'.[3] Years of gruelling struggle and enormous loss of life did not dim enthusiasm. News of the D-Day Normandy landings in 1944 evoked wild rejoicing:

The child excitedly exclaimed 'Daddy – the second front's started'. 'Daddy' rushed downstairs; fumbles with the wireless knob and asks; 'Did we invade? No jokes. You're kidding.' The family sits down to breakfast but are much too excited to eat. We had an urge to rush all over the place, to go knocking at neighbours' doors to find out whether the invasion has started.[4]

Till the end Mass Observation surveys failed to detect war weariness.[5]

Thousands of miles away Dmitriy Loza, a Red Army officer, eulogised the fight against Nazism as a 'Sacred War':

> [W]ar came to us on 22 June 1941, bringing with it blood and tears, concentration camps, the destruction of our cities and villages, and thousands upon tens and hundreds of thousands of deaths ... If it would have been possible to collect all the tears ... that flowed during the four years of the war and to pour them out on Germany, that country would have been at the bottom of a deep sea... .[6]

Even with 70 years' distance, fascination with the Second World War endures. As Loza predicted 'ten or even a hundred generations of true patriots will not forget this war'.[7] No other military event has spawned so many works of history, fiction, or drama. Nearly half of all war films made deal with the Second World War. The shares taken by the First World War, Vietnam and Korea are 12 per cent, 2 per cent and 2 per cent respectively. The rest – from Ancient Rome to science fiction – make up the remaining third.[8]

The Second World War's popularity is surprising given its enormous destructiveness. In comparing casualty figures the warning of this Japanese commentator should be remembered: 'We shouldn't make deaths into numbers. They were each individuals. They had names, faces ... My brother might just be a fraction of several millions, but for me he's the only Elder Brother in the world. For my mother he was the only Eldest Son. Compile the dead one by one.'[9]

Nevertheless the statistics are staggering. The 1914–18 war generated up to 21 million deaths.[10] The tally for 20 years of fighting in Vietnam was five million,[11] while in three years the US-led war on Iraq cost 655,000 lives.[12] Although firm figures for 1939–45 are lacking, one source suggests 50 million people died, of which 28 million were civilians. Chinese losses alone matched figures for Germany, Britain and France in the First World War combined.[13]

Why did such carnage not dent the Second World War's reputation? The answer lies in the widely held and enduring belief that it was a 'good war', when righteousness triumphed over injustice, democracy over dictatorship, tolerance over racism, and freedom over fascism. Terkel's oral history of America captures this spirit:

> 'It was not like your other wars,' a radio disk jockey reflected aloud ... It was not, most of us, profoundly believed, 'imperialistic'.

Our enemy was, patently, obscene: the Holocaust maker. It was one war that many who would have resisted 'your other wars' supported enthusiastically. It was a 'just war', if there is any such animal.[14]

On the Eastern front, Loza concurred: 'The people put up a wall against suppressors, aggressors, thieves, torturers, debauchers, and fascist scum, the dregs of humanity. They threw all their antipathy into the face of this detested, hated enemy!'[15]

So one essential aspect of the Second World War was that millions upon millions were inspired to resist or fight against fascist genocide, tyranny and oppression and did not come to feel they were duped into this belief. Their absolute revulsion at the methods and aims of Hitler and his collaborators was completely justified. Frank Capra's famous US propaganda film *Why We Fight* (1943) explained that the Axis powers 'were out for world conquest'.[16] This was true, whether it was *Lebensraum* for Germany, a revived Roman Empire for Italy, or the cynically misnamed Japanese Greater East Asian Co-Prosperity Sphere.

A few examples demonstrate what a victory for the Axis powers would have meant for humanity. The Nazis used racism as the ideological cement for their movement, and the result was that Jewish women arriving at Treblinka death camp were shaved, so their hair could be sent off to Germany to make mattresses, before being cast into gas chambers, at a rate of 10,000–12,000 per day. The time from arrival to extermination was intended to be just ten minutes.[17] However:

> [B]ecause little children at their mothers' breasts were a great nuisance during the shaving procedure babies were taken from their mothers as soon as they got off the train. The children were taken to an enormous ditch; when a large number of them were gathered together they were killed by firearms and thrown into the fire ... When mothers succeeded in keeping their babies with them and this fact interfered with the shaving a German guard took the baby by its legs and smashed it against the wall of the barracks until only a bloody mass remained in his hands.[18]

Though Italian fascism was less overtly racist, the invasion of Abyssinia in 1935–6 saw abhorrent methods employed, including gassing. Mussolini's son, a pilot, described this conquest as:

'Magnificent sport ... one group of horsemen gave me the impression of a budding rose unfolding as the bombs fell in their midst and blew them up. It was exceptionally good fun.'[19]

Japan's attack on China culminated in the notorious 'rape of Nanjing' of 1937. Over a period of two months the army brutally violated as a minimum some 20,000 women (killing most afterwards) and murdered 200,000 men.[20]

However, even if Allied forces ended these particular barbarities, there is a problem with seeing the Second World War unambiguously as a 'good war'. The Axis did not have a monopoly on inhumanity, the US bombing of Hiroshima being just one example. Moreover, it does not follow that those who commanded Allied armies shared the same goals as ordinary people. Their official rhetoric aside, it was preposterous to believe that the governments of Britain, France, Russia or the USA opposed the principle of 'world conquest'.

Consider, for example, the fate of the Atlantic Charter which *The Times* hailed as: 'Marshalling the Good Forces of the World. Freedom and Restoration for the Oppressed Nations'.[21] In August 1941 America's President, Roosevelt, and the British prime minister, Winston Churchill, jointly pledged to respect 'the right of all peoples to choose the form of government under which they will live'. Stalin too had no difficulty declaring Russia's 'full adhesion of the Soviet Union to the principles of the Atlantic Charter'.[22]

Yet when Churchill presented the Charter to the House of Commons he stressed it did 'not qualify in any way the various statements of policy which have been made [regarding] the British Empire ...'. It only applied to 'the States and nations of Europe now under the Nazi yoke'.[23] Even this narrow interpretation was ignored when implementation became possible. In October 1944 the British and Russian leaders met to take decisions that the former admitted were so 'crude, and even callous [that] they could not be the basis of any public document...'.[24] Churchill's vanity eventually got the better of him and he published this account of the 'percentages agreement':

> The moment was apt for business, so I said ... how would it do for you to have ninety per cent predominance in Roumania, for us to have ninety per cent of the say in Greece, and go fifty-fifty about Yugoslavia? While this was being translated I wrote out on a half-sheet of paper:

Roumania	
Russia	90%
The others	10%
Greece	
Great Britain	90%
(in accord with U.S.A)	
Russia	10%
Yugoslavia	50-50%
Hungary	50-50%
Bulgaria	
Russia	75%
The others	25%

I pushed this across to Stalin, who had by then heard the translation. There was a slight pause. Then he took his blue pencil and made a large tick upon it, and passed it back to us. It was all settled in no more time that it takes to set down ... I said, 'Might it not be thought rather cynical if it seemed we had disposed of these issues, so fateful to millions of people, in such an offhand manner? Let us burn the paper.' 'No, you keep it,' said Stalin.[25]

Although not party to the discussions in Moscow, the USA was equally cynical in its approach to peace. As one leading politician put it: 'As things are now going, the peace we will make, the peace we seem to be making, will be a peace of oil, a peace of gold, a peace of shipping ... without moral purpose ... .'[26] Devoid of moral purpose, maybe, but Hull, Roosevelt's Secretary of State, explained the USA would lead 'a new system of international relationships ... primarily for reasons of pure national self-interest.'[27]

TWO NOT ONE

It is the argument of this book that the gulf between the motivation of Allied governments and those who fought against brutality, oppression and dictatorship could not be bridged. Therefore, the world-shattering events of the 1939 to 1945 period did not constitute a single combat against the Axis powers, but amounted to two distinct wars.

Though unconventional, this premise is based on the well-established dictum of Clausewitz that: 'War is not merely a political act, but also a real political instrument, a continuation of political commerce, a carrying out of the same by other means.'[28]

As 'a policy which fights battles instead of writing notes ... none of the principal plans which are required for a War can be made without an insight into the political relations'.[29] In the case of the Second World War political relations between states generated war between the Axis and Allied power blocks; but political relations between people and governments produced another war fought by the former for their own ends – this phenomenon being particularly evident in resistance movements which operated beyond the control of formal governments.

The thesis of two wars differs from other interpretations of the Second World War. The Allied establishments suggested that they and their populations were as one. For example, when Britain's prime minister (PM) welcomed Russia into the Allied camp he insisted all previous disharmony had been effaced:

> The Nazi régime is indistinguishable from the worst features of Communism [but] the past with its crimes, its follies and its tragedies, flashes away ... We have but one aim and one single, irrevocable purpose. We are resolved to destroy Hitler and every vestige of the Nazi regime ... This is no class war, but a war in which the whole British Empire and Commonwealth of Nations is engaged without distinction of race, creed or party. [It is] the cause of free men and free peoples in every quarter of the globe.[30]

Despite claimed ideological differences, Stalin agreed the sole aim was 'destruction of the Hitler regime',[31] and showed no resentment at the PM's insult. The two men *were* dogged in their opposition to the Axis coalition, not because it threatened 'free men and free peoples in every quarter of the globe', but because Germany and its partners threatened Allied control of every quarter of the globe.

A diametrically opposite account of the Second World War sees it as 100 per cent imperialist. Trotsky was a lifelong and bitter opponent of fascism and understood the 'legitimate hatred of workers' for it: 'By his victories and bestialities, Hitler provokes naturally the sharp hatred of workers the world over.' However, he denied that the Allies were fighting to end fascism. They fought to continue their own domination. Therefore:

> [T]he victory of the imperialists of Great Britain and France would be not less frightful for the ultimate fate of mankind than that of Hitler and Mussolini ... The task posed by history is not

to support one part of the imperialist system against another but to make an end of the system as a whole.[32]

Trotsky's opposition to the Second World War was not on pacifist grounds. He supported 'progressive, just wars ... which serve the liberation of oppressed classes or oppressed nations and thus push human culture forward'.[33] Furthermore, he was not rejecting democracy: 'We Bolsheviks also want to defend democracy, but not the kind that is run by sixty uncrowned kings.' So Trotsky argued that as an imperialist war the Second World War should be opposed, but that it should then be replaced by a people's anti-fascist war: 'First let's sweep our democracy clean of capitalist magnates, then we will defend it to the last drop of blood.'[34] Trotsky was murdered by Stalin's agent in 1940 and so did not live to see that the two processes he discussed ran in parallel rather than being separated in time.

Howard Zinn and Henri Michel adopt a third position that recognises the simultaneous presence of both anti-fascist and imperialist elements in the Second World War. Zinn divides them into short-term and long-term factors.

We can argue endlessly over whether there was an alternative in the short run, whether fascism could have been resisted without 50 million dead. But the long-term effect of World War II on the thinking of the world was pernicious and deep. It made war, so thoroughly discredited by the senseless slaughter of World War I, noble once again. It enabled political leaders, whatever miserable adventure they would take us into, whatever mayhem they would wreak on other people (2 million dead in Korea, at least as many in Southeast Asia, hundreds of thousands in Iraq), to invoke World War II as a model.[35]

Michel's *Shadow War* is an influential work on the resistance that also recognises the complexities of the Second World War, but still asserts its fundamental unity: 'During the second world war two types of warfare were waged. The first ranged the vast regular armies of the two sides against each other ... The second war was fought in the darkness of the underground ... On the Allied side *these two parts of a single whole* were as different as night from day.'[36]

None of these explanations adequately resolve the contradictory character of the phenomenon.[37] The 'single whole' (whether patriotic unity, pure imperialism, a combination of short- and long-term factors, or of official and underground warfare) breaks down when each case is studied in detail. More than unity against the Axis there was an unstable blend of currents that, under certain conditions, could coagulate into separate, mutually exclusive elements. Cabinets and peasants, army HQs and barracks, boardrooms and workers: each fought a different war – one imperialist, the other a people's war.

These terms are used here to cover many different situations, and so they require definition and historical context. Imperialism encompassed both the state policy of foreign domination, and the internal economic and political structures that sustained and generated this foreign policy. With these in mind, one remarkable feature of the run-up to the Second World War was the degree to which Allied and Axis camps *shared* imperialist motivations. This does not mean that they were symmetrical. An individual chess player is involved in the same game as their opponent, even though, after a few moves, the pieces are arranged differently.

Consider first the Allies. In 1939 Britain possessed the biggest agglomeration of land and people in history, covering a quarter of the world's population and land area, an empire upon which 'the sun never sets, but the blood never dries'.[38] France had the second largest overseas empire at 10 per cent of the world's surface. The USSR covered a sixth of the globe, the majority of its population being non-Russian. Under Stalin, as in Tsarist times, it was once more a 'prison house of the peoples', and afterwards it would add most of Eastern Europe. The heyday of US imperialism still lay in the future, but in 1939 it was busy establishing the economic pre-eminence with which to dominate the world and fund a military machine that today has 737 overseas bases, and over 2.5 million personnel across the globe.

Compared with Britain, France and Russia, the Axis powers were latecomers to the imperial game. Japan emerged from self-imposed isolation in 1867; Italy only unified in 1870; and Germany a year later. The globe had already been parcelled out and so they could only affirm their international status by aggressively dislodging established competitors. Germany tried, and failed to do this during the 1914–18 war and was punished by the peace treaty of Versailles afterwards. Italy and Japan had supported the Entente during the First World War in the hope of gaining scraps from the table of the victors, but were sorely disappointed. The Second World War would see a repeat effort by all three to gain imperial power.

The face of imperialism on the national plane was less ruthless on the Allied side than the Axis. Britain and France played on the democratic instincts of their citizens because they were protecting the fruits of earlier aggression, and thus could adopt a defensive stance. The governments of the USA and Russia also pointed to external attack as the cause of their involvement.

This was not the case for the Axis. The ruling classes of Germany, Italy and Japan knew that a renewed bid for world power needed an even more extreme right-wing and authoritarian ideology than before to mobilise their populations. This requirement was only intensified by lack of empire which left the Axis governments unable to shift the burden of inter-war economic crisis onto colonial peoples. They therefore faced huge stresses and severe class struggles exacerbated by the international Communist movement that followed the 1917 Russian Revolution. Consequently, all the Axis powers acquired some form of fascist or militaristic regime. In Germany and Italy the establishment had to accept sharing hegemony with populist outsiders, such as Hitler or Mussolini. In Japan power emanated from within the military. All three Axis governments felt that to seize and consolidate land in the face of recognised imperialist powers left no room for a humanitarian facade either at home or abroad. Axis rule would be brutal. Britain, France and Russia had built their empires at a far more leisurely pace and so could deploy more sophisticated ideologies, whether religious, racial or political, to cover their actions.

Stripped of rhetoric, from this angle the Second World War was not a fight against world domination. It was a quarrel between Allied and Axis governments about who should dominate. So the belief of ordinary people, that the issue was fascism versus anti-fascism, was largely irrelevant for rulers on both sides of the Axis/Allied divide. Events before, during and after the war, confirm this. The Axis powers' intentions and methods were obvious, but their opponents did not form an order of chivalric knights dedicated to rescuing the world from the dragon of fascism. They were an accidental, and indeed unlikely, combination that only coalesced some two years *after* the war had begun. The very concept of the Allies actually being allies was a chimera.

Before the Second World War the US was diplomatically isolationist and followed Coolidge's motto that 'The business of America is business'.[39] President Roosevelt was 'indifferent to the rest of the world'[40] until it became obvious what an Axis victory might signify. Nazi control of Europe could not be confined to that continent. Furthermore, Britain, which had been almost bankrupted by the First World War, was now dependent on US aid to survive the Second and could thus be made to cede its world-power status to America. In Asia Japan was in direct competition with the USA for influence. Zinn cites a State Department memorandum which warned that Japanese expansion meant 'our general diplomatic and strategic position would be considerably weakened' leading to 'insurmountable restrictions upon our access to the rubber, tin, jute and other vital materials of the Asian and Oceanic regions'.[41] Accordingly, Roosevelt placed an embargo on oil to Japan forcing it to choose between abandoning its imperial ambitions or retaliating. It took the latter course at Pearl Harbor in December 1941.

Until 1939 Britain saw communism as a greater danger to its power than Nazism. So it rejected Stalin's pleas for an anti-Nazi alliance and consistently appeased Germany. It stood by while Hitler defied all the military provisions of the Versailles Treaty from 1935 onwards. First Britain signed an agreement approving an enlarged German navy; then acquiesced when, flouting restrictions on numbers, the Wehrmacht was increased five-fold and the banned Luftwaffe airforce was founded; and merely grumbled when Austria was annexed. In 1939 the British Prime Minister, Neville Chamberlain, simultaneously compelled Czechoslovakia to cede territory to Germany and declared 'peace in our time' with the Führer. Britain was reluctantly compelled to fight after the invasion of Poland showed a Nazi appetite for expansion that was insatiable. A pragmatic friendship with Russia only developed when Hitler invaded the USSR and gave both countries a common enemy.

For his part, by 1939 Stalin had concluded that Britain and France were too prone to appeasement to assist him in opposing Nazi *Lebensraum* – a German empire occupying Russian soil. So that year he signed a notorious peace pact with Hitler and told the 18th Communist Party Congress that in a future conflict he would 'allow the belligerents to sink deeply into the mire of war ... to allow them to exhaust and weaken one another; and then, when they have become weak enough, to appear on the scene with fresh strength ...'.[42]

The shared ordeal of the Second World War did nothing to overcome Allied tensions in the long run. This band of hostile brothers only lasted while the battles raged. After 1945, unable to retain its far-flung possessions Britain reluctantly accepted a role as an imperialist junior partner to the USA. That country, with its nuclear bombs, now asserted superpower status because, in the words of Roosevelt's successor Truman, the USA was 'in a position to dictate our own terms at the end of the war.'[43] Its former friend in Russia was now branded 'the evil empire', and a generation was subjected to fears of nuclear holocaust and the rigours of Cold War. This left Moscow racing to develop its own nuclear arsenal to both fend off and threaten its erstwhile allies.

The concept of imperialism applied to more than just the chief protagonists. Many states without empires must also be included because they acted as satellites for the chief powers. Indeed, several governments-in-exile operated from places like London or Cairo. Furthermore, imperialism was a system of society in which capitalism was closely intertwined with state policy. Occupied France provides one example of the ways national and international policy could intersect during the Second World War. From his exile in London de Gaulle stood for restoration of his country's imperial grandeur through the expulsion of the Nazis, whereas the Vichy regime preferred collaboration with German imperialism in order to suppress its working class. Each represented a different aspect of imperialism. Imperialist war also had its own distinctive methods: the use of formal, conventional methods of warfare (often of the most barbaric kind). This was quite different to those employed by resistance movements.

'People's war' is more problematic as an idea and might appear insufficiently rigorous. One only needs to recall that Stalin dubbed the East European states he controlled after 1945 'People's Democracies', to see how the word 'people' can be misused. Therefore, to hone down the definition of people's war a number of searching questions must be asked.

The first is, who exactly were 'the people'? Such war did not entail universal activism. Under occupation the hurdle of contacting a necessarily secretive movement, plus the risk of arrest by the Gestapo or its equivalent, meant only a minority were directly involved. Nevertheless, organised resisters enjoyed the sympathy of wider layers for their heroism and self-sacrifice. In unoccupied Allied countries vast numbers enthusiastically fought for freedom and a better society, even if they were following the orders of those in authority who thought quite differently. In Asia populations battled to end colonialism (against both their European and Japanese masters). The key point is that whether or not the war was fought *by* the people to a greater or lesser extent, it was fought *for* the people.

A second question is: what distinguishes people's war from class war or national war? The Marxist definition of class – a social group who share a common relationship to the means of production – did not apply to the people's war, even where workers' action was prominent such as Italy. Resisters came from across the social spectrum. Yet equally, people's war was not national war. It was not limited to the goal of independence but always strove to go beyond merely preserving or resurrecting the old state and society.

So neither class war nor national war, people's war was *an amalgam*. As a class phenomenon its ideology was one of radical rejection of the pre-war social system and in favour of the lower classes (irrespective of individuals' social origins). As a national phenomenon the people's warriors insisted that the masses, rather than the old, discredited elites, represented the nation. The failure of Allied ruling classes to stand up to foreign oppressors, and their readiness to collaborate with the Axis (either through appeasement before the war, or after occupation) strengthened this conviction.

Of course, it would be convenient to neatly separate class war from national war, but that was not possible, for the reasons given above. Similarly, it would be helpful if liberation struggles could be neatly split away from imperialist influences, but the two were often entangled in such a way as to rule this out.

Although the idea of parallel wars is hinted at in a number of excellent national studies, such as Angus Calder's *The People's War* (on Britain), the analysis has not been applied to the Second World War in its entirety because on the conventional battlefield those giving commands and those performing them acted in concert, however different their thinking. Thus the two wars were indistinguishable even to those involved. There were, however, particular instances where the split was illuminated, as if by lightning. In Axis-dominated countries mass resistance movements developed independently, to the dismay of Allied imperialists; in Asia colonial authority was undermined by the war in Europe or uprooted by Japanese invasion. Another revealing moment came in 1945. Allied governments wanted a settlement based on their victory in the imperialist war which meant reinstating the pre-war *status quo*, but local populations wanted a post-war world based on the successes of their people's war.

It is not possible to write a full standard history in the confines of this short work. Unlike books that concentrate on the Second World War's battles, technology, generals and armies, or those that treat individual leaders (like Hitler, Stalin, Roosevelt and Churchill), or nations, the focus here is on places where the two conflicts can most readily be discerned. Inevitably many countries have been omitted.[44]

The most significant exemption is Russia. It played a decisive role in defeating Hitler, but did not experience parallel wars for two reasons. Firstly, the murderous policies of the Nazi invaders rallied the population to the Stalinist regime in its frantic struggle for survival. Unlike resistance movements elsewhere, the hundreds of thousands of Soviet partisans who fought courageous battles behind German lines never posed an alternative to Moscow. Secondly, the Russian state was intensely repressive. For example, entire ethnic groups which it believed might pose a threat, such as the Chechens, were deported eastwards under appalling conditions. That left no room for an independent expression of people's war. The only sizable forces opposed to Moscow, such as the renegade soldiers who joined General Vlassov's outfit, were passive tools of Nazi imperialism. This lack of people's war would have doleful consequences for those who fell under the thrall of the Red Army when it drove the Nazis from Eastern Europe.

Although this book therefore offers no in-depth study of Russia itself, that country had a huge influence on the parallel wars. The foreign Communist Parties were prominent in almost every resistance movement, and they led, inspired, and died, for the people's war. However, loyalty to Stalin's Russia meant they were strongly influenced by its imperialist foreign aims. This led them to accept dramatic twists in policy. Until the mid-1930s the USSR advocated a 'Third Period line': open class struggle was the only issue of the moment, and all other parties – from fascist to left-wing reformist – were tools of capitalism to be opposed equally. When this disastrous analysis assisted Hitler's accession to power the Popular Front policy was adopted. Class was now utterly irrelevant and everyone who was not a self-declared fascist (including right-wing supporters of imperialism in Britain, France and elsewhere) should unite in the national interest and also defend the Soviet Union.

With a brief interruption occasioned by the Hitler–Stalin Pact in 1939, Popular Frontism continued throughout the Second World War. It produced some extraordinary situations. More than any other grouping, communists organised and led mass resistance to fascism, and encouraged the hope of workers and peasants for a better post-war world. But they simultaneously constrained struggles so as not alarm the imperialist states with which Russia was allied. They both created and castrated the mass movements, assisting the defeat of fascism but allowing discredited ruling class groups to regain power at the expense of ordinary people. That communists represented an intersection of the people's war and the policies of an imperialist power shows the supporters of imperialism did not line up uniformly on one side, and those of the people's war on the other. Both mingled together and co-existed within movements, organisations and individuals. So the notion of parallel wars cannot be treated simplistically.

Another major country not dealt with here is China. Its three-cornered fight between Japanese, Nationalist Chinese and Communist Party armies bore features discussed elsewhere in this book. However, the key events, which culminated in the victory of Mao's People's Liberation Army in 1948, lie outside our time frame.

Hopefully, despite these omissions, the examples covered, taken from a variety of contexts, are sufficient to justify seeing parallel wars as a valid general description of the Second World War.

1
Spanish Prelude

To the extent that the Second World War was truly a fight for democracy against fascism, then it did not begin in 1939 in Poland, but in Spain three years earlier. This was when a people's war against General Franco's Nationalist rebellion was launched. He acknowledged as much in 1941, telling Hitler that in the Second World War 'the first battle was won here in Spain'.[1] From the opposite camp an American anti-fascist volunteer wrote: 'To me, World War Two started on July 18, 1936. That's when the first shot was fired in Madrid.'[2] This is not the conventionally accepted starting point merely because Allied governments were yet to take up arms. Thus Americans who returned from the Civil War were dubbed 'premature anti-fascists' and hauled in front of the forerunner to McCarthy's House Un-American Activities Committee.[3] Their crime: opposing a coup which, according to the Nationalist daily, *El Correo Español*, 'was working ... to liberate Europe from the filth of democracy.'[4]

Although Franco was more a military figure than a classic fascist leader on Italian or German lines, his link with fascism and Nazism was visible from the outset. Without Hitler's Junkers 52 transport planes to fly soldiers from Morocco the rebellion might have fizzled out.[5] Mussolini was also quick to provide planes, arms and ships.[6] The Nationalists remained heavily dependent on the Axis throughout, receiving munitions supplemented by 16,000 German and 80,000 Italian military personnel.

If Franco declared his movement 'not exclusively fascist', he nonetheless admitted that fascism was a component part and the 'inspiration of the new State'.[7] Nationalists echoed the Nazi slogan – *Ein Reich, ein Staat, ein Führer* – substituting the Spanish equivalent – 'One fatherland, one state, one *caudillo*'.[8] Thus Francoist ideology has been dubbed 'an amalgam of fascist corporatism and religious obscurantism'.[9]

Moreover, Nationalist methods prefigured the murderous policies enacted by the Axis elsewhere. One Falangist admitted: 'The repression in the nationalist zone was carried out in cold blood, purposefully and methodically.'[10] In Malaga, a city that surrendered without resistance, 4,000 were shot in one week.[11] So extreme and violent was this process that:

> Even the Italians and Germans criticised such blanket repression as 'short-sighted' and suggested the Nationalists should recruit workers to a fascist party instead of slaughtering them ... The decline in the number executed in the Nationalist zone during 1937 has also been attributed to the fact that there was simply no one relevant left to kill.[12]

When the fighting eventually stopped on 1 April 1939, 300,000 people lay dead.[13]

Though Spain did not join the Axis coalition and remained officially neutral, this was only because the country was utterly exhausted and Hitler was unwilling to pay Franco's price for entry. The latter did, however, send the 47,000-strong Blue Division to fight alongside the Wehrmacht in Russia.[14]

The Spanish Civil War did not conform to the standard model of army versus army, but to army versus revolution.[15] An anarchist who spent 20 years in Franco's jails described how the people's war took shape in Barcelona, not only to defeat the Nationalists but in opposition to the elected Republican government Franco wished to overthrow:

> For months, the coup of the generals had been expected. Everyone knew they wanted to turn out their paymasters in the Republic and establish their own dictatorship, modelled on the lines of the Fascist powers. 'The government can't get out of it,' everyone had said. 'Now it has got to arm the people'. Instead, the Popular Front Government had called on the army to be loyal. When it had finally revolted, we had hit back. Barcelona was ours in twenty-four hours![16]

This was therefore a people's war combining resistance to Franco at the front *and* class war behind the lines. Militia columns marched off to fight the rebel army, but confronted their bosses on return. In Barcelona 80 per cent of enterprises were collectivised[17] under a decree that said: 'The victory of the people will mean the death of capitalism'.[18] In December 1936 George Orwell experienced the results:

the working class was in the saddle ... Every shop and café had an inscription saying that it had been collectivised; even the bootblacks had been collectivised and their boxes painted red and black. Waiters and shop-walkers looked you in the face and treated you as an equal. Servile and even ceremonial forms of speech had temporarily disappeared... Tipping was forbidden by law ... .[19]

One aspect of civil war was a transformation in the status of women, one of whom reported: 'Women were no longer objects, they were human beings, persons on the same level as men ... [This] was one of the most remarkable social advances of the time ... .'[20]

The conflict that began in 1936 was, in one sense, already a world war. For alongside the Spanish working class who battled against Franco, Hitler and Mussolini, were the International Brigades, totalling some 32,000 from 53 different countries.[21] The largest contingent of volunteers came from neighbouring France, but significant numbers of anti-fascist exiles from Italy and Germany were enrolled. Formed in response to a call from the Communist International.[22] Sympathy for the Spanish cause inspired liberals, socialists and democrats, although 85 per cent of Brigaders were Party members.[23] In Britain, for example, the Labour Party initially pledged 'all practicable support ... to defend freedom and democracy in Spain,'[24] while opinion polls showed an 8:1 ratio in support of the Republican Popular Front government over Franco.[25]

Yet the future Allies of the Second World War had no need of this anti-fascist people's war. Instead of siding with the democratically elected government, the French and British promoted a Non-Intervention Committee. Formally backed by all European countries[26] it was supposed to deny weapons and combatants to both sides in Spain. Neville Chamberlain, claimed 'we have no wish or intention to interfere with the internal affairs of any other nation.'[27] In fact, such pretended neutrality assisted Franco because the Republic had lost its main armaments to the rebels and was now denied the chance to purchase weapons on the international market, even though it was the legitimate government.

Furthermore, when Italy and Germany openly flouted the rules, nothing was done to stop them assisting France because even before 1936 the British establishment had concluded that in Spain 'the foundations of civilization are being undermined [because] the revolution is beginning ...'.[28] France had elected its own Popular Front government in 1936 under Blum and he originally wanted to assist the Spanish Republic. However, not only did he fear provoking domestic right-wing forces,[29] he needed Britain as an ally against Hitler. Warned of 'strong pro-rebel feeling in the British Cabinet', it was Blum, who initiated the non-intervention process.[30]

The USA could have sold arms to the Republic as its Neutrality Law did not apply to civil war. However, Washington declared that it would: 'of course, scrupulously refrain from any interference whatsoever in the unfortunate Spanish situation'.[31] Roosevelt described events in Spain as 'a contagion [and] when an epidemic of physical disease starts to spread, the community joins in a quarantine ...'.[32] Some sources suggest he regretted a policy which favoured Franco[33] and dabbled in an abortive plan to send covert military supplies.[34] Perhaps so. Yet in practical terms everything was done to discourage support to the Republic. For the first time in American history, restrictions were put on travel, with 'Not Valid for Travel in Spain' stamped on US passports.[35] While the US government obstructed assistance to the Republic, its big businesses backed Franco with 3 millions tons of fuel, and thousands of trucks essential for his war machine.[36]

The Spanish civil war gave hints of the attitude Russia would adopt towards people's war in the future. Communist International Brigaders volunteered from a commitment to socialist interna-tionalism, but Stalin was motivated by the needs of Russian state capitalism. He hoped to curb Hitler's ambitions through an alliance with Britain and France that threatened war on two fronts. A Spanish Republican victory that brought 'the death of capitalism' would alienate these western powers; a victory for Franco, with Nazi backing, would be equally damaging. Hugh Thomas concludes: 'With crablike caution, therefore, Stalin seems to have reached one conclusion, and one conclusion only, about Spain: he would not permit the Republic to lose, even though he would not help it to win.'[37]

Apart from Mexico, the USSR was the Republic's only significant military backer, and to match fascist supplies to the Nationalists Stalin should have supplied six times more men and three times more tanks[38] than he did.[39] Even so help of any sort was manna from heaven, so Russia's influence grew to the point where it could engineer the downfall of the beleaguered Republic's leader, Largo Caballero, and his replacement by the more pro-Moscow Juan Negrin. Russia's line was for 'democracy' (of the parliamentary sort acceptable to Britain and France), but opposed to the revolution that inspired the mass fight against Franco.

The interaction of imperialist war and people's war was to be found in this clash between Stalin's foreign policy needs and popular revolution. Herbert Matthews, the *New York Times* reporter, was no doubt justified in denying the communists 'were mere robots obeying orders (except for the few Russian leaders involved). I still say they fought against Fascism and – at the time – for the democracy we know.'[40] Nevertheless their loyalty to what they considered the world's only socialist state trapped them in a contradictory stance: following Stalinism to extol conventional capitalist democracy, and yet fighting and dying for a people's war that went so far beyond it. This position was brilliantly summed up by a Scottish communist Brigader:

> at that time I literally worshipped the Soviet Union. And when one finally had a rifle on which one could depend for killing Fascists, and not killing yourself, with a hammer and sickle emblazoned on it, then one felt a real thrill of pride. Here was the great Workers' Republic coming to the aid of the Spanish people in their effort to preserve democracy inside their own country. Because please bear in mind this fact: the struggle in Spain was not a struggle to establish communism.[41]

There was a technical, military, aspect to the interaction of the two wars in the Republican effort. Preston argues that: 'After the early defeats of the enthusiastic and heroic, but untrained and disorganized, workers' militias, many moderate Republicans, Socialists, Communists and even some anarchists advocated the creation of conventional military structures.'[42]

However, the fundamental issue was political. Should the war be conducted in a way that did not alienate the western powers (who sympathised with Franco), or defeat the rotten system which had given rise to so many Francos over the years? These two conceptions came to blows in Barcelona during May 1937. Communists, in alliance with socialists and bourgeois Republicans, repressed the anarchist CNT and the POUM (a movement loosely linked to Trotskyism). Hundreds died, the NKVD Russian secret police pursued the survivors, and the revolutionary hopes of the early civil war were crushed.

It was always going to be difficult for the Republic to triumph given its continuing isolation, the calculations of Russia, the malevolent indifference of the Western Allies, and Axis aid to the enemy. But quashing the revolution sapped popular enthusiasm for the fight, and proved no more effective in defeating the Nationalists. They won in 1939.

Although Britain and France were officially at war with fascism from that year on they did not change their attitude towards the fascist-backed Spanish government. As Glyn Stone writes: '[The Allied governments] had gone to war in September 1939 to challenge Nazi Germany's intention to dominate the European continent rather than to create a new democratic order in Europe and, accordingly, as long as Spain maintained its neutrality Franco's regime had nothing to fear... .'[43]

In 1940 Churchill still waxed lyrical about the Nationalists: 'As in the days of the Peninsular War, British interests and policy are based on the independence and unity of Spain and we look forward to seeing her take her rightful place both as a great Mediterranean Power and as a leading and famous member of the family of Europe and of Christendom.'[44] Franco greeted these overtures by enthusiastically supporting Hitler's war against 'Russian Communism, that terrible nightmare of our generation'[45] and despatching the Blue Division to assist. He warned the USA that entry into the war would be 'criminal madness' and affirmed that the Allies 'have lost'.[46]

The British and French governments were unperturbed. They concluded trade treaties and continued to support the weakest of the fascist regimes because, in the words of the British ambassador, any change 'would only lead to greater confusion and danger'.[47] The civil war had left the country heavily dependent on food imports, and while Indians starved the Western Allies rushed to supply Spain's shortfall with hundreds of thousands of tons of wheat,[48] as well as sending large quantities of industrial goods and oil. One American commentator concluded that Spanish civilians enjoyed the highest level of petrol consumption in Europe.[49]

Allied policy may conceivably have been justified on purely strategic grounds. Formal Spanish neutrality left Gibraltar in British hands, safeguarding entry into the Mediterranean. However, that reasoning could not hold after 1945 when, as Britain's ambassador commented: 'With the elimination of other totalitarian governments in Europe the Spanish anomaly becomes more and more conspicuous.'[50] When Russia called for Franco's removal[51] and US and British experts talked of using dependence on Allied oil as a lever to moderate his tyranny, Churchill weighed in with this tirade: 'What you are proposing to do is little less than stirring up a revolution in Spain. You begin with oil, you will quickly end in blood ... If we lay hands on Spain ... the Communists become masters of Spain [and] we must expect the infection to spread very fast through both Italy and France.'[52]

Leaving Franco untouched allowed the gruesome judicial murder of Republicans to continue unabated. In 1945 they were running at about 60 death sentences a week, with 23 carried out in Madrid on one day alone.[53]

One possible objection to the concept of the Second World War involving a people's war might be that, in propaganda terms, *all* modern imperialist wars are presented as 'progressive' and 'democratic'. The Spanish experience shows that the current of people's war that manifested itself during the Second World War had independent origins, and indeed developed in the face of antipathy from Allied governments.

Part I

Yugoslavia, Greece, Poland and Latvia – Between the Blocs

2
Yugoslavia – Balancing Powers

At first glance Yugoslavia does not appear to conform to a pattern of parallel wars. In the final stages of combat Tito's resistance army, supplied by Britain and assisted by the Red Army, took on and defeated the Axis. The appearance belies the reality, however. Before the triumphant conclusion there was a bitter armed struggle between Tito's partisans and Mihailovich's chetniks. It was a fight over the very meaning of the Second World War.

In conquering Yugoslavia in March 1941, Hitler was entering one of the most backward and oppressed countries in Europe. Eighty per cent of its 16 million people were peasants. Land distribution was highly unequal: a mere 7,000 landowners owned twice as much land as a third of the rural population. The country's 1.1 million workers worked the longest hours in Europe, while 500,000 were unemployed. All this was presided over by an authoritarian royal government that banned the Yugoslav Communist Party (YCP) as early as 1921.[1] Eight years later King Alexander abolished parliament and seized full power. He was assassinated and was succeeded by Peter II who, being too young to rule directly, ceded power to his cousin, the Regent Prince Paul. In the run-up to the Second World War the country balanced uncomfortably between the Allied and Axis power blocs.[2] In 1940 this led a British official to suggest bribing the General Staff because: 'Rumour has it that several Yugoslav Generals have built themselves villas with money supplied by the Germans. Perhaps we could help them to add wings?'[3]

At the outbreak of the Second World War the authorities were keen to be found on the winning side, but no-one knew which that would be. Eventually, in 1941 Prince Paul's cabinet gambled on Axis victory and opted to sign its Tripartite Pact. Another section of the establishment, doubting the value of this alignment, launched a military coup. Prince Paul was deposed and replaced by the still under-age King Peter. Mass anti-fascist demonstrations welcomed this outcome, but, in a sign of its lack of conviction, the new government tried to play for time by adhering to the Pact and simultaneously negotiating with the Allies.[4] British representatives lamented the 'somewhat puzzling and rather discouraging news from Belgrade. Government seems to have put out a statement that their foreign policy isn't changed!'[5] In this chaotic situation Hitler showed a typically brutal decisiveness and launched 'Operation Punishment' to conquer the country.

Military defeat was swift because the regime refused to arm the population or accept left-wing assistance. It was privately admitted that the government feared the occupiers less than the people, something shown by its treatment of the population in Belgrade.[6] Djilas, a leading communist, described how under a hail of bombs:

> The police and the [Serbian nationalist] Chetniks, roaming the streets in trucks, were trying to establish 'order' in a city that had been reduced from 300,000 to 30,000 inhabitants. They were shooting people, allegedly purging the city of its 'fifth column' and its deserters ... The very same policemen who had manhandled students and workers in recent years were rushing all over the city with Chetnik insignia. We Communists had to hide, even though we were the staunchest defenders of the country.[7]

Djilas added that when King Peter's government fled to London it left a feeling of 'great bitterness': 'There was something rotten in this government. A profound moral disintegration that was seeping down from the state apparatus, from the top military ranks.'[8]

The Axis then dismembered Yugoslavia. A puppet state was established in Croatia/Bosnia-Herzegovina under the ferocious rule of Pavelic's Ustasha militias; Slovenia was split between German and Italian zones of influence; Italy took Montenegro. Serbia, under full German occupation, and ruled by the quisling Nedic regime,[9] lost territory to Hungary, Bulgaria and Albania.

Out of this turmoil emerged two resistance forces. The chetniks of Serbia were a group of army officers who took their name from squads who fought the Turks during the First World War. They were led by Colonel Mihailovich, who was duly appointed Minister of War by the exiled royal government.[10] Although he claimed that as a soldier 'politics never interested me',[11] he soon adopted the slogan: 'With faith in God, for King and Fatherland!'[12] A fuller programme emerged later:

1. Struggle for the freedom of the whole country under the sceptre of His Majesty King Peter II;

2. To create a great Yugoslavia and in it a great Serbia, ethnically pure within the frontiers ...

3. The cleansing of state territory from all national minorities and non-national elements.[13]

Like pro-imperialist currents elsewhere, the logic of the chetnik programme was to recover national independence, so as to restore the pre-war social order with its divisive ethnic contours. However, military collapse and flight into exile had discredited the old state machine. This both emboldened its domestic opponents and decreased the ability of the chetniks to suppress them. Mihailovich, like King Peter, dared not fight for independence by mobilising the home population. Without that option his only hope of success was to wait for the Allies to expel the invaders. Such a policy, which appeared in many countries, has been labelled 'attentism'.

In 1941 Mihailovich had reason to expect large-scale British aid. With the Hitler–Stalin pact in force, France defeated, and the USA neutral, Britain was isolated and unable to conduct military operations on the Continent. So Churchill created the Special Operations Executive (SOE) to encourage resistance movements which might 'set Europe ablaze'.[14] Reports of Mihailovich's activity, which reached Britain in the spring of 1942, were the first news of guerrilla warfare behind Axis lines. This made the Serb a 'hero of European resistance, and ... a shining example to the rest ...'.[15]

Churchill had an additional motive for helping the chetniks. When Hitler launched Operation Barbarossa (the invasion of Soviet Russia) Stalin pleaded for a second military front to be established in France, to relieve German pressure on the eastern front. The British PM needed an alibi for refusal. He told Roosevelt: 'The paramount task before us is, first to conquer the African shores of the Mediterranean [from which] to strike at the under-belly of the Axis in effective strength and in the shortest time.'[16] The Balkan area was that under-belly and it also lay conveniently on Britain's strategic route to India.

Tito's partisans were a rival resistance group to the chetniks. Views of this movement tend to be sharply polarised. For example, one American historian has recently ridiculed their claim to be a 'coalition of all democratic and progressive parties' and suggested their aim was 'the imposition of a Communist regime on the people of Yugoslavia.'[17] At the time an opposite view of the partisan movement was expressed by Jones, a Canadian major who parachuted into their camp as a liaison officer: 'It was the unity of the community, symbolised in the local committee that was the strength of the Freedom Front Movement in Jugoslavia. It was democracy at its best. People in any free community were absolutely free to do as they wished ... .'[18]

The partisans were communist-led so an understanding of the YCP is essential. Djilas has described his conversion. It began with 'a deep dissatisfaction with existing conditions and an irrepressible desire to change life...'.[19] '[We] began by gossiping and spreading inflated news of insignificant and serious matters alike: the cost of the Queen's evening dress, gold teeth in the mouth of a government minister's dog ... Should my country be ruled by such people? Should I live like a slave all my life? ... At every step one faced misery and luxury, brute force and despair... .'[20]

Despotism only strengthened the feeling of 'solidarity, a fighting spirit, dedication to the ideals of the working people and to the efforts to improve their lives.'[21]

The YCP's secret conference of 1940, demonstrated how much its 8,000 members had sacrificed. Pijade, who had recently completed over 14 years in prison and concentration camps, opened proceedings. Of the 101 delegates 80 per cent had been arrested and 40 per cent had served average sentences of two years.[22] War brought no respite. When Belgrade was liberated in October 1944, by a combined Red Army/partisan operation, the latter encountered:

> not one – literally not one – member of the party. There were thousands of sympathizers, even wildcat non-party groups, but the party members had been wiped out in camps, in gas extermination trucks, and on execution grounds. At the execution ground in Jajinici night after night – every night in the course of three and a half years – hundreds of hostages and patriots, mostly communists and the sympathizers, were executed ... .[23]

The communists had a unique attitude to the thorny issue of ethnicity. When Yugoslavia was formed in 1918 the monarch and army command were Serbian, a tradition Mihailovich wished to continue. However, as its formal name indicated – 'the Triune Kingdom of the Serbs, Croats and Slovenes'[24] – Yugoslavia contained many groups, the main ones being Serbs (39 per cent) and Croats (24 per cent). One reaction to Serbian dominance was to assert ethnic autonomy, here expressed by the leader of the Croatian Peasant Party: 'the whole Croat peasant people are equally against your centralism and against militarism, equally for a republic...'.[25]

Tito and his supporters rejected the ethnic exclusiveness of both Serb chetniks and Croat Ustashi. He himself was the son of a Slovenian mother and Croatian father,[26] and in the most diverse region – Bosnia – the partisan rallying cry was: 'neither Serbian nor Croatian, nor Moslem, but Serbian and Moslem and Croatian.'[27]

Strengthened by a desire to urgently draw Axis forces away from the Russian front, Tito also opposed the chetnik strategy of waiting for a British/American landing. The importance of the USSR for communists cannot be underestimated. As Djilas put it:

> We were not taught the Biblical 'truth' that a just life in this world prepares a man for the next. We were taught something far greater: to expect a paradise in this world... that was what people who had been to the Soviet Union and seen the 'truth' in practice told us. And we believed it. Misery and despair were all around us, and the more unbearable life became, the closer we were to the new world.[28]

This adulation had a contradictory result. Although the partisans rejected **both** Axis occupation **and** a return to pre-war conditions, the YCP swallowed the Russian line that social demands must be laid aside until the defeat of the occupiers and their quislings. Tito was explicit: 'It was incorrect to call the National Liberation Struggle an antifascist revolution'.[29] The struggle was 'not on class lines but on the lines of the National Liberation struggle.'[30] If that limited the role of people's war, in the sense of discouraging social and economic demands, it was nevertheless true that beneath a shared rhetoric of unity against the invader, chetnik and partisan movements struggled for fundamentally different goals.

This emerged at the first meeting between Mihailovich and Tito, when the communist leader held out the hand of friendship. He explained later: 'Our idea, desire and intentions were to unite all forces in the struggle against the invaders. Mihailovich was an intelligent and very ambitious man. I offered him the supreme command.'[31] Mihailovich ostentatiously refused the offer, rebuking the partisans for destroying land ownership records and supporting disorder.[32]

Even military co-operation was rejected. Mihailovich claimed there was little point in mounting joint chetnik/partisan operations. Firstly, Axis defeat appeared so far off.[33] Secondly, though he was forced to defend Serbs from Ustasha violence, he justified inaction against the Nazis by referring to Hitler's vow that one hundred Yugoslavs would be sacrificed for every German loss. He could point to the 5,000 civilians massacred at Kraljevi and Kragujevac in retribution for 20 German casualties.[34]

The fact that Tito brushed aside such fears has led one critic to accuse him of using Nazi atrocities for his own ends: 'people escaping from such fearful retribution made useful recruits and the breakdown of normal society is one of the keystones of revolution …'.[35] This charge is unfounded. The communists were involved in all-out combat with the Axis because the longer they ruled the more innocent civilians would die. Mihailovich's refusal to act alongside Tito arose because he feared partisan victory would threaten the social order, something which took precedence over his desire for national liberation.

Mihailovich is reported to have said: 'His main enemies were the partisans, Ustasha, Muslim and Croats – in that order – and only when he had dealt with them would he turn his attention to the Germans and Italians.'[36] This policy was confirmed in chetnik practice and justified the suspicion expressed by Djilas in March 1942 that:

> To protect their privileges, the Greater Serbian gentlemen in London have begun a class war, their tactic being to destroy the most dangerous opponent – that is, the Communist Party and the partisan movement – while temporarily collaborating with the remaining opponents … The adherents of the London government have had to take the path of open collaboration with the invader because of the force and scope of the national uprising against that invader.[37]

An important difference between chetniks and partisans was the backing for their movements. If Mihailovich looked to the exiled government in London, Tito's forces depended on mass support from below. The process began with a spontaneous uprising in Montenegro during July 1941. Djilas was on the spot:

> The entire population – those with rifles and those without – rose up against the invader. Gathering at customary meeting grounds, the men came – young and old, grouped by families, villages and clans – and set out against Italian garrisons in towns. Poorly organized but enthusiastic, they were given leadership by the Communists. Not everyone agreed to Communist leadership, but

no one was strong enough to challenge it. The Communists were not only the sole organized force, but a new one, uncompromised. Their propaganda concerning the rottenness of the ruling parties had been confirmed in the recent war. No other political movement could have waged the struggle, for all were confined by regional bounds or carried away with excessive ethnic nationalism.[38]

In September 1941 further attempts to bridge the widening gap between Tito's and Mihailovich's positions failed. On 1 November chetnik forces attacked the partisans' headquarters at Uzice. The counter-attack came within 1km of Mihailovich's base at Ravna Gora on 12 November.[39] The very next day his representative sat down with the head of German Intelligence to ask for aid to fight Communism.[40]

The die had been cast and soon the Mihailovich camp was sending out messages like this:

> The attempt of the Communists to penetrate into Serbia has been repulsed by us and now we are to further our operations until their extermination, which can be accomplished if our units are not in conflict with outer forces. German forces have not interfered with us in this last operation even though we do not have any contact or agreement with them. So that we will not make difficult or jeopardise the arranged operations against the Communistic group, it is necessary to stop all operations against the Germans, but the propaganda must continue.[41]

The 'extermination' of the partisans required arms, and the chetniks were not fussy about where these came from. An officer of the Office of Strategic Services (OSS – the US equivalent of Britain's SOE) attached to the chetniks reported instances where the Wehrmacht left them truckloads of weapons.[42] Another alleged that chetniks were 'fighting with the Germans and Italians against the partisans'.[43] Intercepts proved that 'the Germans were receiving intelligence on a routine basis from some chetnik units in relation to the location and movement of Partisan forces' and identified 'particular chetnik commanders in joint operations with the Germans against the partisans.'[44]

Despite this, it is important not to bracket Mihailovich with quisling figures like France's Marshal Pétain or Yugoslavia's own Nedic. The chetnik leader reflected the interests of an Allied government-in-exile, and was driven to collaborate by the logic of the parallel wars. The Germans may have worked with the chetniks against the partisans, but they did not want the 60,000 chetnik soldiers[45] to increase in number. So not long after the 1941 meeting with German intelligence Mihailovich faced a near fatal German assault.

Far from turning to action against Nazism, this only strengthened his determination to wait for the Allies and he directed his followers either to return to their villages and await orders, or take cover among Nedic's forces. Historians have debated whether this move signified open collaboration or self-protection. Apologists talk about how bearing arms for Nedic was necessary 'camouflage'[46] and 'most of the men in these units were loyal to Mihailovich'.[47] Critics see it as a policy that 'the chetniks and Nedic government should cooperate in the struggle against the partisans ...'.[48] Whatever the correct interpretation, the chetniks were not primarily anti-fascists, but fought to re-establish the old order in league with the imperialist Allied powers.

What of the partisans? They were involved in a fight whose savagery was shocking even for the Second World War. The overall death toll in Yugoslavia exceeded 1.7 million victims or 11 per cent of the population.[49] In a partisan stronghold he visited, Jones found women scarred by: 'the memory of their menfolk being enticed to the local church by appeals for labour from Italian officials, and there locked in, petrol poured in through the windows and the church set on fire, with machine-guns surrounding the pyre that none might escape'.[50] The murderous Croat Ustashi exhibited 'a ferocity that horrified even the German and Italian authorities'.[51]

By the end of 1943 the 300,000 partisans were holding down some 200,000 Germans and another 160,000 auxiliary troops.[52] But the cost was high. The partisans lost 305,000 men and more than 400,000 were wounded.[53] Yet they should not be portrayed as whiter than white. For example, Djilas himself felt uneasy about some of their methods, because: 'imprudent, hasty executions, along with hunger and war weariness, were helping to strengthen the chetniks. Even more horrible and inconceivable was the killing of kinsmen and hurling of their bodies into ravines ... .'[54]

Furthermore, Tito himself was not above negotiating with the occupiers, who were always ready to use divide and rule tactics. In the spring of 1942 discussions of a prisoner exchange with the Germans developed into something more ambitious. The partisans had been on the run and just survived a crucial battle with chetniks on the Neretva River. They were hoping that the Wehrmacht might accept a ceasefire that would allow them to return to Serbia, their original base. Djilas was one of the negotiators and he describes Tito's approach in these terms: 'There was not a word about the cessation of fighting between the Germans and ourselves, but this was understood.'[55] In the end no truce materialised and only the prisoner exchange took place because: 'The Germans couldn't permit our stabilization and expansion, and we couldn't permit them to gain strength ... .'[56]

Discussing the strengths and weaknesses of the partisans, Basil Davidson, an SOE officer who spent time in Yugoslavia, has argued that:

I am not saying that they were saints, nor even extraordinary people in the general run of events, nor that fearful things were not done ... [But] participation in the companionship of resistance to evil became, of itself and out of its own nature, more than a mere joining of wills. It became the shaper of a new state of mind. It became a mental and moral commitment to the good that opposes evil.[57]

In spite of Nazis, chetniks, quislings, and Ustashi, the partisans triumphed because they were a genuine liberation movement. Many accounts attest to their popularity:

Poverty, backwardness, and the devastation of war were everywhere. But the local peasants were proud to receive their own army, though it meant depriving their children of milk and corn meal, and their sheep of lambs. The old men and young girls in the local government and organisations – the young men were all in the army – worked hard and competently. Everyone obeyed them without coercion, which kept the community together and carried on the war.[58]

As with all resistance movements facing organised state machines, the supply of weapons was crucial, and this depended on Allied recognition. One obstacle was Mihailovich's reputation as the representative of a legitimate government-in-exile, a status which even Russia accepted. Tito found this infuriating and protested to Moscow: 'Incessant fighting has left our Partisans exhausted ... they have no ammunition left. The whole people curse the Yugoslav government in London which through Draza Mihailovich is aiding the invader. On all sides the people are asking why the Soviet Union does not send aid.'

The communist leader objected to the BBC talking about the 'common fight' of partisans and chetniks against the invader: 'That is a horrible lie. Please do all you can to expose this terrible treachery and tell the whole world about it ... .'[59]

Gradually, however, the Allies understood the relative contributions made by each resistance movement. In 1943 General Donovan, who led the OSS, concluded the partisan's record stood 'in favorable contrast to Mihailovich's relative lack of activity and narrow field'.[60] That same year an OSS liaison officer reported the partisan movement was of 'far greater military and political importance than is commonly realized in the outside world' and their struggle against Axis forces was 'at times almost beyond the imagination'.[61]

But this was already old news in London. In the summer of 1942 the British SOE cynically reported: 'As we know, any activities in Yugoslavia should really be attributed to the Partisans. But for public consumption we can see no harm in a certain amount of this going to the credit of Mihajlovic.'[62] During the winter of 1942/3 that line was still maintained even though, as the Foreign Secretary readily admitted, Mihailovich was 'not fighting our enemies'.[63] He should be backed 'to prevent anarchy and Communist chaos after the war.'[64] An official added that: 'This support must, we feel, be given *independently of whether or not he continues to refuse to take a more active part in resisting and attacking Axis forces in Yugoslavia* ... .'[65]

The central issue of defeating the Nazis only displaced anti-communism when British plans for a Balkan landing matured. This made Mihailovich an increasing liability. He was given a last ditch opportunity to prove himself and was asked to mount anti-German sabotage operations. The chetnik leader briefly went through the motions but soon returned to inaction, using Allied military supplies against the partisans rather than the Axis. At last the Foreign Office concluded that people's war was preferable to no war at all: 'The only way we can put ourselves right, is to free ourselves at once from our commitments in connexion with Mihailovich for which we cannot possibly find any justification which we could put to the British public ... .'[66] The point was reinforced by a 'blockbuster' report from Churchill's envoy Fitzroy Maclean, a Tory MP. In contrast to the chetniks, he painted the partisans as 'a far more considerable military and political force than we had imagined'[67] who had the 'whole-hearted support of the civil population' and dominated 'the greater part of Yugoslavia'.[68]

So in November 1943 the Allies meeting in Teheran finally announced: 'The partisans in Yugoslavia are to be assisted to the greatest possible extent in supplies and materials... .'[69] That decision had been a long time coming.

From this point on the partisans received increasing military support from Britain. The shifting fortunes were reflected in arms drops. Mihailovich was the sole recipient between 1941 and June 1943, when 23 tons were provided.[70] From July and September 1943 107 tons were delivered to Mihailovich and 73 tons to Tito.[71] In 1944 only the latter was supplied. A belated attempt was made to salvage the political situation by encouraging an accord between Tito and the Yugoslav King, but despite formal agreements the royalty was not to be re-established.

If the British took their time to break from Mihailovich and back the active resistance, the US prevaricated for even longer, maintaining a mission with him until November 1944. Once again, the determining factor was not which movement fought the Axis most vigorously. When British support tilted towards Tito's communists the US State Department stuck with the chetniks because now 'both the Russians and the British may have interests in the Balkan and Mediterranean area which we would prefer not to support.'[72] It added later: 'we disapprove of any plan for building up Tito forces at the expense of the Serbs' [i.e. chetniks].[73]

While British and American policy was influenced by a heavy dose of anti-communism, one would not have expected Russia to show the same hesitation in respect of the partisans. Yet the history of its relations with the Yugoslav CP confirms the two-war thesis also. Stalin had a purely instrumental attitude towards the foreign Communist parties. In the late 1930s he had the emigré Yugoslav leadership in Moscow all but wiped out by purges, and its total dissolution was canvassed.[74] Tito, the sole survivor, found that 'during the war it was easier because at least during war you know where your enemies are'. 'When I went to Moscow I never knew whether I would come back alive.'[75]

Tito judiciously hailed 'the victories of the Red Army' and set his party tasks such as 'a greater popularization of the USSR and the building of socialism'.[76] But a problem remained. Stalin's calculations were driven not by general political principles but the need for good relations with the Allies, and so he had recognised King Peter's administration the day before the Nazi invasion. For his part Tito realised that victory depended on popular struggle against both the monarchy (including its Minister of War, Mihailovich) and the fascists:

> Our struggle would not be so stubborn and so successful if the Yugoslavia peoples did not see in it not only victory over fascism but also victory over all those who have oppressed and are still trying to oppress, the Yugoslav peoples ... if it did not have the aim of bringing freedom, equality of rights and brotherhood to all the peoples of Yugoslavia.[77]

Moscow found this approach inconvenient. In August 1941 the Kremlin criticised the formation of a partisan Liberation Committee.[78] Further, Dimitrov, Tito's Kremlin link, instructed him to 'not raise the question of the abolition of the monarchy' or 'put forward any republican slogans'.[79] For a long period the Moscow-run Free Yugoslavia radio station refused to mention chetnik collaboration with the Axis or publicise partisan struggles.[80] When the First Proletarian Brigade (composed of mobile shock troops from the core of the partisan army) was established, Russia complained that this would provoke British suspicions of 'the partisan movement taking on a Communist character aiming at the Sovietization of Yugoslavia'.[81]

It was not as though the pain of Moscow's criticisms were assuaged by any practical aid. An exasperated Tito radioed Dimitrov that: 'Hundreds of thousands of refugees are threatened by death from starvation. Is it really impossible after twenty months of heroic, almost superhuman fighting to find some way to help us?' The reply was evasive: 'The moment there are conditions we shall do all that is most urgent. Can you possibly doubt this?'[82] In August 1942 Tito asked why nothing was broadcast about 'the traitorous role of the Yugoslav government and of the superhuman sufferings and hardships of our people, who are fighting against the invaders, the Chetniks, the Ustashi etc.? Don't you believe what we are telling you daily?'[83]

It took until the Teheran conference, when the worst of the Yugoslav fighting was over, for the Kremlin to go beyond carping from the sidelines. At last supplies were forthcoming and the Red Army joined partisans in liberating Belgrade. At that moment the parallel wars temporarily converged with Britain, the US and Russia all supporting the partisans' efforts in the final act of liberation.

The fact that Tito was not dependent on a single imperialist power, but could balance them off against each other, proved significant in the long run combined with the success of a massive and dogged people's war, that provided the basis for a genuinely independent state after 1945. Yugloslavia was able to steer clear of Cold War entanglements and stay outside of both Western and Russian-dominated blocs. In the 1990s this balancing act came to an end and the country was torn apart once again by internal crisis and inter-imperialist rivalry.

3
Greece – Allies at War with the Resistance

Although, like Yugoslavia, the Greek resistance successfully challenged German occupation, the result could hardly have been more different. While the Allies were celebrating Tito's triumph, they were bombing Athens to destroy the main resistance movement – EAM (the National Liberation Front) and its military arm ELAS (the National Popular Liberation Army). This stark contrast originated in the different ways imperialism interacted with people's war.

Today oil makes the Middle East the world's chief battleground. In the nineteenth and early twentieth centuries it was the Balkans which saw the fiercest conflicts. Here the tectonic plates of the Russian, British, Austro-German and Turkish empires overlapped. Greece held a unique place within this unstable zone. In 1821, inspired by liberal revolutions in America and France, it won a fragile independence from Turkey. However, to withstand the pressure of its Russian-influenced Slavic neighbours, it always depended on a close alliance with Britain. Support was willingly provided because Greece was a key transit point on the route to India, and so London defended the puppet monarchy in Athens even if this included suppressing its own people.[1]

In 1936 the Greek King appointed a fascist dictator, General Metaxas, to forestall a general strike. He, like rulers before him, proceeded to detain some 50,000 Communist Party (KKE) sympathisers.[2] The autobiography of one Central Committee member for the inter-war period records 15 separate arrests, often accompanied by long jail sentences, beatings and torture.[3] Metaxas consciously emulated the Third Reich with his promotion of the 'Third Hellenic Civilisation', and maintained that 'if Hitler and Mussolini were really fighting for the ideology they preach, they should be supporting Greece with all their forces'.[4] Woodhouse, an articulate liaison officer sent into wartime Greece to promote British interests, considered Metaxas had 'benevolent' and 'high-minded' motives for undertaking supreme power'. The dictator died in 1941, much to Woodhouse's consternation: 'his five years were not enough'.[5] Woodhouse must have been relieved when the King declared that 'all fields of activity, political and military ... shall continue in the same spirit as before'.[6] The British supported dictatorship because, as another liaison officer explained in 1944, Greeks 'are a fundamentally hopeless and useless people with no future or prospect of settling down to any form of sensible life within any measurable time ... [They] are not capable of being saved from themselves nor for themselves worth it. This is also the unanimous opinion of all British liaison officers who have been long in the country.'[7]

Despite its fascist government Greece entered the Second World War on the Allied side because Italy invaded what it thought was a target for easy conquest. Here was further evidence that, despite the rhetoric, rulers did not consider the Second World War to be a war between fascists and anti-fascists. Britain's General Wilson was aware of the irony. It 'was really a paradox in that in our struggle against totalitarianism we should be supporting one Fascist government against another'.[8] However, in the first major setback any fascist army had experienced Mussolini's forces were repulsed. To prevent further humiliation Hitler stepped in,[9] whereupon the Greek monarchy fled to Cairo under British protection.

The Nazi occupation of Greece produced suffering comparable to Russia, Poland and Yugoslavia. It cost the lives of 8 per cent of the population (550,000 people), and 34 per cent of national wealth. 402,000 houses and 1,770 villages were destroyed, leaving 1.2 million homeless. Furthermore, 56 per cent of roads, 65 per cent of private cars, 60 per cent of trucks and 80 per cent of buses were put out of action.[10] One particularly harrowing episode was the famine of 1941/42 that claimed some 250,000 victims and struck Athens particularly hard.[11] An EAM spokesperson, Dimitros Glinos described how many 'have been turned into skeletons ... Suddenly they have all aged and black worry and mortal agony is etched in their eyes. The gap between their income and the most necessary expenditure has become fearful. [An] entire wage is not enough to buy food... .'[12]

The Greek ruling class was divided in its response to foreign occupation. There were open collaborationists like the quisling Prime Ministers Tsolakoglou and Rallis. More cautious members of the ruling class acted to 're-insure themselves by discreetly financing every possible winner'.[13] The King and his ministers turned to attentism. Glinos, wrote that:

the kindest interpretation that could be placed on the stand of these leaders is passive fatalism and biding one's time. 'Let us wait for others to liberate us ...' [For] above all they fear the people itself. They fear its awakening, they fear its active participation, they fear perhaps, as the people takes its liberties in its hands, that they will no longer be the leaders of its future political life. For they are used up to now to ruling from above... .[14]

Unlike their leaders, the ordinary people of Greece could not enjoy the luxury of passive contemplation, and resistance movements emerged. The largest was EAM/ELAS. It found even less sympathy from the British than had Tito, who was eventually allowed to establish an independent republic, despite being less compliant than EAM/ELAS. This discrepancy is at first sight perplexing. Tito, an acknowledged CP leader, never accepted British orders. ELAS's leadership, on the other hand, comprised three people of whom only one (the EAM representative) was closely tied to the KKE.[15] The others were Stephanos Sarafis, (initially) a non-communist army officer, and Aris Velouchiotis, a *kapetan*. The *kapetans* were a group of 'bold, charismatic and fiercely independent [chieftains who] had appreciated the possibilities of armed resistance earlier than anyone else'.[16] Aris was nominally communist but spent the war in revolt against its orders, being described by the KKE General Secretary as 'an adventurist and suspect person [who is] helping the forces of reaction ... '.[17] Furthermore, unlike Yugoslavia's partisans, ELAS, signed an agreement putting itself 'under the orders of the Greek Government [and] the Supreme Allied Commander'.[18]

Britain accused ELAS of brutality, as exemplified by Aris, who has been described as a 'sadistically violent man'[19] who executed people for stealing chickens,[20] cattle-thieving,[21] seduction and rape.[22] In mitigation, however, one British liaison officer recognised that Aris's tactics instilled martial discipline and were 'his effective way of putting life into the growing movement of resistance against the enemy'.[23] People's war inevitably had its share of excesses and cruelty, though these paled against the inhumanity of the imperialists at Auschwitz or Hiroshima.

Woodhouse voiced another objection to ELAS. He stated the chief aim of ELAS was to destroy rival resistance movements in a bid to monopolise post-war power. Stalinist methods were indeed ingrained and ELAS did compel smaller resistance groups like EKKA (National and Social Liberation) to merge with it or disband.[24] Yet this criticism should not be taken too far. In relation to its largest rival, EDES, ELAS proposed unity by offering its leader the post of joint commander-in-chief.[25] He refused. Ignoring this fact, Woodhouse concluded that for ELAS 'fighting the Germans was a secondary, though not a negligible, consideration ...'.[26] The truth was rather different. British antagonism to ELAS did not arise because it was ineffective against the Germans, but because ELAS was part of a much bigger enterprise.

It was just the military wing of EAM, a broad-based political movement established in October 1941. This took resistance right into the heart of society. Glinos reported its 'fight is daily and embraces all levels of existence. It takes place in the people's market, in the soup kitchen, in the factory, on the roads and in the fields, in every kind of work.'[27] By the end of the war EAM claimed up to two million members,[28] and the support of about 70 per cent of the seven million population.[29]

As we have seen, opponents accused EAM/ELAS of being no more than a KKE front. Though less directly tied to communism than the Yugoslav partisans, EAM/ELAS was certainly associated with the KKE. That Party began the war with just 5,000 members, but possessing a national organisation, knowledge of operating illegally, and above all a belief in mass struggle, the Party's membership rose to 350,000 by 1945.[30] However, to suggest the KKE simply manipulated the population for its own ends was unfair. Comprising just a fraction of EAM's total membership[31] the Party could only lead it if the masses freely accepted the Party's policies. Furthermore, EAM included several other parties, such as the Union of Popular Democracy and Greek Socialist Party. Though the KKE was the largest component at EAM's foundation in September 1941, by 1944 the Agrarian Party had overtaken it.[32]

Finally, the EAM was, as one writer puts it, an umbrella organisation for a vast network of other bodies 'in each village, town, and orchard, it seemed'.[33] Collectively this made up a resistance state which operated right under the noses of the Nazis. One entity was the Workers' National Liberation Front (EEAM). Woodhouse, by no means a sympathiser, writes that 'wherever there was a working population, EEAM inspired it against the occupying authorities'.[34] The most dramatic example of this came when Germany attempted to conscript labour for the Reich. Eudes's account captures the spirit of the moment: 'The Athenian sea was flowing into the centre of the city from all directions ... 200,000 men, a quarter of the population of Athens, marching empty-handed through a hail of bullets ... The Athenians charged, insane but irresistible, transported towards their objective with a battle-crazy momentum that could not be touched by mere blood, by a scattering of deaths ... .'[35]

As a result of the demonstration Greece became the place where Nazi conscription of slave labour suffered its most comprehensive defeat.[36] EAM took up other issues of immediate concern that connected with resistance to occupation. According to an eyewitness: 'The first goal EAM had set was to fight for life – against hunger ... The first song that was heard was "For life and freedom, bread for our people".'[37]

Another feature which might, by comparison, seem a surprising distraction in the middle of a world conflagration, was the transformation of gender relations. Before the Second World War women were regarded as virtual slaves.[38] Their lives were strictly regulated (with honour killings not unknown), and in the countryside three quarters were illiterate.[39] One participant, commenting in the 1990s, recalled that thanks to the resistance: 'we women were, socially, in a better position, at a higher level than now ... Our organization and our own government ... gave so many rights to women that only much later, decades later we were given.'[40] For the first time, women voted and shared in the clandestine election of a provisional government for Free Greece.[41] This body announced that: 'All Greeks, men and women, have equal political and civil rights.'[42] Women deputies and judges were elected, and equal pay decreed.[43]

This was practical politics. EAM/ELAS could not afford to overlook the contribution of half the population and once involved, women changed themselves:

> I couldn't go anywhere without my parents knowing where I was going, whom I was going with, when I would be back. I never went anywhere alone. That is, until the occupation came and I joined the resistance. In the meantime, because we were right in the midst of the enemy, we had an underground press, there at the house ... It was very dangerous [but my parents] had to support us.[44]

Equality was not a paternalistic gift:

> The minute you confront the same danger as a boy, the minute *you also* wrote slogans on the walls, the moment *you also* distributed leaflets, the moment you also attended protest demonstrations along with the boys and some of you were *also* killed by the tanks,

they could no longer say to you, 'You, you're a woman, so sit inside while I go to the cinema.' You gained your equality when you showed what you could endure in terms of the difficulties, the dangers, the sacrifices, and all as bravely and with the same degree of cunning as a man. Those old ideas fell aside. That is, the resistance always tried to put the woman *next* to the man, instead of behind him. She fought a double liberation struggle ... .[45]

Thus the partisans (known in Greece as *andartes*) included a women's regiment.[46] This perturbed Woodhouse who complained to London that 'many weapons are wasted in the hands of women ... .'[47] But the new role of Greek women reflected a recurrent aspect of people's war. It was also seen in Yugoslavia, as elsewhere, because the fight was not only against Nazism but also for a different world.

The Greek resistance generated mass activism in other arenas too. Areas under EAM control organised self-government on a grand scale. Villagers elected municipal councillors and judges in mass assemblies. A very popular move was to have courts dispense with expensive lawyers: both sides presented their own case, and natural justice prevailed.[48] In the public administration of Free Greece *demotic,* literally the language used by ordinary people, replaced the formal Greek of the educated elite – *katharevousa.*

One of the most spectacular achievements was a general election involving one million voters[49] conducted under the noses of the Nazi occupiers. Mazower warns against 'idealising' this event since 'voting procedures bore little relation to peacetime practice'.[50] Polling stations and ballot boxes were impossible so votes were collected door to door. But the ballot was remarkable nonetheless. It created the Political Committee of National Liberation (PEEA) which, unlike pre-war official parliaments, was a representative cross-section of society. Its 250 delegates included two bishops and two priests, 22 labourers, 23 farmers, 10 journalists, 10 scientists, 9 school teachers, and so on.[51]

The resistance struggle was costly in terms of food and taxes. So there is no reason to doubt one writer's claim that, 'Under the thumb of andartes it must have seemed to many that one form of state had replaced another in the struggle for control of food supply'; and 'you do not argue when you are faced with men with guns'.[52] Yet even Woodhouse admitted: 'The success of the rebel movement is bound up with the support of the villages: if the villages were disloyal to the movement it could not have made a successful start ...'.[53] The benefits were reciprocal. EAM reforms encouraged villagers to furnish ELAS, the military wing, with the wherewithal to exist, and this sustained the defensive shield that enabled EAM reforms to be implemented.

In a much-quoted passage, Woodhouse later wrote in grudging admiration that:

> The initiative of EAM/ELAS justified their predominance, though not their tyranny. Having acquired control of almost the whole country, except the principal communications used by the Germans, they had given it things that it had never known before. Communications in the mountains, by wireless, courier, and telephone, have never been so good before or since ... The benefits of civilisation and culture trickled into the mountains for the first time. Schools, local government, law-courts and public utilities, which the war had ended worked again ... All the virtues and vices of such an experiment could be seen; for when the people whom no one has ever helped started helping themselves, their methods are vigorous and not always nice. The words 'liberation' and 'popular democracy' filled the air with their peculiar connotations.[54]

If EAM represented political struggle, the work of ELAS embodied the military side of people's war. A German report on 'The Political Situation in Greece' in July 1943 described ELAS as 'the main bearer of the entire resistance movement against the Axis powers [and] represents the greatest danger to the occupying forces'.[55] Woodhouse agreed:

> [B]etween October 1943 and August 1944, apart from purely punitive reprisals, nine operations serious enough to warrant codenames were launched [by Germany], all in northern Greece. Except for the last case (in August 1944), all these operations ... [were] mainly directed against ELAS, because the Communists ignored the instruction of [Britain's] General Headquarters Middle East to refrain from offensive operations.[56]

ELAS suffered four-fifths of all the casualties inflicted by the Axis.[57] The Nazis themselves counted 19,000 dead and had to commit about 10 per cent of all their anti-resistance forces to ELAS alone.[58] This was all the more impressive in that ELAS received little aid. Its commander affirmed that he could have doubled the 50,000 andartes deployed if properly equipped,[59] and Woodhouse's predecessor as chief British liaison officer, Myers, calculated that London provided less than one-sixth of ELAS's arms.[60] He wrote that despite 'getting virtually no war supplies', ELAS liberated four-fifths of the Greek mainland.[61]

London hoped that in EDES (the Greek National Republican League) they could find an alternative resistance movement to help with its war. Unlike ELAS, EDES eschewed social radicalism and mass mobilisation and claimed to focus exclusively on the military struggle. Thus it evaded the key question of the monarchy and its fascist past. According to EDES's political adviser, attempts to formulate a programme were always met 'with stubborn opposition ... Nothing was heard but the slogan "Faith in the leader. All for the leader. All from the leader".'[62] That leader was Napoleon Zervas who, according to Britain's Military Mission, needed 'persuasion' to take to the field. After 24,000 gold sovereigns proved insufficient[63] tactics 'little short of blackmail' had to be employed to make him fight.[64]

EDES's 12,000 guerrillas were totally dependent on Britain's generous assistance.[65] When ELAS complained about inequality of treatment, one British officer replied: 'It's only natural that we should reinforce Zervas as he is our servant.'[66] Although EDES did mount some serious anti-German operations,[67] like the chetniks of Yugoslavia it was willing to collaborate with the occupier. One letter to the Wehrmacht read: 'We are not fighting you Germans, we are fighting the Communists. We are ourselves true Fascists',[68] and Woodhouse found EDES harboured 'downright collaborators' in Athens.[69] So unsurprisingly EDES made little headway against the Germans. By the time ELAS drove them from Greece EDES held only 'a tiny strip thirty-five miles long and twenty-five miles wide ... a Greek San Marino'.[70] Despite EDES's Allied backers, it took just a fortnight for ELAS to rout Zervas's force in a short civil war. His troops finally retreated to Corfu on board British ships.[71]

The difference in the treatment meted out by London to Tito's partisans and ELAS arose from the calculations that produced the 'percentages agreement'[72] between Stalin and Churchill. This assigned respective British/Russian influence as 50/50 in Yugoslavia, but 90/10 in Greece. So its very strength as a resistance movement made London determined to crush ELAS. *It was too effective!* The strategy unfolded in two phases. At first ELAS and EDES were treated on a relatively equal footing. A spectacular operation to blow up the Gorgopotamos rail viaduct in November 1942 was carried out by four British agents, 45 EDES and 115 ELAS andartes.

They cut the supply line to Rommel for six weeks, depriving him of crucial deliveries during the battle of El Alamein.[73] The greatest level of co-operation came in the summer of 1943 during 'Operation Animals', a resistance offensive which fooled the Nazis into expecting Allied landings in Greece rather than Sicily.

However, the British attitude was governed by a cynical calculation, so well described by Brigadier Barker-Benfield that it is worth quoting at length:

> Our long-term policy towards Greece is to retain her as a British sphere of influence and that a Russian dominated Greece would not be in accordance with British strategy in the Eastern Mediterranean ... Our present Political and Military policies are at first sight contradictory. The former, by propaganda and public speeches is designed to indicate our disapproval of EAM. Therefore, should EAM reach power we can expect them to be anti-British. Military considerations, however, demand that we should give maximum support to ELAS, who are the only resistance organisation in a position seriously to support our attempts to harass the enemy. Thus our military policy is bolstering up EAM.
>
> Although these two policies appear to be diametrically opposed, this is not the case, as it is solely a question of timing.
>
> Our immediate policy should be the purely military one of giving support to the guerrilla organisations to enable them to assist in liberating their country and ensuring that Greece continues as a British sphere of influence. This should give way to the political policy of no support to EAM as soon as liberation is achieved.
>
> The changeover from one to the other is certain to cause opposition from ELAS and can only be carried out successfully if British troops are sent to Greece at the appropriate time. These troops would have two roles, firstly that of hitting the Germans where they are weakest, and secondly, that of ensuring a British military control of the whole country.[74]

The 'change-over' from 'military policy' to 'political policy' can be dated to mid-1943. Before that time General Wilson welcomed ELAS help, saying 'Bravo to the guerrillas!' Afterwards he ordered that: 'all operations cease immediately [and] all guerrillas remain quiet ...'.[75] Churchill's shift in attitude was equally marked. Once he described ELAS as 'gallant guerrillas containing thirty enemy divisions.' Now they were 'in many cases indistinguishable from banditti...'[76]

In April 1944 the exiled Greek army in Egypt were subjected to the new policy. Britain and the US insisted the King would be re-established, although they knew full well that apart from republicans there were 'no other organisations in Greece visible without a microscope'.[77] When the Second Brigade protested[78] Churchill accused them of an 'undignified, even squalid, exhibition of indiscipline, which many will attribute to an unworthy fear of being sent to the front.'[79] The reverse was true. They had long been asking to be sent into action and instead were now threatened with being disarmed. They replied: 'We hold our weapons to liberate our country. We do not wish to surrender these arms which we glorified with our blood in Albania, in Macedonia, in Crete, and at Alamein. We request that the order for our disarming be rescinded and that we be sent immediately to the front to fight.'[80]

However, imperialist politics outweighed defeating fascism. Churchill ordered that the Brigade be 'rounded up by artillery and superior force and let hunger play its part'.[81] Starved into submission, up to 20,000 men were sent to North African concentration camps.[82] The rest of the Greek army was then purged of all dissidents.[83]

The lengths to which Britain would go to secure the defeat of ELAS were revealed when the Wehrmacht began to withdraw in late 1944. Neubacher, the chief German official in Greece, was perplexed by the strategy the Allies adopted:

[T]hey have hitherto allowed our forces to be moved from the islands to the mainland with almost no opposition by sea or in the air, but they mobilise the red bands against our escape routes on the mainland. By this they apparently intend to keep German forces on the Greek mainland until the moment when their own operation is possible, and in this way they hope to prevent a general revolution.[84]

The commander of Germany's Army Group F reported 'repeated offers of negotiations concerning the evacuation of Greece'.[85] In what Mazower calls 'one of the most extraordinary and potentially explosive episodes of the whole war'[86] an Allied officer, with the full knowledge of SOE Cairo, met the head of the German Secret Field Police to canvas possible joint action (though nothing came of this).

German reports were confirmed by statements from British officials: 'it would be very awkward if the Germans in Greece were anxious to surrender immediately, since we do not want them to collapse until we ourselves are ready to send in British troops to Greece. Otherwise, there will be a hiatus of which EAM will take full advantage.'[87]

Ultimately, this delicate plan almost broke down because the Germans beat an ignominious retreat. ELAS controlled large areas by September 1944 while the British reached Athens only on 14 October.

That the British nevertheless attained their goal is very revealing of the politics of EAM/ELAS and the KKE. Like many wartime movements they had mobilised vast numbers to fight, not only against occupation, but for a different post-war world. Why, having succeeded with the former, did the leadership fail to implement the latter? The answer lay in Moscow where foreign policy was shaped by its Anglo-American alliance, and local communist parties knew it. The KKE's leader, Zachariadis, saw Greece as between 'two poles: the European Balkans with the Soviet Union at its centre, and the Middle East with its centre in Britain. A correct policy would be to tie together these two poles.'[88] After Zachariadis was shipped off to Dachau concentration camp, it fell to Siantos to implement the updated line of 90/10 shares: 'Greece belongs to a region of Europe where the British assume all responsibilities ... .'[89] On his release in 1945, Zachariadis took charge once more and was proud to declare: 'From the very first day, the people's liberation movement invested sincere efforts, trying to achieve understanding and co-operation with Great Britain ... to help that country master its great difficulties, the crisis through which it was going in the Mediterranean.'[90]

So leaders of the Greek people's war were mentally disarmed before British imperialism. This was exemplified by the PEEA, the body created by the clandestine general election. It spoke in conciliatory terms, declaring support for the Atlantic Charter and the Allies' Teheran Conference, and asked only that it be included in a future Greek coalition government.[91]

At this point face-to-face encounters between the royal government-in-exile and the guerrillas became possible when a mountain airstrip permitted resistance representatives to travel abroad. When they met the government-in-exile, the Greek resistance (including both EAM/ELAS *and* EDES) discovered each inhabited different worlds.[92] The Greek PM 'was very uncertain about the continuance of the resistance movement at all ... It might be better to urge the guerrillas to return to their village [and] cultivate the land.'[93] British officials on hand agreed: 'There has never been any doubt that our long-term political interests would be better served by an inactive sabotage policy.'[94] After hearing this the resistance delegation was abruptly dismissed. Even the EDES delegate was outraged: 'We were transported like prisoners to the airport... Because we disturbed British policy and the plans of the King, we were "undesirables".'[95]

EAM/ELAS now had to choose between continuing its Free Greece government, based on the aspirations of the people's war, or co-operation with Britain. It chose the latter.[96] The way was smoothed by a marginal shift from the monarchy. To regain any support at home it would have to temporarily work with the guerrillas. The result was the Caserta agreement, whereby PEEA members joined the government-in-exile (now renamed 'Government of National Unity'). In return the resistance had to agree that: 'All guerrilla forces operating in Greece place themselves under the orders of the Greek Government of National Unity, [which in turn] places these forces under the orders of [Britain's] General Scobie who has been nominated by the Supreme Allied Commander as General Officer Commanding Forces in Greece.'[97]

To prove its sincerity EAM/ELAS forbade 'any attempt by any units under their command to take the law into their own hands. Such action will be treated as a crime and will be punished accordingly.'[98] Russia played its part. EAM/ELAS had awaited a Soviet military mission with great anticipation, not just because of apparently shared political beliefs, but as an alternative source of military aid.[99] When it arrived the mission delivered an 'abrupt shock'.[100] It offered no support but ordered the resistance to enter the government of the detested King.[101]

This sacrificing of the people's war was criticised from within the resistance itself. At a crisis meeting in the summer of 1944 even the communist Secretary of EAM denounced the betrayal.[102] Woodhouse recounts that: 'Inside the KKE, the apostles of direct action under Aris Velouchiotis were openly spoiling for a new fight; the apostles of political infiltration under Siantos were wondering whether to persevere with the government-in-exile'.[103]

In Eudes's account the argument has been interpreted as a division between imaginative partisan tactics and doctrinally correct urban struggle policy. The andartes and kapetans were 'unorthodox ... by comparison with the Stalinist ideal' and 'recoiled spontaneously from the centralism and quasi-industrial organization of the orthodox Revolution'. The KKE's Central Committee was 'prepared to renounce [the guerrillas] at the decisive moment to preserve an abstraction'.[104] There may have been an element of this in play. One of the built-in tensions in all anti-fascist resistance was between its social driving forces and the demands of military strategy. Though Clausewitz's axiom is correct, politics and their military expression are not identical. In many parts of Europe communist organisation was based on the urban working class, but, until the final showdown, partisan warfare avoided Wehrmacht concentrations, which were located in towns. So there was a disjuncture between the two, which meant guerrilla resistance did not follow a conventional proletarian model. This was true in mainland Greece where the andartes operated in the mountains.[105]

However, this town/country split was not paramount. A more important factor was the contradictory position of the KKE leaders caught between people's war and imperialist war. That proved a fatal weakness at the moment of Nazi withdrawal.

When the British arrived in Athens, just 48 hours after the German departure, the royal Government had virtually no representation on the ground. Apart from a tiny enclave controlled by EDES and disputed border areas, 'the rest of Greece was in the hands of EAM/ELAS, who occupied the towns, the villages and the provinces'.[106] The Nazi collapse had been rather too sudden for the Allies. Nevertheless, they had meticulously planned for this moment. As early as May 1944 Churchill was organising the despatch of thousands of British troops, ostensibly to 'restore law and order'.[107]

George Papandreou, the Greek Prime Minister, wished to participate in this enterprise. He wrote to Churchill that he was 'seriously disturbed' by the success of EAM/ELAS. 'Only the immediate appearance of impressive British forces in Greece, and up to the Turkish frontier, will suffice to alter the situation.'[108] This telegram was sent just three weeks after the formation of the 'Government of National Unity' with EAM members included as ministers!

However, such was their contempt for all Greeks that the British decided to carry off the coup alone. Churchill's view was that: 'It is most desirable to strike out of the blue without any apparent preliminary crisis. It is the best way to forestall the EAM: the Greek Government know nothing of this plan and should on no account be told anything'.[109] Though Churchill threw up a smokescreen of democratic rhetoric to justify 'Operation Manna', General Alan Brooke was clear that the role of Allied forces 'was to ensure the setting up of a Government which we consider the most suitable, but there was no guarantee that the Greek people would be of the same opinion'.[110]

This was not a simple policing operation as claimed, but classic imperialism. The British wanted to physically dominate a foreign land. The Allied commanders would have liked to emulate Nazi methods but feared opposition from their own soldiers. As one put it: 'We could go quicker if we stormed our way through the streets with tanks and "Rotterdamed" the whole quarters by air bombardment as the Germans and Russians in a similar position would probably do. But, apart from other disadvantages of such a policy, the troops would refuse to do it.'[111]

Nevertheless, Churchill told General Scobie: 'Do not hesitate to fire at any armed male in Athens who assails the British authority or Greek authority ... [A]ct as if you were in a conquered city where a local rebellion is in progress.'[112] Even the Greek PM was appalled[113] and threatened to quit. Churchill told his ambassador in Athens: 'Force Papandreou to stand on his duty ... Should he resign he should be locked up till he comes to his senses.'[114]

To consolidate their hold the British forces and their Greek assistants employed the 'Security Battalions'. One reason that ELAS agreed to disarm was this clause of the Caserta Agreement: 'The Security Battalions are considered as instruments of the enemy [and] will be treated as enemy formations.'[115] It was not honoured. These repressive forces came straight out of the era of Nazi occupation. Recruited by the previous quisling Government they had been equipped and commanded by Germans. The Battalion pledge of allegiance ran: 'I swear by God this sacred oath, that I will obey absolutely the orders of the Supreme Commander of the German Army, Adolf Hitler'.[116]

Churchill's private view of these militias was extraordinary: 'It seems to me that the collaborators in Greece in many cases did the best they could to shelter the Greek population from German oppression... .'[117] In public he was no less forthcoming, telling Parliament: 'The security battalions came into existence ... to protect the Greek villagers from the depredations of some of those who, under the guise of being saviours of their country, were living upon the inhabitants and doing very little fighting against the Germans.'[118] In other words he preferred collaborators to anti-fascists, and Nazi's auxiliaries to the people's resistance! Other reactionary forces used included what remained of the Greek army after its purge – the far-right Sacred Company and Mountain Brigades.[119] While these forces ran rampage, ELAS was ordered to dissolve as a 'private' militia (that just happened to have the support of 70 per cent of the population).

The head of EAM pleaded: 'The British must give the Greeks at least the impression that they are a free people ... .'[120] but the KKE understood that the new government was deploying 'Fascists, disguised Fascists or supporters of the Metaxas dictatorship'.[121] Nevertheless it still hoped to avoid confrontation, and in the face of open violence from the British and Greek governments told its members: 'Communists. You stood as champions of the national and popular uprising. Stand now as ... patriots, united in the struggle for the completion of the liberation of Greece along with the ELAS and *our allies under our United Government.*'[122]

Operation Manna was fully unleashed when a mass demonstration protested at the violation of the terms regarding new security forces. At least ten people were shot dead by police, the victims including unarmed children.[123] In the uproar the British army indeed acted as if 'in a conquered city where a local rebellion is in progress'. During the first 24 hours it fired 2,500 shells into residential areas of Athens causing 13,700 casualties.[124] Scobie dropped the following leaflet:

All civilians are informed that as from 9am tomorrow all rebel guns firing, whether in the town or in the environs will be hit with all the arms at my disposal – that is to say, with land artillery, naval guns, aeroplanes, rockets and bombs. This attack will continue until the guns are destroyed. For their personal security all civilians in the areas concerned must immediately evacuate to a distance of 500 metres (545 yards) from the position of any rebel guns. No further warning will be given.[125]

By the time the 'December events' were over Scobie had been as good as his word. There were 50,000 Greek dead and 2,000 British casualties.[126] Incredibly, Churchill claimed 'our troops are acting to prevent bloodshed'.[127]

The clash between the two wars was so stark that it caused an outcry in Britain. One MP pointed out that: 'British soldiers and Greek patriots lay dead side by side, each with an allied bullet in his heart [because] British policy seemed inclined to support many of the worn-out regimes in Europe, as against the popular forces which had emerged.' Another suggested the Government backed 'reactionary and often even quisling elements to delay recognition of the genuine democratic movements in Europe'.[128] Even *The Times* found it 'inconceivable that the British liberation armies ... should be asked to coerce or conquer a section of a liberated and allied people which, only a few weeks ago, was engaged in active and gallant resistance to the Germans'. Repression in Athens came 'at the expense of the war against Germany' because its forces were, at that very moment, making a daring breakthrough in the Ardennes during 'the Battle of the Bulge'.[129] While the Gorgopotamus raid had assisted British efforts in North Africa, the attack on Athens drew numerous troops from Italy and hampered the Allied offensive there.[130]

The Americans later adopted the role of imperial arbiter in Greece, but at the time they were horrified. In Athens Ambassador McVeagh accused Churchill of handling 'this fanatically freedom-loving country (which has never yet taken dictation quietly) as if it were composed of natives under the British Raj ...'. He also understood that behind the conflict stood those 'with possessions, on the one hand' and those 'without possessions but hungry, homeless and armed on the other'.[131]

The battle for Athens was not as straightforward as Churchill had hoped. On 21 December *The Times* reported RAF headquarters 'overrun after an all-night battle ... by a force which, it was officially announced to-day, included fully armed women, boys and girls'.[132] According to Woodhouse, 'ELAS at one time held almost the whole of Greece but for a few square miles of Athens'.[133] At home a beleaguered Churchill lamented: 'there is no case in my experience ... where a British government has been so maligned and its motives so traduced in our own country by important organs of the press or among our own people.'[134] Facing a vote of confidence in Parliament he turned rhetorically to Stalin, his one remaining significant source of support, by suggesting that Britain was locked in 'a struggle to prevent a hideous massacre in the centre of Athens, in which all forms of government would have been swept away and naked, triumphant Trotskyism installed'.[135]

Eventually Churchill had to fly to Greece himself to sort out the mess. Still EAM did not press home its military advantage. A Guy Fawkes style plot to blow up his hotel was therefore abandoned and ELAS battalions gave up their weapons.[136] EAM's Central Committee sent this grovelling message to the British PM: 'Your Excellency, the Greek people experienced on the happy occasion of your coming to Athens a feeling of deepest relief ...The Greek people has never ceased for a moment to look with unshaken faith and deep regard on our great allies and, in particular Great Britain... .'[137]

Unlike Yugoslavia, in Greece the issue of the two wars was settled decisively in favour of imperialism. It is true that the

British postponed the return of the King for a time, and under the Varkiza agreement of 12 February 1945 promised a regime of 'free expression', 'an amnesty for political crimes', a 'purge' of collaborators, plus a 'plebiscite and elections' to be 'conducted in complete freedom'. But, in return, 'the armed forces of resistance shall be demobilised and in particular ELAS, both regular and reserve ...'.[138] ELAS carried out its pledge, surrendering more guns than the agreement had stipulated.[139] The other side failed to reciprocate. In the year following Varkiza a right-wing reign of terror murdered 1,289, wounded 6,671, arrested 84,931, and tortured 31,632 Greeks.[140] Promises of a free election became a hollow joke. A delegation of British MPs reported that:

> Throughout our visit we found that, with the exception of the extreme right wing, everybody said that the election was carried through by means of forgery, perjury, terrorism, assassination, and every possible form of corrupt practice... [T]he giving of official positions in the state, gendarmerie and police to notorious collaborators with the enemy [means] no such thing as a fair election or fair plebiscite is a possibility.[141]

Women who had glimpsed liberation in the ranks of EAM/ELAS now faced rape, torture and death. Between 1948 and 1950, for example, 17 were executed for subversion, the youngest being 16 years old.[142] Others were in jail right up until the 1960s. Their persecutors, now working with US counter-insurgency forces, had flourished under the British, and previously under the Axis. A US Senator described what they were doing: 'We had to back not the good guys but the bad guys in Greece, to put it simply in the vernacular. We did not back the people.'[143] On the ground a resistance woman confirmed this: 'After the liberation ... we, who had *fought* the occupation, *we* were the bad guys, and those who had collaborated with the Nazis, they were now the good ones. The government rewarded them and punished us'.[144] The civil war eventually cost 158,000 Greek lives,[145] but it meant that in 1947 a US paper could report: 'Churchill's victory is complete – and neatly underwritten by hundreds of millions of American dollars. It could only be slightly more complete if Hitler himself had engineered it!'[146]

What happened in Greece was not a difference of opinion within a single world conflict. It was two types of war clashing to such an extent that bombs, tanks, torture, rape and prisons decided the outcome.

4
Poland's Warsaw Rising

Greece's experience might seem to indicate the key conflict on the Allied side during the Second World War was primarily between communists and non-communists, rather than involving parallel and sometimes opposed wars. The Warsaw Rising of 1944 provides a useful testing ground for such arguments because the chief protagonist of Allied imperialism was Russia itself.

In the early seventeenth century Poland was an important European power with a population comparable to France and a territory rivalling that of Russia's. However, as one historian puts it:

> she lacked the asset of a peripheral geographic position such as had permitted Spain and Sweden, for example, to withdraw into hard and relatively immune shells once their bids for expansion had been defeated. Poland's location being more central and pivotal, she was doomed to obliteration as a state in the second half of the 18th century ... .[1]

The country was partitioned no less than three times (1772, 1793 and 1795) with Russia, Prussia and Austria sharing the spoils. Despite a series of heroic revolts (in 1794, 1830, 1848, 1863 and 1905) partition continued until the First World War.[2]

Modern Poland only began to emerge after the Russian Revolution in 1917, when Lenin applied the principle of 'self determination': 'to recognise not only complete equality of rights for all nations in general, but also equality of rights in forming independent states, i.e. the right of nations to self-determination, to secession ... .'[3] This policy attracted criticism from an unexpected quarter. The Polish revolutionary, Rosa Luxemburg, argued that pursuing national independence, in which rich and poor combined to oppose foreign control, was less progressive than socialist internationalism – the uniting of Russian and Polish workers against a common capitalist enemy. Lenin agreed the latter was the ultimate goal, but asserted it would not be achieved if Polish workers felt their former imperialist oppressor denied them the right to independence.[4]

Whoever was generally correct, Luxemburg's warnings about the reactionary potential of Polish nationalism bore fruit when the country was fully re-established, following the collapse of the German and Austrian empires. Marshal Pilsudski, its first ruler, aided by France's General Weygand (of later notoriety for capitulating to the Nazis), attacked Soviet Russia and seized an area inhabited by six million Ukrainians, land far beyond the 1772 borders originally claimed.[5] It even took advantage of the German invasion of Czechoslovakia in 1939 to grab Cieszyn.[6] Thus, at the outbreak of the Second World War one third of Polish citizens were from national minorities.[7] On the domestic front Pilsudski founded *Sanacja* (Political healing), a dictatorship which outlived him and still ran Poland at the outbreak of the Second World War.

Ironically, sharing in the dismemberment of Czechoslovakia was but the prelude to Poland itself becoming a target for Nazi aggression. At that point Britain and France resolved to back Polish independence, by war if necessary. Stalin distanced himself, however, saying he would not 'be drawn into conflicts by warmongers who are accustomed to get others to pull the chestnuts out of the fire for them'.[8] His reserve had nothing to do with the Bolshevik anti-imperialism. The Stalinist counter-revolution had destroyed all traces of that. Instead Moscow was signalling its readiness for the Hitler-Stalin Pact of August 1939, a deal whose secret protocols divided Poland between Germany and Russia.[9]

Doubtless Anglo-French appeasement had convinced Moscow there was no alternative but to conciliate Berlin. Nonetheless, the Pact was an act of breathtaking audacity. Nazism and Bolshevism were polar opposites. The Nazis had murdered many thousand German communists. All this was brushed aside, the Soviet Union providing Hitler with vital raw materials in return for weapons.[10] On hearing the Pact was signed a jubilant Hitler 'began to hammer on the wall with his fists, uttering inarticulate cries, and finally shouting exultantly "I have the world in my pocket!"'[11]

When the re-conquest of Poland commenced, the Russians left the Wehrmacht to carry on the fighting, thus minimising their own risks and masking their avarice.[12] The Nazis were asked to indicate 'as nearly as possible when they could count on the capture of Warsaw' as this would be the signal for Russia to grab its share.[13] But they misjudged and Moscow attacked ten days too early. Embarrassingly, the joint Nazi-Soviet victory parade at Brest-Litovsk preceded the capital's fall on 27 September.[14] Nevertheless, Stalin still made the outrageous claim that the Red Army had only intervened to 'extricate the Polish people from the unfortunate war into which they have been dragged by their unwise leaders, and to enable them to live a peaceful life'.[15] In private he boasted that German-Soviet friendship had been 'sealed in blood'.[16] It was the blood of 216,000 Poles. In the campaign Germany lost 60,000 soldiers, and Russia 11,500.[17]

Once the fighting was over, Stalin held 52 per cent of Polish territory, and Hitler 48 per cent.[18] Both agreed that they would tolerate 'no Polish agitation which affects the territories of the other party', and 'suppress in their territories all beginnings of such agitation...'.[19] A powerful fight-back developed despite this. It was distinct from both the Greek and Yugoslav resistance because *the gap between the local imperialist government and anti-fascist resistance was minimal.* The root of the difference lay in the unusual roles played by Poland's communists and its ruling elite.

While the Greek and Yugoslav CPs were central to the people's war, Poland's communists were not. In 1938 they had been physically liquidated by Moscow, and the Party was formally dissolved once Poland itself was extinguished.[20] For good measure a quarter of the one million ethnic Poles in the Soviet Union were shot before the war began.[21] The picture changed in 1941, when Hitler seized Stalin's portion of Poland and invaded Russia itself. Now Moscow supported a surrogate CP, the Polish Workers' Party (Polska Partia Robotnicza – PPR), though it made little progress due to its close association with a former occupying power.[22]

In other occupied countries elites shunned people's war and favoured collaboration or attentism. In neither the German nor Russian sectors was this an easy option for the Polish ruling class. Hitler regarded all Poles as 'more like animals than human beings'.[23] In colonising Western Poland he eliminated or enslaved the inhabitants. A near genocidal approach involved Wehrmacht 'housecleaning' – the displacement of some 900,000 people. Even speaking Polish in public was banned in some areas.[24] Children were to learn only how to write their names, count up to a maximum of 500 and know: 'It is God's command that they should be obedient to Germany ... .'[25]

Eastern Poland experienced the brutality of Russian rule. Here Stalin was driven by a desire for absolute control not racist fanaticism. But, as with Nazi-occupied Poland: 'No political distinctions were made, and Polish communists ... worked and perished alongside Catholic priests and university professors, farmers and railwaymen ... .'[26] The most notorious incident of the

Russian occupation was the execution of several thousand Polish officers at Katyn.[27] Up to two million people (9 per cent of the population) were deported as forced labour.[28] Many never returned.

A recent study comparing the German and Russian occupations concludes that though the latter was less violent, 'similarities persisted, particularly in the application of targeted collective terror'.[29] Indeed the Nazi SS and Russian secret police (the GPU) co-ordinated their approaches.[30] Between Scylla and Charybdis, Poland suffered over six million killed, the highest proportion of death for any country during the Second World War. Of these 90 per cent were civilians[31] and half were Jews. As a resistance leaflet of 1940 put it: 'History has taught the Polish nation a dreadful lesson. For us, now, the road to freedom leads through the torture chambers and the Gestapo and the [Russian] GPU.'[32] The Poles could therefore claim 'the presence of Quislings, collaboration, and compromise [was] impossible'.[33] A common calamity engulfed all sections of society.

Poland's resistance therefore began in the key institution of the pre-war Sanacja dictatorship – the military.[34] Major General Tokarzewski, a Pilsudskiite, organised what became the underground Home Army (Armja Krajowa, or AK).[35] This shaped its future development. As one author puts it: 'throughout its existence [the AK was] commanded and officered mainly by the members of the Polish pre-war military establishment [who] brought with them into the resistance ideas, attitudes, traditions and professional doctrines and standards acquired during their service in the pre-war army... .'[36] In other words, the AK command was tied to a tradition of reactionary dictatorship and imperialist policies.

While rightly emphasising the importance of the AK, Norman Davies goes so far as to subsume the entire anti-fascist movement into this military formation: 'Europe's largest Resistance movement, which in January 1940 adopted the name of the Union of Armed Struggle (ZWZ), and in February 1942 the Home Army... was a branch of the regular Polish armed forces ... .'[37] Its achievements were outstanding. 380,000 fighters[38] carried out 25,000 acts of sabotage in just three years,[39] and by 1945 had killed 150,000 Germans.[40]

However, if this were the whole story there would have been little room for a people's war. Yet there were two other elements of considerable importance. One was the Underground State led by General Sikorski, an opponent of the Sanacja.[41] Sikorski argued: 'The movement must not be confined merely to the function of [military] resistance, but must take shape as an actual state. All the apparatus of a state must be created and maintained at all costs, no matter how crude it is.'[42]

The results were impressive. Although its Headquarters were in London, a full suite of government institutions were reproduced in Poland. The Ministry of Education, for example, educated one million children, as well as operating universities in Krakow, Lwow and Vilno. Thirty per cent of available funds went to social welfare.[43] The state had a shadow parliament – the 'Political Representation'. A 'Directorate of Civilian Resistance' functioned as a court system that tried and sentenced collaborators.[44] A vast clandestine press with numerous titles also operated.[45]

The third bloc in the resistance was made up of the Socialist, Peasant, Christian Labour and National Democrat parties. While the first three had been to the left of the Sanacja, the National Democrats were followers of Dmowski. He was a right-wing anti-Semite who denounced 'the menace of Socialism inside the nation, as well as the threat coming from the Jewish element [who] represented international forces which could do no good, but might well do much harm'.[46] It was a sign of Dmowski's continuing influence, that even after the horrors of 1939–45 Bor-Komorowski, the commander of the AK, could pander to anti-Semitism in his memoirs, writing Jews 'had undoubtedly been a foreign body within the Polish community'.[47] These political parties together represented the bulk of politically active Poles.

Even taking into account those elements of resistance outside the Sanacja-controlled army, it might still appear that Poland's resistance did not include people's war. A recent history counters this impression:

> Hundreds of underground organisations ... were established 'from below' in conjunction with existing ties of family, job, friendship, and neighbors. Hundreds of conspiratorial networks thus emerged as an expression of a spontaneous rebellion against this humiliation, and were not created 'from above', [though] the numerical ratio between the two types of organizations will never be clear.[48]

A direct participant reported that: 'anybody who had some imagination, a little ambition and initiative, and a great deal of courage could, and often did, start an outfit of his own ... .'[49]

It is a sign of the complex inter-mixing of imperialist and people's war elements that the balance between right and left in the resistance has been hotly debated. One Jewish woman declared: 'I wasn't afraid of the Germans, I was afraid of the Poles.'[50] At the same time members of the resistance assisted the Jewish Warsaw Ghetto uprising of April 1932, and sheltered survivors.[51] Some 15,000–20,000 Jews were hidden in Warsaw beyond the Ghetto walls[52] and the Zegota organisation (for rescuing Jews) was linked closely to the Polish Government-in-exile.[53] One book concludes that 'there is no national group about which there are as many (frequently contradictory) reports and judgments as there are about the Poles'.[54]

Poland was unique in having the active involvement of upper- and lower-class forces in its resistance, yet there were powerful internal stresses in play.[55] The overlap of people's war and imperialist war was never comfortable or complete. As well as the split between left and right parties, and movements from 'above' and 'below', army supporters of the Sanacja sat uneasily alongside civilians who blamed that system for Poland's ignominious defeat.[56] An example of the tension occurred at a critical point in the development of the Warsaw Rising. Poland's military Commander in Chief, Sosnowski, absented himself in order to plot a coup against the head of the civilian Government, Mikolajczyk. Sosnowski feared a compromise with the Russians was in preparation.[57] Another issue was the emphasis of the resistance on Polish nationalism which alienated the non-Polish third of the population living within the pre-1939 borders.

Despite the obstacles to attentism mentioned above, the AK was tempted to try it, and for the same reasons as other 'official' resistance movements: primarily fear that mass actions would unleash dangerous social forces, but also to avoid Nazi reprisals (which were especially horrendous in Poland). Thus Bor-Komorowski based his initial strategy 'on the assumption that sooner or later the German western front would crack, giving us a favourable opportunity for a successful insurrection'.[58] In other words Anglo-French success must precede serious action. He felt France's defeat in 1940 to be 'the end of our organisation [as] all our plans were collapsing' and determined on 'a long-term policy. Our main task would be intelligence work and Press and propaganda action.'[59]

Attentism proved untenable, however. When the Nazis began clearing all Poles from the Lublin and Zamosc regions to make way for ethnic German colonists there was no choice but to authorise the formation of partisan units. Their action stopped the expulsions. Yet the AK still resisted more drastic steps.[60] It was eventually dragged into adopting the tactics of people's war by the pressure of events.

One factor was betrayal of the Polish cause by Britain, the country where the government-in-exile resided, and in whom the attentists placed their hopes. Although defending Polish sovereignty was the ostensible reason for war in 1939, Britain was more concerned to woo Moscow, a fellow great power, the Hitler-Stalin pact notwithstanding. As early as October 1939 London indicated its belief that Russia should keep 90 per cent of its ill-gotten gains.[61] When Russia joined the Allied camp, Churchill pressured Sikorski into signing a treaty with Stalin that implicitly recognised this conquest.[62] News of the massacre at Katyn scuppered the enforced friendship, but brought no change in overall British policy.

Would Roosevelt back the resistance, given the USA's large Polish electorate? He was even more solicitous of Stalin than Churchill. Until 1944 no assistance at all was forthcoming. As the Warsaw Rising drew near the US allocated $10 million (the Poles had asked for $97m), on condition that they collaborated with the Red Army. It was not until the Rising was in its third week that any money at all was released.[63]

An emissary of the Underground State, Karski, who reached the West at great risk to reveal its existence to the Allies, commented bitterly on their lack of sympathy: 'I soon realised that the outside world could not comprehend ... It never could understand or estimate the sacrifice and heroism entailed in our nation-wide refusal to collaborate ... The whole notion of the underground state was often unintelligible to them.'[64] This incomprehension was not caused by a lack of imagination, but by the common interests of the Allied imperialists.

The negative attitude of the Allies weakened the fighting potential of the Polish resistance. Although the underground army acquired some equipment from its own secret workshops,[65] in 1944 its hundreds of thousands of volunteers held no more than 32,000 guns.[66] As Russia was unlikely to provide additional weaponry, the AK turned to Britain. Geographical distance was the excuse given for refusal, but direct discussions between the British and Russian secret services were probably more decisive. Thus, in the period up to the Warsaw Rising, the tonnage of supplies the AK received was one tenth and one eighteenth of that sent to Greece and France respectively.[67]

Such disdain for Polish aspirations led to disagreements between the London exiles, who were closely tied to the Allied powers, and the AK's commanders who were subject to popular pressures at home. Compare government pronouncements to those made in Warsaw on the eve of the Rising. The former were squarely in the Anglo-French camp: 'Free Poland ... will become an effective prop to the Western-cultured Slavonic countries and other small nations situated between Germany and Russia.'[68] This statement deliberately distanced itself from radicalism.

In Warsaw, General Bor-Komorowski might have been expected to speak in similar tones. He had been selected as AK commander because he was an aristocratic cavalry officer known for right-wing views.[69] Furthermore, until fairly late on he tried to incorporate the fascist NSZ into his forces, even though they had been murdering left-wing supporters of the Government-in-exile, as well as communists.[70] However, Bor-Komorowski had to contend with the fact that, as time passed, Red Army successes created a sense of impatience which allowed the communist PPR to begin making headway.[71] One historian writes that Poland was experiencing a 'surge of radical feeling ... sharing the longing of all European resistance movements for a cleaner world after the war, for social equality and full employment.'[72] A sign of the mood was that in August 1943 the right-wing National Democrats, of all people, agreed to a statement proposing 'a planned economy ... with the state having the right to nationalise public utilities, transport, key industries and banking ... The requisitioning of all private estates over fifty hectares ... full employment, health, education, and social services.'[73]

General Bor-Komorowski followed suit. He feared a rift between his 'self-contained professional group' of right-wing officers, and the AK rank and file – 'people of all walks of life and professions ...'.[74] In July 1944 Bor warned London against inaction because 'the initiative for fighting the Germans is liable then to be taken by the PPR (Communist) and a considerable fraction of the less-informed citizens might join them. In that case the country is liable to move in the direction of collaboration with the Soviets and no one will be able to stop it.'[75]

To place himself at the head of the people's war, Bor-Komorowski called for a Poland 'governed in the interests of the wide working masses'.[76] He did not ask people to risk their lives to make Poland an 'effective prop to the Western-cultured Slavonic countries' like the exiles. Instead he called for expropriation without compensation of large rural estates, a welfare state, nationalisation of industry, and workers' councils.[77]

As Ciechanowski explains, by 1944 the AK was confronted with 'a dangerous and explosive situation. They tried to prevent the PPR from gaining ground and to maintain the loyalty of the masses by increasing their anti-German operations. They regarded as their supreme task the preparation of an anti-German insurrection.'[78]

Bor now stressed: 'the only chance of gaining anything was a constant demonstration of our will to fight Germany to the last, sparing no effort, in the teeth of every adversity.'[79] With Russia unfriendly and Anglo-American forces too far away to mount a D-Day style landing, attentism, that refuge of governments-in-exile, had run its course in Warsaw.

Conjuring up active mass resistance, however, put the domestic Polish leadership on a collision course with Allied imperialism, as represented by Russia. This first became apparent during Operation Burza ('Tempest'). AK units were to emerge from underground the moment the Red Army entered Poland and greet Soviet commanders with these words: 'Acting on the orders of the Government of the Polish Republic I approach you ... with a proposal to coordinate military operations against the common enemy with the Soviet forces entering the territories of the Polish republic.'[80]

General Bor-Komorowski explained that Burza would demonstrate: 'Our will to manifest our struggle against the Germans', and 'Our will to manifest to the Soviets the presence of elements representing the sovereignty of the Republic'.[81] The relative importance attached to a people's anti-fascist war or restoration of pre-war Poland was unclear in this formulation. Bor still balanced uncomfortably between the two.

Burza was launched in the Volhynia region, which Borodziej has discussed in detail. Here the population was five-sixths Ukrainian and only one-sixth Polish. This unfortunate area had endured centuries of imperialism – mainly Tsarist, then Polish, and now German. To win local co-operation Berlin cleverly exploited Ukrainian hostility to their Polish neighbours, of whom 50,000 were killed. Before Burza the AK's role in Volhynia had not been to attack Germans but to defend the Polish minority through counter-terror – 20,000 Ukrainians perished as a result.[82] It was here, and after these appalling events, that the AK proposed to re-establish the 'sovereignty of the [Polish] Republic'!

A genuine people's war, imbued with internationalism and emphasizing the common interest of ordinary people in opposing *all* ruling classes (or at least a Titoist emphasis on multi-ethnic resistance) could have generated mass support for Burza in Volhynia.

The AK was not about to go that far, and so when it appeared on the scene the Red Army easily brushed the resistance fighters aside.

The pattern set in Volhynia reappeared elsewhere: Red Army commanders welcomed AK assistance during the fight against the Germans, but the instant the battle was won they demanded the resistance dissolve or join a puppet Polish army under General Berling. Those who refused were interned or executed.[83] Stalin wanted Eastern Poland back after the war; he did not want rival factions under arms. Not only was the AK weak in terms of military hardware, in the Eastern regions it could not appeal to Polish nationalism. So Burza failed wherever it was attempted.

Warsaw was another matter. The capital was less ethnically diverse, especially after the elimination of its considerable Jewish community. Yet throughout Operation Burza, and indeed up until the very moment when the Warsaw Rising erupted, no-one proposed large-scale fighting there.[84] Bor-Komorowski was explicit: 'I have issued directives aimed at preventing our diversionary activities from becoming a spontaneous attempt at an armed insurrection launched under unfavourable conditions.'[85] Proof the AK leadership did not pre-plan the Rising was the fact that precious armaments were sent out of Warsaw in the preceding weeks.[86] On 14 July Bor said: 'In the current situation of the German forces in Poland and the preparations against the Uprising [it] has no chance of success. We can only rely on the case that the Germans collapse and the army falls apart.'[87]

A kaleidoscope of pressures rather than one single element changed this line. It was believed the Germans were about to deport large numbers of young Varsovians which would have crippled the AK. The Red Army was approaching the city, and on 29 July broadcast a Polish communist statement: 'the hour of action has already arrived'. It appealed for 'direct active struggle in the streets' so that the moment of final liberation will be hastened and the lives of our brethren saved'.[88] The next day the language was even stronger: 'Warsaw is shaking to the foundations from the roar of the guns. Soviet forces are advancing forcefully and approaching Praga [the district facing central Warsaw on the other side of the Vistula River]. They are coming to bring you freedom ... People of the Capital! To arms!'[89] Colonel Monter, Bor's subordinate, reported the same (as it turned out false) claim at a crucial meeting of the AK leadership.[90] The decision for a rising in Warsaw was made, and on 1 August 1944 it began.

That day the Home Army and civil population threw themselves into the biggest insurrection of the entire Second World War. Historians disagree on its wisdom. Davies sees it as a justified attempt to throw off the German yoke, on the reasonable expectation that Allied anti-fascist rhetoric would translate into concrete assistance. Kolko suggests the AK leadership and Government-in-exile were manoeuvring to preserve their role within the system of state powers: 'The uprising was in reality against both the Germans and Russians, and therefore doomed to failure from the beginning. It was a ghastly outcome of the logic which the Poles, both in London and in the Home Army, attempted to employ for years as part of their diplomacy of grandeur.'[91]

There is evidence for both interpretations. For example, General Bor-Komorowski believed: 'The general lust of revenge for the years of tragedy and humiliation suffered under the Germans was overwhelming and practically impossible to check. The whole town was waiting breathlessly for a call to arms ... .'[92] But he also hinted at 'the diplomacy of grandeur' when describing the insurrection as 'the last trump card we had in that game in which the stake was the independence of our country.'[93]

The AK had weapons for only a fraction of its 40,000 troops and could hold out for little more than a week.[94] However, with the Red Army nearby and the Polish Premier having arrived in Moscow just two days before, it was believed that Russian assistance would soon be forthcoming.[95] The AK's need for external help was obvious. On the very first day of fighting it lost 10 per cent of those mobilised, at a cost of four fighters for every German.[96]

This did not dim popular enthusiasm for a reckoning with the Nazis. An eye-witness would write of the:

> joy which we felt at the time. It arose as a result of the torment of the occupation, as a result of the pain and humiliation suffered for nearly five years. We were prepared for anything ...The years of the occupation had taught us to be indifferent to the dangers that threatened us with every step. But above all the belief that the Polish armed movement would hasten the moment of the crossing of the Soviet Army to Warsaw and immediately force the Germans to leave the town invigorated us.[97]

An AK officer described the:

> fervour with which the inhabitants built anti-tank barricades, organised soup kitchens at short notice to feed soldiers and

those people not able to return to their homes, caught where the
Uprising had surprised them. The mood in the street reminded one
of a continuous holiday … Everyone in their own way and within
the limits of their ability took part in this decisive struggle.[98]

Three days into the Rising Bor-Komorowski reported how
women and men were rushing to join the AK, volunteering for all
sorts of roles such as extinguishing fires, feeding the fighters, and
producing homemade petrol bombs that compensated for the lack of
armaments.[99] Amongst many others, the 'Grey Ranks' – the Polish
scout movement – played a prominent part and paid the price.[100]

Whatever the different factors behind the decision to act, an AK
officer witnessed in Warsaw a crucial aspect of the people's war:
'the boundary between fighters and participants has been erased.'[101]
This was echoed by a British observer: 'Today, a battle is going on
that I think is very difficult for the British nation to understand. It
is a battle that is being carried on by the civilian population as well
as by the AK.'[102] One in seven combatants were women, and, in
Bor-Komorowski's words, 'the majority were workers, railwaymen,
artisans, students and clerks in factories, railways and offices'.[103]
So AK methods could not 'be compared with the attack of any
regular army. It had all the drive and enthusiasm of a revolutionary
uprising [and] we attributed our success of the first few days to the
impetuous fervour of this first onslaught. It more than made up for
the poor quality of our arms.'[104]

This does not mean that the union of the movement 'from
above' and 'from below', cemented by universal hatred of Nazi
rule, was incapable of dissolving. A report to the Government-in-
exile from within Warsaw indicated that large numbers were less
concerned with whether the Polish Government was associated with
the Western Allies or Russia, than whether it could deliver social
reforms. The report therefore warned that the radical promises
must not be dropped.[105]

Everything now turned on the Russians' attitude. With Poland's
fate not yet pre-determined by the notorious blue-pencilled paper
and its percentages, would they make common cause with the
insurgents and promote people's war, like communists elsewhere,
or would Stalin treat Warsaw with the same hostility as Churchill
did Athens? In comparing the two men we will use the British PM's
insider account from his *History of the Second World War*.

On 4 August Churchill informed Stalin of British aid to the AK
as this 'may be of help to your operation'.[106] Stalin's reply the next

day was that the Rising was 'greatly exaggerated and does not inspire confidence' because 'they have neither artillery nor aircrafts nor tanks.'[107] Precisely the point. The Rising was timed to coincide with the anticipated arrival of Red Army artillery, aircraft and tanks. The deadline of a week that the AK had foreseen as the limit of their endurance came and went, with no sign of any Russian advance or aid. So the insurgents improvised a host of ingenious techniques, and because guns were recovered from those who fell, the high death toll actually served to increase the proportion of AK troops with weapons. Meanwhile the strength of popular feeling maintained morale.[108]

But Nazi resolve strengthened too. German orders now read: '1. All rebels were to be shot after capture; 2. The non-fighting part of the population would be massacred indiscriminately.'[109] The local Nazi ruler, Hans Frank, added: 'Warsaw merits the fate of being utterly destroyed.'[110]

On 12 August Churchill tried to soften Stalin's position by presenting an appeal delivered from Warsaw:

We receive from you only once a small drop [of supplies]. On the German-Russian front silence since the 3rd. We are therefore without any material or moral support, as with the exception of a short speech by the Polish Vice-PM (from London), we have not had from you even an acknowledgement of our action. The soldiers and the population look hopelessly at the skies, expecting help from the Allies. On the background of smoke they see only German aircraft. They are surprised, feel deeply depressed, and begin to revile...I repeat emphatically that without immediate support, consisting of drops of arms and munitions, bombing of objectives held by the enemy, and air landing, our fight will collapse in a few days.

Churchill pleaded: 'Can you not give them some further help?'[111] On day 16 came Stalin's response: 'I am convinced that the Warsaw action represents a reckless and terrible adventure... .'[112]

It was true that Rokossovsky, the Red Army commander on the Polish front, faced stiff resistance from the Wehrmacht at this time. Even Davies, the historian most sympathetic to the Rising, finds that initially there was 'a determined German counter-attack to the east of the Vistula ... [and] little chance that Rokossovsky could easily have crossed the Vistula in force'.[113] However, the Rising continued until 2 October and in that time numerous opportunities arose for the Russians to provide assistance.

Air drops were an option and Churchill and Roosevelt sent this joint appeal to Stalin: 'We are thinking of world opinion if the anti-Nazis in Warsaw are in effect abandoned ...We hope that you will drop immediate supplies and munitions to the patriot Poles in Warsaw, or will you agree to help our planes in doing it very quickly?'[114] The Soviets put no obstacle in the way of British and US supply planes flying the 1,250km from their nearest bases in Italy, but they were not permitted to land or refuel in Russia. Equally, the Russians had no intention of flying the 30km from their positions to aid Warsaw.[115] The Western Allies mounted a series of virtually suicidal missions but it could not radically alter the outcome.[116]

In mid-September the Russians eventually deigned to provide limited aid. Churchill saw through this belated manoeuvre: 'They wished to have the non-Communist Poles destroyed to the full, but also to keep alive the idea that they were going to their rescue.'[117] Harriman, the US ambassador in Moscow was appalled by the Kremlin's approach: 'These men are bloated with power and expect they can force their will on us and all countries to accept their decisions without question ... .'[118]

After two months the insurgents finally capitulated. The Polish Government explained the disastrous outcome in these terms: 'We received no effective support... We have been treated worse than Hitler's allies in Romania, Italy and Finland ... [Our] Rising is going under at a time when our armies abroad are helping to liberate France, Belgium, and Holland... .'[119]

Without any sense of irony the British PM, who bombed Athens to break the Greek resistance, echoed their argument:

Immortal is the nation that can muster such universal heroism... These words are indelible. The struggle in Warsaw had lasted more than 60 days. Of the 40,000 men and women of the Polish Underground Army about 15,000 fell. Out of a population of a million nearly 200,000 had been stricken. The suppression of the revolt cost the German Army 10,000 killed, 7,000 missing and 9,000 wounded... When the Russians entered the city three months later they found little but shattered streets and the unburied dead. Such was their liberation of Poland where they now rule.[120]

The tragic end of the Warsaw Rising was the result of many factors, including miscalculations by the AK, and the unexpected strength of the Wehrmacht. However, there is no doubt that Deutscher's accusation against Russia was accurate. The blocking of aid to Warsaw 'sent a shudder of horror through the allied countries [as] a demonstration of callousness [that] shocked even Stalin's admirers in the West'.[121]

Poland saw a repetition of the pattern seen in Greece, in spite of the very different political context. Irrespective of the formal ideological position of the Allied governments involved, imperialists opposed resistance movements when these did not suit their purpose. This reinforces the idea that the Second World War experienced parallel imperialist and people's wars which could find themselves in direct opposition. In Greece Britain attacked the population. In Poland Russia allowed the Nazis to do their dirty work for them. The outcome was the same in each case. It was a bitter consolation, as one Polish broadcast put it, that 'at least the Germans cannot take Warsaw again. All that is left is a heap of rubble ... Warsaw no longer exists.'[122]

5
Latvia – Standing History on its Head

Although the Second World War encompassed two distinctly different conflicts, they were not manifested everywhere. Latvia experienced only imperialist war and so, as one writer has put it: 'the good war narrative simply will not work'.[1] It is an informative case because, when taken alongside Yugoslavia, Greece and Poland, the prerequisites for people's war are revealed.

The peculiarity of Latvia's role is confirmed by the quagmire contemporary historians fall into if they apply the conventional categories of the Second World War to their country's past. Thus a recent anthology by 'the Commission of the Historians of Latvia' states the only party 'that came near to being a resistance movement in the West European sense' was the Perkonkrusts. This word is Latvian for Swastika,[2] and in a country where a quarter of the population were from ethnic minorities, the policy of its leader, Celmins, was: 'in *a Latvian Latvia* there will only be Latvians [because] the question of minorities will not exist ... '.[3] Perkonkrusts members sought that goal by organising the notorious auxiliary police battalions and Commando squads at the behest of the Nazis. These butchered 70,000 Latvian Jews.[4] Is it not strange to describe the Swastika Party as 'a resistance movement in the West European sense'?

Valdmanis is presented as another resister. As a minister in Latvia's Nazi-appointed quisling regime, he publicly invited his compatriots 'to participate in the war for the liberation of Europe and put the fate of the Latvian people in the hands of Adolf Hitler.'[5] In private he wrote: 'we would prefer to receive our Latvian independence from Germany instead of from other powers ...'.[6] Valdmanis's biographer finds 'collaboration became increasingly indistinguishable from resistance'.[7] An official history concurs: 'One could simultaneously be both a collaborator and an active member of the resistance.'[8]

Such a bizarre, indeed chilling, approach is only explicable (though not any more justifiable) because Latvia was occupied by Russia from 1939 to 1941, and 1944 to 1991. Accordingly, these historians regard those who opposed Russia as the true 'resisters'. Conversely,

Latvians who fought Nazism are dubbed 'collaborators rather than members of the resistance movement'.[9] The historians reject the 'Nuremburg consensus', believing the trial of Nazi war criminals represented a 'winners' position' that ignored the Soviet misdeeds.[10]

This topsy turvy argument has repercussions even today. One dissident Latvian historian warns that: 'The truth about the Holocaust and mass murders that took place also in Latvia during the German period is still being ignored deliberately or unintentionally'.[11] As recently as May 2010, at the urging of the Latvian government, the European Court upheld the conviction of Kononov, the only anti-Nazi partisan to be successfully prosecuted as a war criminal. He led an attack on a village suspected of harbouring German collaborators, in which nine people, including a pregnant woman, were killed. The state of Latvia argued that 'the Court should take into account the broader historical and political events before and after the Second World War' including Soviet occupation.[12]

The confusion arises from the absence of a people's war in Latvia, which was rooted in its geographical and historical position. With a landmass one-264th the size of Russia's, and one-seventh that of Germany, it was long oppressed by these powerful neighbours. Teutonic knights took control in the thirteenth century, and though Baltic Germans formed a mere 4 per cent of the population by the start of the twentieth, they still dominated economically and socially. Above them was an authoritarian Tsarist regime which pursued aggressive Russification policies. Even after independence in 1918, ethnic minorities controlled over three quarters of private enterprise.[13]

In this situation one's attitude to imperialism was critical. The approach adopted by the country's first and largest political party, the Latvian Social Democratic Workers' Party (LSDWP) was left internationalism. The LSDWP had a policy akin to Luxemburg's. It argued that so long as Russian or German imperialism existed the demand for independence was impractical in a country as weak as Latvia. Only an alliance with revolutionary workers fighting to overthrow these imperialist powers from within could succeed. So Stucka, the LSDWP leader, did not want 'the struggle of nationalities but of classes'.[14] This policy meant that during the 1905 Russian Revolution workers in Riga joined in mass strikes that shook Tsarism. Simultaneously peasants (the most numerous social group) challenged the power of the local German landowners.[15]

But imperialism recovered, and during the First World War Latvia became a battleground fought over by Germany and Russia. It only escaped the carnage when the 1917 Bolshevik insurrection brought Russia's withdrawal from the War. During this episode Latvian riflemen played a key role as Bolshevism's 'praetorian guard'. However, at the Treaty of Brest-Litovsk in 1918 Moscow was forced to cede the Baltic States of Latvia, Lithuania and Estonia to Germany. While the Bolsheviks were too weak to do anything else, this act probably prevented a successful revolution in Latvia with broad popular backing.[16]

In 1918, with left-wing influence on the wane, the initiative shifted to Latvia's nationalists, who tended to be middle and upper class. They feared the Latvian workers and their internationalism and would ally with whichever capitalist power guaranteed them a state with the jobs, status, and power to restrain domestic opponents. Britain was hostile to both communism and the Kaiser and so in October became the first country to accord Latvia diplomatic recognition.[17] Full independence was granted by the victors of the First World War just days after Germany's capitulation.

Latvia began the inter-war period with a parliamentary democracy, but after President Ulmanis visited Nazi Germany in 1934 fascism was introduced.[18] His first target was the communists, whose support for a foreign government was styled 'unpatriotic'. Eventually all political parties (including the Perkonkrusts and his own formation) were banned. While Ulmanis avoided virulent anti-Semitism, he clearly aligned himself with the Perkonkrusts general motto by promoting slogans like 'Latvia for the Latvians'[19] and 'Latvia is a Latvian State'.[20]

The Hitler-Stalin pact granted the Baltic States to Russia, and in 1940 Soviet troops toppled Ulmanis. In a statement worthy of Orwell, the newly founded 'People's Government of Free Citizens of Latvia' asserted: 'The Red Army being in the territory of Latvia, and the happy reception that our inhabitants gave the Red Army, is solid proof and a guarantee of our stable relations and our brotherly friendship with the USSR... .'[21] An election produced a resounding 98 per cent vote of confidence for the 'Working People's Bloc'. However, this was the Latvian Communist Party's grouping and the only one allowed to stand. At the time the Party had just 400 members, of whom only 50 were themselves ethnic Latvians.[22] In August 1940 Latvia was admitted into the USSR and its 'community of brother and great socialist lands and fortunate nations'.[23]

Some Latvians swallowed the rhetoric. Swain's excellent history of the town of Daugavapils shows how they believed Russian control was a green light for soviets – workers' and soldiers' councils. At the Italia works the soviet cut hours, reinstated a worker victimised under the fascist regime, and ensured payment of wages for the days of the 'revolution'. In the barracks food quality improved, 'fascist elements' were purged, and equal rights for all nationalities to promotion and holidays were promulgated.[24] However, the illusions were swiftly destroyed. Russian Latvia was given what Swain calls 'a five year plan in five months'.[25] The power of factory managers was restored and party committees replaced broad-based soviets.[26] Rationing accompanied a 300 per cent rise in food prices. Through the Stakhanovite movement workers were enjoined to multiply productivity and spied on by the secret police.[27] While the Hitler-Stalin Pact held communists were told: 'their task was no longer to be part of the world wide struggle of communism against fascism, but to persuade a sceptical populace of the benefits of incorporation into the Soviet Union... .'[28]

The Baltic economies were to be rapidly integrated into the USSR's war preparations. In July 1940 the government seized ('nationalised') all major enterprises and banks.[29] Changes to land ownership followed, which, though they fell short of full collectivisation, made many peasants suspect the state would soon confiscate their farms.[30]

As the Baltic States were close to Leningrad and contained German minorities which Hitler might use to justify invasion[31] the decision was taken to remove them, and any other 'dangerous elements'. Thousands of citizens were deported causing intense bitterness. The process came in four waves,[32] culminating on 13/14 June 1941 when 15,000 people (including 2,400 children under the age of ten) were shipped off to Siberia in appalling conditions.[33] This was the regime's last major act.

Official Latvian circles today class the period of deportations as 'the year of horror',[34] and some implicitly blame the Jews for what happened. One writes: 'part of the Jewish population, especially members of the Jewish socialist movement, welcomed and actively collaborated with the Soviet power'.[35] Given the alternative of Nazi rule this was hardly surprising. Another points to 'the conspicuous position of the Jews in the new regime [which] caused the Letts to identify the whole of the Jewish community with the hated Soviet regime'.[36] A third points out that 'three of the main figures in the security apparatus were of Jewish origin, and this fact created the stereotype common in occupied Latvia ...'. A more measured account notes that 'Latvians in Latvia noticed only that the perpetrators were not just Russians and Latvians, but also Jews – "again those Jews!"'[37]

As usual, the stereotype was false. Latvia's Jews suffered relatively the most. They were 5 per cent of the population, but constituted 11 per cent of the deportees.[38] Their larger numbers were due to their position in the economic structure, which was regarded as an impediment to Russia's monopoly: 'The Soviets viewed all conquered peoples as a possible threat, to be forcibly incorporated into the communist system. With regard to the Jews, who were not granted the status of a nation in Soviet ideology, the aim was to assimilate them as soon as possible, by uprooting Jewish communal and religious organizations.'[39]

Yet the Jews were to be the victims once more when, in the absence of a viable alternative to imperialism, the actions of one oppressor (Russia) pushed many of the Latvian population straight into the arms of another (Germany). One book explains that as a result of the deportations: 'in a very short period the common view of the Germans ("the black knights") as the Latvia's primary enemies – developed over the centuries – was suddenly replaced by the view that the primary enemy was Russia and the Communists. This change of perspective defined the reception the Germans received when they invaded.'[40]

Latvia's Soviet regime collapsed in June 1941, under the Wehrmacht onslaught. As before, when Ulmanis's regime was overthrown, there was a brief transition period when neither imperialism held full sway. However, nothing resembling a resistance to Nazism appeared. Those on the left who had not been broken by Ulmanis's fascist rule were disoriented or discredited by the Stalinist phase. Instead, a 'national partisan' movement spontaneously emerged to harass the retreating Red Army, assist the German advance, and arrest communists and Jews.[41] Nazi sympathisers set up a Centre for Latvian Organisations to take power at the local level, but it was ignored by the new masters.[42]

The Nazis found willing collaborators in most states they conquered, from Quisling in Norway, to Pétain in France, and so on. However, in the swathe of territory that experienced recent Soviet deportations, such as the Baltic States and the Ukraine, this phenomenon was particularly intense. Here, writes the American author, Dean, 'it was relatively easy for the Nazis to recruit people locally who were prepared to carry out their terrible policies ...'.[43] Latvian historians are at pains to point out that their countrymen did not turn to genocide without external encouragement. In most places the 'interregnum' between Russian and German control lasted less than one day, and there seems to be no evidence of spontaneous mass murder of Jews during that brief time.[44] However, the speed of events was nevertheless startling.

The Holocaust is generally dated to the late summer of 1941, becoming large-scale from October. In Latvia, however, the Final Solution was underway on 23 June, just two days after the Germans took charge. By mid-August a high proportion of Jews in rural areas were dead. In the Zemgale region the toll was 100 per cent. This thoroughness was only possible with close collaboration and local knowledge. As Dean asserts more broadly, there was an 'element of the perpetrators personally knowing the victims [which] lends a gruesome intimacy to the massacres'.[45] The (once again Orwellian sounding) 'Latvian Self-Defence Commands' identified and rounded up victims. 700 such units had formed in just a few weeks.[46] Clearly the invaders had little difficulty finding volunteers. A study of the Krustpils area describes how things worked at the micro level:

> Both those who executed and those who gave orders came from Krustpils or adjacent parishes. Germans usually were not present in such operations involving small groups of Jews. Instead they allowed their local henchmen 'initiative' and gave them 'free rein'. In all Latvian regions the local murderers helped to relieve the psychological pressure on the executors from the ranks of 'the supreme race.' Regretfully, they often tried to please the occupation authorities by doing more than they were expected to.[47]

Latvian collaboration was self-organised. Alongside German *Einsatzgruppen* there were bodies like the 1,600-strong Arajs Commando led by a former Perkonkrusts member.[48] It was directly responsible for killing 26,000 people and was implicated with the deaths of 34,000 more.[49] While factors ranging from greed, sadism and anti-Semitism may have motivated the Arajs Commando, the court testimony of one volunteer was telling, and typical. He joined 'to fight against the units of the Red Army that have fallen behind, against Soviet activists and other supporters of the Soviet regime ...'.[50]

The entire population did not necessarily share the genocidal intent of the 'Self-Defence' squads. Another of Arajs Commando suggest that while its members 'realized that a countless number of people would be killed', they also knew that amongst the wider population murdering women and children was not supported, even though anti-Semitism was prevalent.[51] German officials complained that Latvians 'behaved passively towards the Jews' and that contrary to expectations local forces had spontaneously liquidated only 'a few thousand'.[52] Indeed, some 400 individual Latvians have been identified who, at great personal risk, shielded Jews from persecution.[53]

Nazi–Latvian relations were determined by the fact that the Baltic States were the only part of Eastern Europe intended for inclusion in the Reich after 'Germanisation' (a combination of assimilating the 50 per cent considered 'racially suitable', but exile or extermination for the rest).[54] The Nazi authorities therefore privileged Latvians over other East Europeans, but opposed their independence by the same token. Could this blocking of national aspirations be the basis for a people's war?

In Riga the Germans established a 'Self-Administration' under General Dankers. Most historians treat such bodies as quisling regimes, yet some Latvian historians describe the Self-Administration as a source of 'resistance'. Is this the case? When the occupiers called for police battalions to be assembled, minister Valdmanis suggested that the Latvians should demand concessions from the German side in return for co-operation.[55] It is difficult to allege that putting a price on collaboration (as opposed to offering it for free) amounted to resistance as such, but Dankers overruled Valdmanis in any case. By the end of the war 49 battalions, consisting of 15,000 individuals, were in operation. In fact, 'Police battalion' was a misnomer since the duties they performed included fighting on the Eastern front, guarding the Warsaw ghetto, and transporting Jews to the Treblinka death camp.[56]

The craven approach advocated by Dankers did not lessen the exploitation Latvia endured. The Nazis treated it as brutally as the Russians. When Audrini village hid Red Army soldiers all 235 inhabitants were killed and the buildings burned.[57] The anti-partisan Winter Magic operation on Latvia's Russian border involved flattening a 40km no-man's land. All women and children who did not leave went to concentration camps or to Germany, while the men were deported or shot.[58] Economic exploitation was equally shameless. The Germans retained property seized under Soviet occupation 'as spoils of war'.[59] It was subsequently calculated that Germany cost Latvia $660 million (compared to Russia's $1,000 million):[60] 265,000 Latvians were used as labour in the Reich.[61] After willing participants ran out there was, what Swain calls, a 'hunt for people ... Snatch squads would grab whoever was closest and load them on to the lorry at gun point.'[62]

Contemporaries made a direct comparison with the Russian era. One German official considered his country's 'activities were so brutal that the methods used can certainly be compared to the methods of the [Russian] Cheka'.[63] A communist prisoner told his jailors: 'We have treated our people badly, so badly that it would be a true art to treat them worse. You Germans have managed that.' Another suspected the Nazis 'were not German at all but merely Russians who had donned other uniforms'.[64] All this should have given ample reason to fight the Germans.

Yet opposition is difficult to find. In a desperate bid to unearth it, some Latvian historians claim to have discovered the elusive anti-fascist element in a body proposed by Himmler in May 1943 – the 'Latvian SS Volunteer Legion', a 150,000-strong force.[65] This is described as 'the legal centre of resistance to German rule'.[66] Why? Firstly, they insist it was not a volunteer force because the bulk of the Legion was conscripted.[67] Even if correct this does not make the conscripts resisters. The second ploy is to suggest Latvians confronted Germany over its formation. When the Self-Adminis-tration first considered Himmler's proposal it renewed the earlier debate about 'more recruits as a price for concessions, or concessions as the reward for more recruits'.[68] Valdmanis wanted Germany to give Latvia an improved puppet status, in return for drumming up 100,000 soldiers,[69] but the Self-Administration put a more modest proposal – that Latvia's General Bangerskis be given command. This was refused but the Self-Administration caved in and approved the Legion anyway. The Nazis made the smallest concession possible in return. Bangerskis was appointed General Inspector with the rank of SS Gruppenführer and Waffen-SS Lieutenant General.[70]

So what is left of 'the legal centre of resistance'? Only this: 'A Latvian spirit prevailed in the Legion from the outset. For example, orders were given in Latvian, the ranks, roll-calls and prayer hymn were the same as the old Latvian army'.[71] We are supposed to believe fighting alongside Nazi Germany was resistance, just so long as hymns were in Latvian!

A marginally more credible analysis of the Legion is that: 'Though fighting with an unwanted ally, Latvian soldiers fought heroically against their greater enemy, the Communists.'[72] This has been confirmed by a study of foreign veterans of the Waffen-SS which shows that while few Finns and Norwegians were enthused by the

Nazi 'crusade against Bolshevism', 100 per cent of the Latvians cited anti-communism as their motivation.[73]

Does the notion of resistance gain a scintilla of plausibility through the fact that Germany repressed certain leading Latvians? It is true the Nazis disliked those who put a price on collaboration. When Celmins opposed his Perkonkrusts party being banned he was sent to Flossenburg concentration camp. Valdmanis was deported in 1943. But Celmins was treated as 'an inmate of honour',[74] unlike the 1,100 Latvians who were killed at the camp.[75] Valdmanis's deportation meant his being rehoused in Berlin's most prestigious hotel.[76] Surely it is ridiculous to compare these people to genuine resistance fighters elsewhere, who faced torture and death.

Our final candidate for anti-Nazi resistance was the Central Council of Latvia (CCL). Bilmanis, the pre-war Latvian ambassador to the US, affirmed it stood for 'the principles of the Atlantic Charter [and] followed a policy based on the coming victory of Great Britain and the United States … .'[77] Backed by Latvia's four largest pre-war parties the CCL was, according to a current official history, 'the largest and most influential resistance organisation [whose] most important stand… was to fight against both occupying powers – Nazi and Soviet'. Unfortunately, the evidence offered for such even-handed opposition to totalitarianism is scanty. Even those who make the claim admit the CCL did not fight the Nazis[78] because 'military action would only serve to weaken Nazi Germany and therefore hasten the return of the Soviet regime'.[79]

The CCL's policy statement, signed by 190 prominent individuals, is much lauded but rarely quoted. In fact, it was anything but a declaration of opposition to Nazism. The opening warns: 'The enemy from the East is again threateningly approaching Latvia.' It then complains that Nazi blocking of nationalist aspirations was hindering 'complete mobilization of Latvia's inhabitants into the German armed forces'.[80] And the statement was a plea addressed to none other than Latvia's very own SS Gruppenführer and Waffen-SS Lieutenant General, Bangerskis. This was the man to whom the Germans turned in their final hours to head an '"ersatz" administration which could act as a cover for their illegal acts'.[81] It is surely a sign of the weakness of resistance that the Nazis in the Courland (Kurzeme) region of Latvia surrendered a day *after* Germany itself had done so and thus officially ended the Second World War in Europe.

There was another force claiming the mantle of resistance in Latvia – the pro-Soviet partisans. That they were a tool of Moscow, and consequently found recruitment problematic, is suggested by a detailed study showing they had great difficulty striking roots beyond the cities of Riga, Liepaja and the Russian border area of Latgale.[82] When the exiled Latvian CP Central Committee tried to establish bases within the country, partisans on the ground declared this to be impossible, so for a prolonged period operations were launched from neighbouring Belorussia.[83] Eventually Nazi brutality brought recruits, first from the ethnic Russian population, and then more broadly.[84] By 1943 there were more volunteers than arms to equip them because, according to a partisan report: 'in Latgale everyone is waiting for the Red Army to return, because of the taxes, the high prices and the demands of the Germans'.[85] By the end of the war units like the Red Arrow, composed of Red Army paratroops, Latvian communists and deserters from the Legion, were on the offensive in several areas.[86] In the Stalinist era the figure of 20,000 for the partisan movement was quoted,[87] but a more realistic figure was that given by its own staff on its dissolution in October 1944 – 5,900.[88]

Finally, the 40,000 plus Latvians who fought in the ranks of the Red Army's Latvian Riflemen Division and its other units must be mentioned. But they were no more independent of imperialism than the Latvian SS Legion. In that respect the clash of imperialisms and lack of a people's alternative, resulted in a Latvian civil war in which both sides killed their compatriots on behalf of a foreign oppressor.[89]

The pro-Soviet regime that replaced the Nazis after the Second World War so clearly lacked local support that it had serious difficulty finding sufficient native speakers to staff its offices. Half the key postholders in Daugavapils District were Russians and only one in six ethnically Latvian.[90] And its actions did nothing to garner popularity. The deportations started again, with 150,000 people sent to Siberia in the first five months of 1945.[91]

The experience of ordinary civilians makes clear the reason for the lack of a people's war. They were caught between two mighty imperialist blocs. This was brought home to the author by an interview in Riga with a woman who had a grandfather in the SS Legion and another in the Red Army. Her grandmother's farm was overrun by the Soviets in 1940 and by the Wehrmacht in 1941. Each plundered it, and in the last days of the war the partisans joined in. Another woman describes her family history after the arrival of the Nazis in these terms:

[M]y father was put in prison; my youngest brother was deported to Germany at the age of 18 years. After a while he was put into a camp of concentration at Stutthof in Danzig. I was deported to Germany to work on the land at the age of seventeen years. In 1944 the Communists occupied Latvia for the second time. In the confusion of war I did not hear anything about my family. Later I got news that my father had been deported on foot to Russia at the age of seventy-one and died somewhere on the side of the road.[92]

The postscript to the Second World War in Latvia was equally dismal. Without a people's war to counterbalance it, imperialism completely determined the people's fate. Latvian nationalists withdrew allegiance from the defeated Germans at the last minute, in the hope of finding a sympathetic response from the Allies. It made no difference. The Teheran and Potsdam conferences rubber-stamped the gains Stalin made through his pact with Hitler. That undermined the 'national partisans', some 20,000 of whom challenged Soviet control after 1944. Many had been trained by German counter-intelligence and by 1953 had killed 3,242 Red Army soldiers, a number roughly matched by losses in their own ranks.[93]

Latvians who had been fighting alongside the Germans constituted the largest single group of captured non-German enemy personnel.[94] When the Cold War got underway Britain announced that such Baltic Waffen-SS veterans were not war criminals after all, but 'displaced persons'. It accepted the argument of the pre-war Latvian ambassador that people like Arajs 'were great national patriots, men of quite modest means; anti-Bolshevik of course, but certainly not to be described as fascists'.[95] The US employed Valdmanis on the grounds that he had 'never participated in politics and his character and background are excellent.'[96]

Latvian historians have tried to normalise their country's experience by trying to tack a 'resistance' on to its past. This cannot be done because, unlike most other places, there was no movement independent of imperialism of whichever stripe. The result was annihilation for the Jews and devastation for the local inhabitants who remained alive. Latvia is a sort of negative proof for the parallel wars argument. It shows just how bad the Second World War might have been, and just how important people's war was elsewhere.

CONCLUSION

In this section we have seen four very different patterns of interrelationship between people's war and imperialist war. The common context was that each country was occupied by the Axis, though the response to that problem varied enormously.

At one end of the spectrum lay Yugoslavia where the people's war was able to take advantage of splits within imperialism to triumph. In Greece ELAS successfully confronted Axis imperialism, but was robbed of victory by British imperialism. The Polish people's war – the Warsaw Rising – lacked the weaponry to defeat the Nazis unaided, and was cynically abandoned by the imperialist power that could have helped. Latvia's case is perhaps the most tragic, if not the largest in scale. The crushing weight of successive imperialist invasions made it impossible for a people's alternative to emerge. The consequence was a horrific miniature Holocaust in which sections of the local population mistakenly took the side of one imperialist camp – the Nazis, in the belief they could punish Russian imperialism by murdering Jews.

The next examples to be considered are Allied countries. Neither Britain nor the USA endured Axis occupation such as Yugoslavia, Greece or Poland. Yet the phenomenon of the two wars emerged there too.

Part II

France, Britain and the USA – Divisions Within the Allied Camp

The co-existence of imperialist war and people's war in Western Europe during the Second World War was closely linked to the outcome of the First, which saw a monumental struggle between the established powers of Britain, France and Russia, against an ambitious newcomer – Germany. That clash of the rich and powerful caused enormous suffering to ordinary people, so that when proletarians and peasants seized the property of Russia's capitalists and landowners in 1917 it inspired a wave of international revolution. Although working class power was not secured in any other country than Russia, the establishment had been sufficiently frightened to back a right-wing backlash.

In Germany and Italy, where frustrated imperial ambitions and post-war class struggles were particularly concentrated, rabid counter-revolutionary movements came to power. Hitler and Mussolini had a dual goal: to build new empires at the expense of the old ones, and smash working class organisation. Thus in Western Europe the Axis offensive signified both a renewed bid for hegemony and a naked assault on labour. Twin threats inspired a twin response: inter-imperialist war and people's anti-fascist war.

6
France – Imperial Glory versus Resistance Ideology

Germany's stunning defeat of France in 1940 was one of the most dramatic events of the twentieth century. A mighty European power was humbled in just six weeks of *Blitzkrieg*. Much criticism has been made of the conservative mindset of French generals who thought in terms of the First World War trenches rather than the latest technology. Hitler's forces relied on planes and armoured columns that overcame these obstacles with terrifying ease. However, the rout cannot be understood simply in military terms. After all, the opposing forces were evenly matched: Germany fielded 114 divisions and 2,800 tanks; France 104 divisions and 3,000 tanks.[1]

France's fate was also influenced by a history of class war at home. On 6 February 1934 extreme right-wing groups attempted to storm the French Parliament but were blocked by police. In the melée 15 died and 1,400 were wounded.[2] Although the riot failed to reach its target it brought down Prime Minister Daladier. A united left demonstration of protest followed. The movement became unstoppable and a general strike of 4.5 million showed the determination of the working class to resist fascism.[3] This was but the prelude to still larger walkouts. In June 1936 alone there were 12,142 separate strikes. One participant described his feelings: 'Going on strike is joy itself. A pure joy, without any qualification ... The joy of standing before the boss with your head held high ... of walking among the silent machines with the rhythm of human life re-established.'[4] The same year a Popular Front government was elected.

The close linkage of anti-fascism, workers' struggle and communism led significant elements of the establishment to conclude that the threat to French state sovereignty from Hitler was the lesser of two evils. De Gaulle, France's future leader, described the phenomenon in this way: 'some circles were more inclined to see Stalin as the enemy than Hitler. They were much more concerned with the means of striking at Russia ... than with how to cope with the Reich.'[5]

This explains France's hesitancy during the first days of the Second World War. Despite formal declarations of belligerency over Poland in September 1939, both Britain (which had reluctantly given up appeasement only just before) and France fought a 'drôle de guerre' (phoney war). This involved fairly nominal military action against Germany. There was no such timidity when it came to opposing Russia's attack on faraway Finland. General Gamelin's plan to send forces was only thwarted when the Finns sued for peace in early 1940.[6]

Meanwhile the French government witch-hunted the Communist Party (*Parti Communiste Français* – PCF). On the eve of the Nazi invasion 300 Communist municipal councils with 2,778 councillors were suspended. Following 11,000 police raids the mass circulation *L'Humanité* and *Ce Soir* newspapers were banned along with 159 other communist publications.[7] For the first time, elected representatives of the Third Republic were expelled and jailed, and seven communist leaders were condemned to death.[8] Employers used this climate of intimidation to victimise the activists and strikers of 1936.[9]

It was against this background that Germany attacked in the summer of 1940. Its tactics were frighteningly effective, but more importantly, the French government was in a predicament aptly summarised by a refugee from the fighting:

> the ruling class in any democratic country … has to rely on the forces of the whole nation, it has to call upon all classes, it has to appeal above all to the working class. Or else it may try to come to terms with the threatening aggressor, appease him, strike a bargain with him – so as to avoid any shock to the social structure … .[10]

France's leaders were conscious of the choice. General Weygand, Commander-in-Chief, told de Gaulle of his fear that the country's military organisation 'might collapse suddenly and give a free run to anarchy and revolution'.[11] He was ready to capitulate, but one nagging doubt remained: 'Ah! If only I were sure the Germans would leave me the forces necessary for maintaining order!'[12] Finally putting this behind him, Weygand stampeded his colleagues into surrendering by claiming that Maurice Thorez, the PCF leader, had begun the revolution and seized the presidential palace – a pure invention![13]

In the midst of this turmoil Marshal Pétain exhibited a sure sense of French history. Ever since the 1789 revolution governments had had to decide between mass mobilisation to repel foreign threats, or suppressing the population to maintain class rule. In 1871, when the radical Paris Commune refused to compromise with German invaders, Thiers had worked with the latter to drown the Parisian working class in blood. Seven decades later Pétain argued that faced with Hitler: 'the only thing was to end, negotiate, and, if the case arose, crush the Commune [i.e. popular resistance], just as, in the same circumstances, Thiers had already done.'[14]

In an attempt to instil some backbone Churchill proposed a Franco-British Union with joint citizenship for all.[15] The French Cabinet reacted with comments such as: 'Better be a Nazi province. At least we know what that means.'[16] This wish was fulfilled. On 22 June 1940 an armistice with Germany was signed giving the Nazis a northern zone (covering about 55 per cent of the country) under their direct control. Pétain's collaborationist Vichy regime ran the South.

Among the working class a different view had been evident since the demonstrations of 1934 and strikes of 1936. When the British and French governments appeased Hitler over Czechoslovakia this drew a storm of cheers from the Centre and Right in France's parliament. The PCF leader countered: 'France had yielded to blackmail, betrayed an ally, opened the way to German domination, and perhaps irretrievably jeopardized her own interests.'[17] Five hundred and thirty five deputies backed the government position, while 75 (of which 73 were communist) voted against.

However, the left was thrown into disarray by the Hitler-Stalin Pact. While Russia and Germany savaged Poland, the PCF leadership called for peace with Hitler. When this came and Nazi jackboots echoed through the streets of Paris, the PCF wrote:

French imperialism has undergone its greatest defeat in History. The enemy, which in any imperialist war is to be found at home, is overthrown. The working class in France and the rest of the world must see this event as a victory and understand that it now faces one enemy less. It is important that everything is done to ensure that the fall of French imperialism is definitive.

There was a qualification added to this amazing statement:

A question to consider is whether it follows that the struggle of the French people has the same objective as the struggle of German imperialism against French imperialism. That is true only in the sense that German imperialism is a temporary ally.[18]

Not all communists accepted this nonsense. One third of the PCF's MPs rejected the idea that France was now occupied by 'a temporary ally'.[19]

In one respect the PCF was correct. French imperialism had been defeated by German imperialism, though its demise was not 'definitive'. On 18 June, Charles de Gaulle, a young French brigadier-general who had escaped to London, announced the existence of 'Free France' on the BBC: 'Whatever happens, the fire of the French resistance shines and flames.'[20]

De Gaulle's idea of what this resistance would consist of was rather strange. He appealed to the French Commander in Chief of North Africa, the High Commissioner of Syria/Lebanon, and the Governor General of French Indochina to form a 'Council for the Defence of the Empire'.[21] A week later he said 'powerful forces of resistance can be felt in the French Empire'. On 3 August de Gaulle reported: 'at numerous points in the Empire courageous men are standing up and are resolved to preserve France's colonies.'[22]

It is no surprise that Commanders in Chief, High Commissioners and Governor Generals did not rush to respond, and de Gaulle was forced to re-think how he might save French imperialism. He added two new components to his strategy. Firstly, the Nazis must be expelled and there was no alternative to mobilising the masses, but they must be kept from going too far. He did not abandon his initial defence of empire. Here is de Gaulle's own formulation:

> There would be the power of the enemy, which could be broken only by a long process ... There would be, on the part of those whose aim was subversion, the determination to side-track the national resistance in the direction of revolutionary chaos ... There would be, finally, the tendency of the great powers to take advantage of our weakness in order to push their interests at the expense of France.[23]

De Gaulle elaborated on the last point when he called on France's colonial administrators to 'defend her possessions directly against the enemy [and] deflect England – and perhaps one day America – from the temptation to make sure of them on their own account'.[24]

Though the brigadier-general would become its figurehead, in France the resistance developed independently. It began as a 'chain of solidarity' – escape routes for prisoners fleeing the occupier. Then 'networks' appeared to pass on information to the Allies. Movements organised around clandestine newspapers soon followed.[25]

In 1941, after Hitler's attack on Russia, the PCF joined the struggle and the level of direct action and sabotage rose dramatically. In one three month period, for example, the communists alone claimed to have mounted 1,500 actions – 158 de-railings; 180 locomotives and 1,200 wagonloads of materials or troops destroyed; 110 train engines and 3 bridges sabotaged; 800 German soldiers killed or wounded.[26] In 1942 an attempt to draft French labour for Germany drove many young men into joining the *maquis* guerrilla bands. Finally, in 1944 the resistance mounted important diversionary actions to assist the D-Day Normandy landing. This level of action required courage. Resisters were hunted by the Gestapo in the North, and Vichy's vicious *Milice* in the South. Torture, the concentration camp, or execution, were real possibilities: 60,000 PCF members were killed.[27]

The resistance functioned both 'as a movement' and 'as an organisation'.[28] As a movement it had a huge following. The daily circulation of its press was 600,000 in 1944, even though possession of a clandestine newspaper could mean arrest by the Gestapo.[29] Organised resisters were fewer, amounting to no more than 2 per cent of the adult population.[30]

Who were these individuals who, as an influential northern paper put it, were 'totally uncompromised, people who have proved their worth under the German occupation'?[31] Although the French resistance has been thoroughly studied, the question is difficult to answer because no-one carried membership cards. The evidence there is appears to be contradictory. Regarding social composition, Georges Bidault, president of the National Resistance Council (CNR), wrote:

> The Resistance included all types, all classes, all parties. There were workers side by side with peasants, teachers, journalists, civil servants, aristocrats, priests, and many more. For the most part they joined after making an individual choice born from their conscience in revolt.[32]

This diversity seems to challenge the assertion that there was an imperialist war pursued by the ruling class, and a people's war backed by the masses. That conclusion is incorrect, however.

The composition of the resistance was heterogeneous because the fight for national independence, and the betrayal of it by the ruling class, enraged many sections of the population. The national struggle and the class struggle overlapped. But, the social composition and the social outlook of the resistance were not identical.

However wide its membership, it was markedly left-wing in outlook, because the French establishment was thoroughly 'compromised by their solid public adherence to Vichy, and consequently German domination.'[33] Isolated resisters bore right-wing, even extreme right-wing ideas, but fighting fascism came more naturally to left-wing circles:[34]

> because it was a matter of pursuing a battle in which they were already engaged ... Those who had voted for the Popular Front in France and wished for a Republican victory in Spain were immediately hostile not only to Hitler's Europe, but also Pétain's France.[35]

The PCF component would be expected to use radical language, but it was not alone. The rest of the resistance produced documents that, as one historian puts it, 'are virtually unanimous in predicting and declaring revolution'.[36] Time and again the radicalising effect of occupation and capitulation was illustrated by resistance publications. One article entitled 'This War is Revolutionary' explained that it was 'a fight between two conceptions of the world ... authority and liberty'.[37] It went on: 'the masses will not act unless they know what the aim is, and it needs to be an ideal that will justify their efforts and great enough to encourage supreme sacrifice ... THE LIBERATION OF HUMANITY'.[38] This involved much further than expelling the Nazis:

- Liberation from material servitude: hunger, squalor, the machine
- Liberation from economic servitude: the unfair distribution of wealth, crisis and unemployment
- Liberation from social servitude: money, prejudice, religious intolerance
- And the selfishness of the possessors ...[39]

Libération, the paper of d'Astier, an ex-army aristocrat linked to trade union and socialist circles, took a similar position:

We will fight and struggle, with weapons in our hands for liberation from both internal and external enemies war and national imperialism, the power of money and economic imperialism dictatorship of any sort, whether state, social or religious.[40]

Such sentiments could not have been more distant from de Gaulle whose instincts were authoritarian through and through. His self-proclaimed motto was: 'Deliberation is the work of many men. Action, of one alone.'[41] However, he understood the need to blend radical language into his defence of French imperialism if he was to have any hope of controlling the movement. So he peppered speeches with phrases like this: 'In uniting for victory [the French people] unite for a revolution ... For us the ending of the war will mean not only the complete restoration of our national territory and its Empire, but the complete sovereignty of the people.'[42] But his words lacked conviction and a power struggle developed between de Gaulle in exile and the resistance in France.

Until his death at the hands of the Gestapo in 1943, de Gaulle's emissary was Jean Moulin. He commanded respect because, when Prefect of the Department of Eure-et-Loire at the outbreak of war, the Nazis locked him in a room with the mutilated torso of a woman and tortured him to sign a document blaming black French soldiers. Fearing he might succumb to pressure he attempted suicide.[43] De Gaulle wanted Moulin to ensure the resistance would work for the interests of imperial France rather than the people. His instructions were to: 'To reinstate France as a belligerent, to prevent her subversion ... .'[44]

The first step was to gain control. Moulin's orders were to bring the numerous groups of resisters under 'a single central authority',[45] without which they might 'slip into the anarchy of the "great companies" or ... Communist ascendancy'.[46] He first amalgamated southern non-communist groups into the United Resistance Movement (MUR). In May 1943 he formed the National Resistance Council (CNR), which included the communists.

Moulin's second task was to secure de Gaulle's political authority in the military sphere, by excluding ideological debate and discussion: 'the separation of the movement's political and military activities must result in an autonomous military organisation linked to London from whence it would receive and execute orders.'[47] This would be the hierarchical 'Secret Army' with which de Gaulle hoped to neutralise the effectiveness of radical elements.

The resistance accepted a more unified structure in the interests of co-ordinated action, but bitterly opposed the separation of military and political functions. Frenay of the MUR insisted that: 'The Secret Army is an integral part of the United Movement because the latter created all its parts, determined its structure, its orientation, shaped its cadres and recruited its troops.'[48] Frenay's vision of warfare was sharply different to de Gaulle's:

> With us, discipline is achieved through trust and friendship. There is no sense of subordination in the military sense of the term. It is not possible – and we have ample experience of this – to impose officers at any level of our hierarchy. What can be done in a regiment or government office cannot be achieved here.[49]

Different armies use different techniques, as another resistance leader explained:

> On the one hand there were those, usually former officers, who saw it as a point of honour to turn out 'their boys' ... in a classic conventional army ... Others were conscious of participating in a revolutionary war, and for some of them, a veritable international civil war ... and in the area of tactics employed exclusively guerrilla methods.[50]

Neither side won the debate outright and separate militias persisted, ranging from the de Gaulle's Secret Army, to the PCF-led 'Franc-Tireurs et Partisans' (FTP). Others like the MUR sat in between. Each adopted a different strategy. The Secret Army was to serve as de Gaulle's tool and adopted a classic attentist approach. It waited for the brigadier-general to cross the Channel on D-Day ('Jour J' in French).[51] This ran so counter to the spirit of the resistance that Moulin was forced to deny rumours 'that the intention was to forbid any action by Secret Army militants while they waited for Jour J ... which is something that is practically impossible anyway'.[52]

The communist-led movements ignored this wait-and-see attitude and launched high profile actions, often at extremely high cost to themselves.[53] They might well have achieved the 'ascendancy' that de Gaulle feared (and which was obtained in places like Yugoslavia and Greece) had not the US-led invasion of North Africa (Operation Torch) supervened in November 1943.

Torch went smoothly because in Algiers pro-Gaullist officers, in combination with a resistance movement led by the Jewish Aboulker brothers, arrested the top Vichy officials as well as seizing barracks and command posts.[54] No sooner had the Americans landed than they began talks with one of the prisoners, Admiral Darlan. This was an extraordinarily insensitive decision. Even Funk, a semi-apologist for the US's action, has to admit:

> As the chief architect of Pétain's policy, Darlan [had] exerted his utmost skill to convince the Axis of France's willingness to cooperate with the Nazi New Order... he pursued exactly the same policies for which Laval, Pétain and other Vichyites were later indicted and for which Laval was hanged. To the French resister Darlan became the epitome of collaboration and surrender.[55]

Furthermore, Darlan was the anointed heir of Pétain, yet the US freed him and returned the government of North Africa to his hands! Privately Morgenthau, US Secretary of the Treasury, grumbled, if 'we are going to sit back and favor these Fascists ... what's the use of fighting just to put that kind of people back in power?'[56]

The resistance movement was stunned, though this outcome could have been predicted. Roosevelt had maintained close relations with Vichy from the start by signing a trade agreement in 1941.[57] The US enthronement of Darlan infuriated the French resistance: 'In no case will we agree to consider the about-face of those responsible for our political and military betrayal an excuse for their past crimes ... .'[58] Revenge came when the Admiral was assassinated by a resistance fighter.[59] The US now turned to General Giraud, who at least had not courted Nazis and was respected for a spectacular escape from their prison. However, according to Funk, 'Giraud's attitude – toward Pétain, toward Vichy, toward democracy, toward anti-Semitism – did not differ distinguishably from Darlan's'.[60] A charitable interpretation of Roosevelt's actions would be that he hoped to prise Vichy away from Germany. More likely, the US wanted its own clients in place as an alternative to the British protégé de Gaulle. Certainly, Roosevelt refused any dealings with 'dissident groups which set themselves up as Governments',[61] which was code for de Gaulle. Clearly, the US would take anyone who would do their bidding, rather than see a restored a rival imperialism in France.

Operation Torch did not bring about the Atlantic Charter's promise of 'the right of all peoples to choose the form of government under which they will live'. Under Giraud seven million Algerians continued under the yoke of US-backed French colonialism and its 600,000 French settlers.[62] Vichy's anti-Semitic laws remained intact, as did concentration camps containing elected communist deputies. They were now joined by Gaullists, and the very resistance fighters who had assisted the Allied landing.[63]

In mainland France the Nazis responded to Operation Torch by brushing aside the Vichy fig leaf and took control of the entire country.[64] As the same time the shock of the Darlan incident rallied all the resistance groups to de Gaulle. This gave him a powerful enough base to marginalise Giraud and establish a provisional French government in North Africa. The legitimacy conferred by the newly-formed CNR proved crucial in making de Gaulle the national figurehead. But once his hegemony was secure he completely ignored his followers. Moulin was killed by the Gestapo and his replacement, Bidault, recounts that he wrote 'hundreds of coded telegrams to the French government in exile ... I did get one answer and only one: the only reply that ever reached me was "Reduce traffic".'[65]

De Gaulle eventually deigned to communicate with 'his' resistance movement at the time of the Normandy landings in summer 1944. General Eisenhower wanted maximum disruption of the Wehrmacht from within France. At great personal cost all the resistance movements threw themselves into battle. In unequal combat thousands died at places like Vercors. Yet still more joined the fray so that the 'interior forces' rose from 140,000 to 400,000 between June and September.[66] The insurrection was heavily reliant on Allied arms deliveries, but weapons were distributed on a highly selective basis. Even Frenay, a man much closer to Gaullism than communism, complained that until shortly before D-Day only de Gaulle's direct representatives, who were committed to attentism rather than action, received vital radios, money and arms.[67] Furthermore, although parachute drops accelerated[68] supplies were still inadequate, something ascribed to the 'visceral distrust' the US had of the resistance.[69]

Corsica offered a glimpse of liberation by people's war (as opposed to Operation Torch). The island was jointly occupied by German and Italian troops. When Mussolini fell, and the Italian government switched sides, the broad communist-initiated resistance movement moved into action. Partisan bands, in alliance with Italian troops, confronted the Wehrmacht and between 9 September and 4 October 1943, killed a thousand Germans (for a loss of 170 *maquis*).[70] An uprising in the capital, Ajaccio, saw the election by mass meeting of leaders who refused to deal with any Corsican equivalent of

Darlan: 'We can't mount an effective defence of the island unless proven patriots take command of the levers of power. We can't trust a local government that did nothing to resist in 1940 ... Let's kick out the Vichyists!'[71]

De Gaulle was dismayed, not because of the rejection of Vichy, but because he was not in control. He announced that he did not wish to 'see this precedent followed tomorrow in metropolitan France'.[72] This difference between his war and that of the Corsicans, was played out on a grander scale during the liberation of Paris.

By August 1944 Nazi authority was disintegrating in the French capital in the face of a restless population.[73] De Gaulle feared the resistance would free Paris before imperialist forces could reach it. When mass strikes of police, postal and metro workers erupted in mid-August[74] de Gaulle ordered them to: 'Return to work immediately and maintain order until the Allies arrive.'[75] This command was ignored, and on 19 August a general insurrection began. Headed by Rol-Tanguy, a communist veteran of the Spanish civil war, 20,000 fighters (of whom only one tenth were armed[76]) freed the capital over an eight-day period.

The German commander, von Choltitz, was under orders to demolish Paris rather than lose it. Despite being a veteran of Stalingrad, and a man who had wreaked horrific carnage upon Warsaw,[77] he realised this policy could not be implemented and that a more likely outcome would be that his forces would be trapped by the resistance and destroyed. At the critical moment Gaullist representatives threw von Choltitz a lifeline. Despite the Allied policy of unconditional surrender, they offered him a truce. He could evacuate in good order if he promised not to sack the town. Accordingly, the resistance was ordered to 'cease fire against the occupier'. Its leaders were outraged, one writing that: 'It was impossible to imagine a greater divorce between the action sustained by the masses and the coterie which had positioned itself between them and the enemy.'[78]

In the confusion, the Germans regained the upper hand for the first time. On the night of 20/21 August, 99 resistance fighters lost their lives as against five Germans.[79] So the next day the uprising resumed and completed the job that had been so dangerously interrupted. It was only on the evening of 24 August that regular French troops (General Leclerc's Second Armoured Division) reached the heart of the city. The final tally for the liberation of Paris was 1,483 French lives compared to 2,788 Germans.[80]

Now that the hated enemy had been disposed of, would former differences disappear in the glow of national unity? Not at all!

While the triumphant resistance waited for de Gaulle at the Hotel de Ville, the symbol of Parisian revolt for three centuries, the brigadier-general was elsewhere. First he met von Choltitz's aide-de-camp, then leading financiers, and then the Director of the Bank of Indochina, before heading to the War Ministry.[81] Only after greeting the Parisian police, who had helped the Nazis maintain order, did he deign to visit the Hotel de Ville.[82] De Gaulle did not use the occasion to congratulate the fighters, but to complain that Rol-Tanguy had had the temerity to receive the German surrender as an equal alongside the 'legitimate', 'regular' soldier, Leclerc.[83]

This was a foretaste of things to come. Three days later, de Gaulle met the resistance again. According to his own account he told the meeting: 'The militias had no further object. The existing ones would be dissolved [and] after having made note of the accordant or protesting observations of the members of the [CNR] I put an end to the audience.'[84] It was not long before the resistance was disarmed. Although this was less violent than in Greece, the process was essentially the same. With the PCF, the main party of the resistance, accepting Stalin's view that France lay in the Western capitalist camp, its fighters simply accepted de Gaulle's demands.[85]

The different conceptions of the Second World War found further expression on the very last day of the war in the West. Amidst the celebrations on 8 May 1945 French troops opened fire on jubilant crowds in Sétif, Algeria, killing thousands.

It might seem that French imperialism had vanquished the people's war completely, yet the impact of the latter was long-lasting. In the words of a resister, Stéphane Hessel, the CNR programme of 1944 'set the principles and values that formed the basis of our modern democracy' with its wide-ranging reforms in the economy, welfare and education. In 2010 Hessel suggested that despite the passage of 65 years it required the current economic crisis to threaten the final vestiges of that heritage.[86] This statement is true for most of Western Europe, where a post-war 'social democratic consensus' prevailed after 1945, and is today being fought over once more.

7
Britain – The Myth of Unity

Unlike France, Britain was not occupied by the Nazis. Therefore no radical resistance movement developed independently of an official government-in-exile. Hints of class tension were smoothed over. Thus, on the eve of war, when Labour's Arthur Greenwood rose to denounce the arch-appeaser and Tory PM, Neville Chamberlain, dissident Tory MPs shouted 'Speak for England', while Labour MPs shouted 'Speak for the workers'.[1] In 1940 both combined to back a coalition with Churchill, as new Prime Minister. He affirmed: 'This is not a war of chieftains or of princes, of dynasties or national ambition; it is a war of peoples and of causes,'[2] and from Labour's ranks the former union leader Bevin promised that 'British Labour would not fight an imperialist war'.[3] National harmony was also the theme of *Britain Under Fire,* a pictorial record of the blitz. It was fronted by a photo captioned 'their Majesties outside Buckingham Palace ... subject to identical trials and chances'.[4]

This heart-warming picture seemed to be confirmed when their Majesties visited the wreckage of Southampton. Journalists reported: 'excited multitudes [who] lined the wintry streets which re-echoed to volley after volley of cheers and repeated cries of "God save the King".'[5] However, Southampton's indefatigable Mass Observation volunteers, who looked past the media hype to gauge the popular mood, considered this comment more typical: 'If they gave new furniture, good food and no fuss, we'd be truly grateful.'[6]

The nature of modern warfare meant that even without occupation British people experienced the disjuncture between imperialism and their own needs in a way not entirely dissimilar to France. As one writer put it: 'The Front is not a distant battle field [but] part of our daily lives; its dug-outs and First Aid posts are in every street; its trenches and encampments occupy sections of every city park and every village green ... .'[7]

In London the Blitz threatened to dispel the mirage of unity. A senior diplomat noted privately that in government circles: 'Everybody is worried about the feeling in the East End, where there is much bitterness. It is said that even the King and Queen were booed the other day when they visited the destroyed areas.' He was therefore mightily relieved when the Luftwaffe targeted the much wealthier West End: 'if only the Germans had had the sense not to bomb west of London Bridge there might have been a revolution in this country. As it is, they have smashed about Bond St and Park Lane and readjusted the balance.'[8]

To make the myth that everyone, 'however rich or privileged, was in it together'[9] plausible required the cultivation of amnesia. On becoming PM Churchill warned his colleagues: 'If we open a quarrel between the past and the present, we shall find that we have lost the future'.[10] He was right to be cautious. He had selected a Cabinet that included notorious appeasers, such as Chamberlain and Halifax, while 21 of the 36 ministerial posts went to people who had served under the previous PM.

Churchill's cupboard had its own skeletons, too. After visiting Mussolini in 1927 he wrote he 'could not help being charmed, like so many other people have been, by his gentle and simple bearing and by his calm, detached poise'. He told the inventor of fascism that, '[i]f I had been an Italian, I am sure that I should have been whole-heartedly with you from start to finish in your triumphant struggle against...Leninism'.[11] Nine years later, during the Italian aggression against Abyssinia, Churchill opposed sanctions against Italy and described the Hoare-Laval pact (an attempt to appease the fascists by handing much of the country over), as 'a very shrewd, far-seeing agreement ...'.[12] Nothing Mussolini did could dissuade Churchill from his admiration. Despite the bitter fighting in North Africa that culminated in the Battle of El Alamein, when the Duce fell in 1943 the British PM swore that: 'Even when the issue of the war became certain, Mussolini would have been welcomed by the Allies'.[13] Evidently, determined action against fascism was not his primary motivation during the Second World War.

Neither were the rights of small nations a factor. We shall consider his contemptuous dismissal of Indian nationalism later, but what he had said about the demand for Irish independence in 1921 was also revealing: 'What an idiotic and what a hideous prospect is unfolded to our eyes. What a crime we should commit if, for the sake of a brief interval of relief from worry and strife, we condemned ourselves and our children after us to such misfortunes. We should be ripping up the British Empire.'[14] Therefore, Eire 'must be closely laced with cordons of blockhouses and barbed wire; a systematic rummaging and question of every individual must be put in force'.[15]

Yet Churchill *was* strongly against appeasing Hitler and his 'rule of terrorism and concentration camps'.[16] His opposition to the Führer was unwavering, but only because Germany directly threatened Britain's power.[17] Churchill's wartime speeches are justifiably famous, yet the familiar ringing phrases are lifted out of context and key sentences left incomplete. After every stirring appeal there was a reference to Empire. Here are a few examples:

> *I have nothing to offer but blood, toil, tears and sweat* ... for without victory there can be no survival – let that be realized – no survival for the British Empire, no survival for all that the British Empire has stood for.[18]

> *The Battle of Britain is about to begin.* Upon this battle depends the survival of Christian civilisation. Upon it depends our own British life and the long continuity of our institutions and our Empire.[19]

> Let us therefore brace ourselves to our duty and so bear ourselves that if the British Commonwealth and Empire lasts for a thousand years, men will say, *'This was their finest hour'*.[20]

Churchill was not as openly blunt as Amery who declared, once the defensive Battle of Britain had been won, that 'The Battle of Empire comes next'.[21] He did insist, however: 'We mean to hold our own. I have not become the King's First Minister in order to preside over the liquidation of the British Empire.'[22]

The imperialist character of the British government's war was not simply a matter of personal predilection but was structured by grand strategy past and present. For centuries overseas colonies had required a strong Royal Navy, and the military budget was apportioned accordingly.[23] Next in line came the RAF; while the army, the key element in any war with a continental power like Germany, came a poor third. Thus in the decade 1923–1933 the fleet took 58 per cent of spending, the airforce 33 per cent and the army just 8 per cent.[24] When the Second World War began only 107,000 of Britain's 387,000 troops were stationed at home.[25] So the Expeditionary Force sent to the Continent could provide no more than auxiliary support to sit out the phoney war with the French. When this '*Sitzkrieg*' ended in 1940, it had to scramble from the beaches of Dunkirk.

After this there was little choice but to try and wear down the German war machine from afar. One historian suggests it was essential 'to avoid the risk of *any* confrontation with the German Army anywhere'.[26] Skirmishes with the Wehrmacht were therefore by accident rather than design. One example was Norway, which Britain had intended to seize before the Nazis, but found on arrival to be already occupied. London's chief land operation was far away from Europe, in the Libyan desert defending the route to India from Italians. And only when the latter called in Rommel's Panzer divisions did engagement with the German army occur there.

A new opportunity to confront Germany on more advantageous terms arose after 1941 when Hitler attacked Russia and the USA joined the war. With 240 Nazi divisions fighting in the East (as compared to just 50 guarding the West), Stalin begged for soldiers to be sent across the Channel to open a second front. When Britain prevaricated some said it was happy 'to fight to the last drop of Russian blood'. Churchill's petulant, though technically accurate, reply was that the Russians 'certainly have no right to reproach us. They brought their own fate upon themselves when by their pact with Ribbentrop they let Hitler loose on Poland and so started the war... .'[27]

Further, he accused the Soviets of following 'lines of ruthless self-interest in disregard of the rights of small States for which Great Britain and France were fighting as well as for themselves ...'.[28] This was rich coming from a government which postponed the second front on the ground that British troops were 'spread across a distance of some 6,300 miles from Gibraltar to Calcutta',[29] and:

> We have to maintain our armies in the Middle East and hold a line from the Caspian to the Western Desert ... Great efforts will be needed to maintain the existing strength at home while supplying the drafts for the Middle East, India, and other garrisons abroad, e.g. Iceland, Gibraltar, Malta, Aden, Singapore, Hong Kong ... .[30]

No-one was convinced when Churchill tried to pass off Operation Torch, the landing in French North Africa, as a 'full discharge of our obligations as Allies to Russia.'[31]

Britain's chief strategy bore a feature typical of imperialist war – contempt for human life, and civilians in particular. It involved 'area bombing' – the use of the RAF to flatten German cities rather than hit specific military targets. This tactic was predicted in 1932 by the then PM, Baldwin. He declared laconically that because 'the bomber always gets through': 'The only defence is in offence, which means that you have to kill more women and children more quickly than the enemy if you want to save yourselves. I just mention that ... so that people may realize what is waiting for them when the next war comes.'[32]

Despite initial doubts, Churchill turned to this method in 1940 because: 'We have no Continental Army which can defeat the German military power [but] there is one thing that will bring him back and bring him down, and that is an absolutely devastating, exterminating attack by very heavy bombers.'[33] Bomber Command translated this into practice: 'the aiming-points are to be the built-up areas, not, for instance, the dockyards or aircraft factories ... This must be made quite clear ... .'[34] Three-quarters of bombs fell on civilian targets,[35] the ultimate intention being to render 25 million homeless, kill 900,000, and injure one million more.[36]

It has been alleged, in mitigation, that practical factors made area bombing unavoidable. German anti-aircraft defences made daylight raids on military installations too costly, but night-time attacks could not hit precise military targets. Big cities were therefore a more realistic goal.[37] Nonetheless, the technical capabilities of the British military were shaped by Empire and were inseparable from it.

Even if area bombing had been tenable as the only viable tactic, it lost all credence after the Normandy landings in the summer of 1944. Yet it carried on relentlessly under Arthur 'Bomber' Harris of Bomber Command. He boasted that his boys had 'virtually destroyed 45 out of the leading 60 German cities. *In spite of invasion diversions* we have so far managed to keep up and even exceed our average of two and a half cities devastated a month... .'[38] On 13 February 1945 British and US bombers generated a firestorm that destroyed Dresden's cultural centre, the Altstadt, along with 19 hospitals, 39 schools and residential areas. Key military and transport installations remained intact. Between 35,000 and 70,000 people died, of whom just 100 were soldiers.[39]

The bombing campaign only ceased when Churchill realised nothing would be left to plunder after victory:[40] '... we shall come into control of an utterly ruined land. We shall not, for instance, be able to get housing materials out of Germany for our own needs because some temporary provision would have to be made for the Germans themselves.'[41] Belatedly he argued for 'more precise concentration upon military objectives, such as oil and communications behind the immediate battle-zone, rather than on mere acts of terror and wanton destruction, however impressive'.[42]

Could it at least be argued that all this suffering speeded the end of Nazism? It was claimed that area bombing would break morale and slow armaments production. But Germany's output actually rose under the hail of bombs: from an index of 100 in January 1942, to 153 in July 1943, and 332 in July 1944.[43] Far from morale being broken, Germany's population was steeled. Hitler's Armaments Minister wrote that, 'the estimated loss of 9 per cent of our production capacity was amply balanced out by increased effort.'[44] Max Hastings concludes that: 'Bomber Command's principal task and principal achievement had been to impress the British people and their Allies, rather than to damage the enemy'.[45]

When it came, German defeat was largely due to the Red Army, which fought the most crucial battles, at Stalingrad and Kursk (1942–43). Soviet military deaths amounted to 13.6 million out of 20 million under arms (an attrition rate of 68 per cent). British military strength was 4.7 million and its forces endured 271,000 deaths (an attrition rate of 6 per cent).[46] Refusing to open a second front until Russia was winning on its own (and marching towards Western Europe), plus the deliberate slaughter of civilians to minimal military effect, were chilling evidence of the nature of the war being fought by Churchill. His government was driven, above all, by the need to impress friend and foe of Britain's great power status.

The motives of most British people were not the same as their government's. A variety of writers expressed the notion that: 'The world is confronted by a clash between two irreconcilable ideals: humanism and anti-humanism.'[47] The war was about 'accepting a way of life determined by love rather than power'.[48] Mass Observers found people largely free of the jingoism of the First World War: 'There is no gushing, sweeping-away dynamo of "patriotism", no satisfied gush of the primitive, the hidden violent, the anti-hun and "destroy the swines".'[49] This should not be taken as cool detachment – quite the contrary. In 1938, 75 per cent of those asked about foreign affairs were either bewildered or could make no comment. In 1944 85 per cent had definite views and 'an overwhelming majority are in favour of international cooperation …'.[50]

Ordinary people remembered that during the 1930s appeasement abroad walked hand in hand with attacks on living standards at home. Therefore, when appeasement was discredited they wanted to confront the home-grown 'little Hitlers' who had conducted a blitzkrieg against labour.[51] In Glasgow a Mass Observation study of 1941 reported:

The workers do not believe that the employers care a fig for the men, or for anything else than saving their skins now by at last producing the vessels, metals, cargo discharges; and ... a surprising number of men do not even believe that the employers really care about saving their skins, because 'they would be just as happy under Hitler' – here left wing propaganda has certainly had an effect in equating the employer with the friend of Fascism.[52]

Based on experience after the 1914–18 war many feared what the Second World War might bring. *Ritzkrieg*, a satirical book of 1940, warned that if the establishment had its way once more: 'The People's War was to have become the Best People's War, and the peace to follow it... a return to Olde England and the aristocratic regime, without the alteration of one jot or title.'[53] Mass Observation found it was not that 'workers are against the war or for peace. They want it as much as anyone... [but they] are *also* having a war of their own ... .'[54] And this was the crux of the matter. Most were not fighting to defend the Britain of the 1930s or colonial rule. In 1944, a Mass Observer noted, '[t]he things that people want put right *first* are the things that went wrong last time ... Chief among these is certainty of a job, and then certainty of a decent house to live in.'[55]

So in place of area bombing and Empire, ordinary people focused on a fight for justice and decency. Remarkably, the inhabitants of cities most damaged by the Blitz were least favourable to reprisals. In London where 1.4 million (one in six) were rendered homeless, only a minority wanted to fight back in kind.[56] Individual comments recorded by Mass Observers showed how ordinary people's views clashed with the government's approach:

PEACE AIMS: an armed League of Nations to precede Socialism.
RECONSTRUCTION AT HOME: every man who has been a worker should be allowed enough to live in comfort for the rest of his life.
THE END OF THE WAR: financiers... are running the war, and when they have made as much money as they want, the war will stop.[57]

The Labour Party sought to bridge the widening gap between imperial war and the people's war, as this rather confusing contribution by Bevin shows: 'England's experience in the realm of giving liberty is probably the greatest. We have built up a great empire over the last three or four hundred years ... .'[58] However nonsensical, such statements do show an awareness of the two wars.

British communism's position was even more complicated. At the outbreak of war Harry Pollitt was its leader and an enthusiastic advocate of people's war:

> Whatever the motive of the present rulers of Britain and France... [T]o stand aside from this conflict, to contribute only revolutionary sounding phrases while the fascist beast rides roughshod over Europe, would be the betrayal of everything our forbears have fought to achieve in the course of long years of struggle against capitalism.[59]

Since this contradicted the Hitler-Stalin Pact, Pollitt was replaced. The October 1939 CP manifesto called for: 'a united movement of the people to compel the immediate ending of the war ... to bring down the Chamberlain government, to compel new elections and to prepare the establishment of a new government which shall make immediate peace'.[60]

In June 1941 Moscow's line changed again and the Party reverted to supporting anti-fascist struggle, but with all references to 'struggle against capitalism' deleted. Pollitt returned to promote unity with 'all who are for Hitler's defeat. Our fight is not against the Churchill Government...Now it is a people's war.'[61] His definition does not accord with the one used in this book, but these alternating CP interpretations shows how difficult it was to reconcile people's war and imperialist war.

The bosses were divided too. This emerged in a debate over Joint Production Committees, bodies set up to encourage worker-employer collaboration. The director of the Engineering Employers' Federation insisted he 'was not going to be a party to handing over the production of the factory and the problems concerning production to shop stewards or anyone else'.[62] Another managing director took the contrary view: 'If industry doesn't plan for revolution, there'll be revolution ... And we can only avoid it by anticipating it, by meeting the needs of the people and the times, by taking the great changes that are going to be forced on us anyway if we don't do it ourselves.'[63]

On the workers' side the Manchester District Committee of the Amalgamated Engineering Union (AEU) warned perceptively that:

> we are working under a capitalist system, more highly organised for exploitation, even than in peace time. Every advantage that the employers can secure from collaboration and relaxation [of

trade union vigilance] will be, and is being, ruthlessly acquired, throughout the industry ... For the workers it is truly a war on two fronts, or, if you like, back and front.

Despite these misgivings the conclusion drawn was that Joint Production Committees should be supported to increase production and prevent a Nazi victory.[64] The conundrum is perhaps explained by this opinion picked up by a Mass Observation volunteer in 1944: 'Away from selfishness. In the factories of Britain men and women worked long hours, not for a boss, not for any one person's private advantage, but for <u>everyone</u> ... .'[65]

The strong belief that the people's will could be impressed upon the Second World War did not depend on ideas alone. With 30 per cent of the male workforce called up,[66] and an unquenchable demand for industrial output, ordinary people had a new-found economic clout and confidence. The signs of this were everywhere. When homeless Londoners invaded the underground stations to use them as shelters the government objected, but eventually gave in.[67] Calder recounts how:

Father John Groser, one of the historic figures of the 'blitz' took the law into his own hands. He smashed open a local depot. He lit a bonfire outside his church and fed the hungry. There wasn't a cabinet minister or an official who would have dared to stand in his war or to challenge this 'illicit' act. Similarly, in another London borough a local official of the Ministry of Food found a crowd of homeless uncared for. He broke open a block of flats. He put them in. He got hold of furniture by hook or by crook, he got the electricity, gas and water supply turned on, and he brought them food.[68]

It was in industry that the clash between the two wars was most strongly expressed. The CP's drive for maximum production led it to strive 'might and main to avoid stoppages'[69] and industrialists gratefully rewarded it with positive testimonials.[70] There was an alternative analysis expressed. At one shop stewards' meeting a speaker referred to the appeasement of Hitler at Munich in 1938: 'There were Municheers still in the Government and there were Municheers still running business ... .'[71] This distrust was clearly a common view, and the public often took the side of the workers during industrial disputes.[72]

While the CP's links with Russia gave it a rising prestige that more than compensated for losses sustained by opposing strikes, its stance opened the way for other political forces to channel workers' discontent. The Trotskyist movement was miniscule but its position on the war enabled it to lead a series of strikes far beyond its numbers.[73] According to the movement's historians, British Trotskyists 'differentiated between the defencism of the capitalists and that of the workers, which "stems largely from entirely progressive motives of preserving their own class organisations and democratic rights from destruction at the hands of fascism".'[74]

There were 900 strikes in the first months of war. By 1944 the figure had risen to 2,000 (with 3.7 million days of lost production). This was in spite of the combined efforts of Labour, the CP, and Regulation 1AA which, by virtually outlawing stoppages has been described as '... the most powerful anti-strike weapon possessed by any government since the 1799 Combination Acts'.[75] One historian writes that: 'the tempo of activity and discussion increased dramatically, sometimes giving a toehold to some extreme left political agitators [though] it was at this point too early to speak, as some of these agitators did, of a "second front at home".'[76]

Radicalism never matched that seen in the First World War because of the 'contradictory duality' of the Second World War.[77] Nevertheless, the very idea of a 'second front at home' spoke volumes.

Britain's Middle East Army also experienced war in parallel. The mission was to protect Egypt and the sea route to India, the 'jewel in the Crown' of the Empire. Its commanders have been described in these terms:

> Almost to a man the officers were tall, upper-class Englishmen who came to a formal dinner wearing the same skin-tight crimson trews that had seen service in the Crimea. They had almost all attended the same top six English public schools ... The Nottingham-based Sherwood Rangers under the Earl of Yarborough had even tried to take with them to Palestine a pack of foxhounds belonging to the Brocklesby Hunt.[78]

The playing fields of Eton proved a poor preparation for total war. The fall of Tobruk was, after Singapore, the largest British capitulation in the Second World War,[79] and German panzers came within 10km of Cairo. The morale of Britain's 'desert rats' had to be rapidly reconstituted, so Field Marshal Montgomery motivated his troops by giving them a purpose for risking their lives. This was explained to them by the newly founded Army Bureau of Current Affairs (ABCA), a body largely run by radically-minded tutors committed to making the Second World War a people's war.[80] The King's Regulations forbad political activity by soldiers, but in the highly charged atmosphere of the time the borderline between current affairs and politics was easily blurred.

A rank and file soldier's movement developed and found its voice in a profusion of information sheets and wall newspapers. They were for a people's war as opposed to an imperialist one. For example, the founding statement of the Soldiers' Anti-Fascist Movement said:

> We shall campaign for a maximum war effort, expose slackness and reactionary influences in the fighting services. Our news on international affairs will be from the anti-fascist viewpoint... We shall do all we can to speed victory over fascism, victory that must be followed by a People's Peace.[81]

The very fact of soldiers openly discussing military policy was insubordination, as was the widespread demand for a second front in opposition to Churchill's foot-dragging.[82]

However, it did not stop there. Allied rhetoric asserted this was a fight for democracy. If so, some soldiers concluded, democracy could and should be practiced by those doing the fighting. A mock soldiers' parliament was set up in Cairo in late 1943. Although others appeared elsewhere, what made the Egyptian experiment unique was the lack of officer influence. It was a 'parliament of Other Ranks in the tradition of the English Revolution'.[83]

The tenor of the proceedings can be gauged from the Bills it 'passed'. The first called for public ownership of businesses. On 1 December the distributive trades were nationalised. An Inheritance Restriction Bill followed.[84] There were also plans to grant independence to India, abolish private schools and nationalise coal, steel, transport and the banks.[85] An 'election' by mass meeting was held. The joint Labour/CP ticket won 119 seats, Commonwealth (a new party opposing the Churchill-led coalition from the left) 55, Liberals 38 and Conservatives just 17.[86] Simultaneously, in the 'real' parliament at Westminster, a move to permit off-duty soldiers to engage in politics was proposed by no less than a Tory MP. He argued it 'could do no harm and might do a great deal of good, and which ought to be his by right – that is to say if we are indeed fighting for democracy'.[87]

Unsurprisingly this 'real' proposal was defeated. An imperial war requires a tame army that unquestioningly follows ruling class orders. The advocates of people's war had to be silenced. In February 1944 the Commander in Chief of Middle East Forces ordered: 'that the name of parliament must not be used; that there must be no publicity of any kind, even war correspondents being excluded, and that the proceedings must be supervised and directed by an Army education officer.'[88]

When this was read out to the Cairo Parliament the soldiers protested 600 to one. That one vote was the brigadier who had presented the order. Members of the organising committee were immediately transferred, as was the new 'Prime Minister'. The man who moved bank nationalisation, Leo Abse, was spirited away under 'open arrest', and deported back to Britain.[89]

This Forces Parliament was broken up and the old order restored. However, discontent bubbled up again. When news of Labour's election victory in Britain reached Egypt in 1945, soldiers stopped saluting officers for about ten days.[90] Real fury erupted after Victory over Japan Day, August 1945, when soldiers realised that defeating the Axis had not ended the war. If the government had considered the Second World War an anti-fascist war, demobilisation should have begun the day the enemy capitulated. However, Labour refused to bring its weary troops home. Bevin told the Commons in November 1945 that: 'It is the intention of his Majesty's Government to safeguard British interests in whatever part of the world they may be found.'[91] British troops must continue to fight for the British Empire, and for the empires of those yet unable to fight for themselves – France and Holland. Their Vietnamese and Indonesian colonies would have to be violently restored to the 'rightful' owners.[92]

Some servicemen had other ideas. They struck rather than sail Dutch soldiers to Indonesia.[93] 700 RAF briefly mutinied at Jodhpur, India.[94] By the end of 1945 protests had occurred in Malta[95] followed by Ceylon, Egypt and again India[96] where a new Forces Parliament had been reconstituted.[97] In March 1946 a radar operator was sentenced to ten years in connection with RAF strikes in Singapore, and in May there was a full-scale mutiny in Malaya which resulted in a string of court martials.[98]

Britain's industrial strikes and military mutinies, while revealing the existence of parallel wars, were limited affairs. More often the conflict between those giving orders and those carrying them out was masked, existing as divergent ideas held in people's heads. Indeed, many ordinary citizens just wanted to muddle through without choosing between either of the two wars. Rather than politics or strategy, the driving force for the 'poor bloody infantry' has been described as frequently a combination of 'coercion, inducement and narcosis'.[99] And the sentiment of this Yorkshirewoman was doubtless commonplace among civilians:

> We used to watch our bombers going out, hundreds at a time at regular intervals … I would say, 'They've gone over the edge of England and many won't ever come back. They are just going out there to die.' And then we thought of all the innocent people over there who were going to be destroyed by us. When was it going to end? It was all so hopeless – and for what? You felt the futility of it all and the sorrow for all the human beings involved in this hellish war, and wished with all your heart it was over.[100]

Nonetheless, there were clear proofs that large numbers, probably the majority, saw the war very differently to the establishment. One example was the reception accorded to the 1942 Beveridge Report that laid the basis for the post-war welfare state and National Health Service. Calder is correct to argue that 'the scheme was nothing like so revolutionary as Beveridge, and some of his admirers, liked to present'.[101] For example, contributions to the scheme were flat rated so the poor paid as much as the rich, and it provided no more than a safety net. Nonetheless, 'after the first glare of limelight, the Government went to extraordinary lengths to stifle all official publicity for the report'.[102] A summary written by Beveridge for servicemen was withdrawn two days after being issued[103] on the grounds that the Report had become 'controversial and therefore contrary to King's Regulations',[104] while Churchill regarded the report as a distraction from the fighting.

The fascinating thing is that in spite of all this, as Mass Observation discovered, ordinary people took it to be 'a symbol of Britain's war aims'.[105] No other official government publication has sold 635,000 copies or had the approval of 90 per cent of those polled.[106] Even *The Times* pointed out that the public 'refuses to accept the false distinction between these aims and the aim of victory'.[107]

The ultimate purpose of the war – a better, more equal, fairer world as embodied in a welfare state, or a return to pre-war structures – was the main issue of the 1945 general election. Churchill plainly hoped for a 'khaki election' such as the one that returned the First World War's Prime Minister, Lloyd George. Churchill called on the public to 'Vote National'. The brunt of his keynote speech was directed in veiled terms against welfare: 'Here in old England ... in this glorious island, the cradle and citadel of free democracy throughout the world, we do not like to be regimented and ordered about and have every action of our lives prescribed for us.' Labour's welfare state, he predicted, 'would have to fall back on some form of Gestapo'.[108]

In his reply Attlee appealed to the concept of a 'people's war'.

I state again the fundamental question which you have to decide. Is this country *in peace as in war* to be governed on the principle that public welfare comes before private interest?... Or is the nation to go back to the old conditions...? I ask you, the electors of Britain, the men and women who have shown the world such a shining example of how a great people in the face of mortal danger saved itself, to give Labour power to lead the way to a peaceful world and a just social order.[109]

Even if Labour failed to deliver on many of its promises, the significant point is that it claimed the mantle of a people's war. And the results were eloquent. Churchill's Conservatives dropped to 213 MPs, while the Labour Party romped home with 393 MPs, to form its first majority administration. The coalition government (including Labour) had fought an imperialist war, but in the minds of millions of voters the goal of the conflict had been quite different.

8
USA – Racism in the Arsenal of Democracy

The USA made a major contribution to the outcome of the Second World War. 405,000 Americans lost their lives and a staggering $330 billion was spent.[1] If the death toll pales in comparison with that of the Soviet Union, the USA's role as a source of arms was outstanding. Through lend-lease it supplied mountains of military equipment and food. The Soviet Union gained about one tenth of its hardware from the US,[2] and Britain twice as much.[3]

In some respects the position of the USA did appear different to its Allies. It lacked extensive colonies[4] and more readily spoke the language of people's war. In 1940 President Roosevelt made a famous speech claiming the USA was the 'great arsenal of democracy'. He castigated the Nazis for having 'proclaimed, time and again, that all other races are their inferiors and therefore subject to their orders'.[5] A week later he declared 'national policy' was 'without regard to partisanship' and involved 'the preservation of civil liberties for all'.[6]

However, the differences between the USA and its Allies should not be exaggerated. Washington's involvement in the Second World War was part of what Ambrose has called its 'rise to globalism':

In 1939 ... the United States had an Army of 185,000 men with an annual budget of less than $500 million. America had no military alliances and no American troops were stationed in any foreign country ... Thirty years later the United States had [a defence budget of] over $100 billion. The United States had military alliances with forty-eight nations, 1.5 million soldiers, airmen, and sailors stationed in 119 countries.[7]

If, prior to the Second World War, America had followed a different path to the European powers, it was one of internal rather than external colonisation, not just through the drive West and obliteration of Native Americans, but through the exploitation of enslaved Africans shipped to its soil. Therefore, on the question of whether the US war effort took on an imperialist or people's character, a crucial test was the domestic issue of race, which has been called 'the American obssession'.[8]

THE JAPANESE

This first arose in relation to the Japanese. Although the December 1941 attack on Pearl Harbor was the brainchild of Tokyo, Federal authorities turned on the Japanese in America. Roosevelt's Executive Order 9066 (March 1942) interned 'all persons of Japanese ancestry' in the Western Defense Command area (California, Oregon, Washington and Arizona).[9] This affected 120,000 people of whom 70,000 were American citizens.[10]

Asians had been exploited on America's western seaboard since the mid-nineteenth century, and racism was encouraged to both keep their wages down and divide all workers, white and non-white, amongst themselves. The Japanese were a common target. When running for President in 1912 Woodrow Wilson declared that the Japanese could 'not blend with the Caucasian race,' and a few years later the Californian governor insisted on 'the principle of race self-preservation'. In a notorious court case one man was refused naturalisation simply because he was 'clearly of a race which is not Caucasian',[11] and by 1924 that precedent had solidified into national law. To maintain 'racial preponderance' only 'free white persons' were now eligible.[12]

The architect of Order 9066, Western Defense Commander DeWitt, was clear his motivation was genetic:

> The Japanese race is an enemy race and while many second and third generation Japanese born in the United States soil, possessed of United States citizenship, have become 'Americanized', the racial strains are undiluted. To conclude otherwise is to expect that children born of white parents on Japanese soil to sever all racial affinity and become loyal Japanese subjects.[13]

Administrators of Order 9066 thought it an over-reaction, but they accepted the view that: 'the normal Caucasian countenances of such persons enable the average American to recognize particular individuals by distinguishing minor facial characteristics [but] the Occidental eye cannot readily distinguish one Japanese resident from another.' This made the 'effective surveillance of the movements of particular Japanese residents suspected of disloyalty' virtually impossible.[14]

The public justification for Order 9066 was military necessity. DeWitt loudly claimed that the US Japanese were broadcasting sensitive US intelligence, though he knew it to be untrue,[15] and the notoriously reactionary FBI boss, Hoover was aware the claim was pure fiction.[16] To get round the lack of evidence an amazing proof, worthy of Donald Rumsfeld, was advanced: 'The very fact that no sabotage has taken place to date is a disturbing and confirming indication that such action will be taken.'[17] Although the authorities suggested internment was popular, secret polling in the areas affected showed only 14 per cent favoured the strategy.[18] People could see through the scare-mongering of politicians and press.

Order 9066 was implemented using methods reminiscent of Nazi 'aryanisation'. Japanese were herded into former stables, cattle stalls and pigpens before transfer to longer term 'relocation centers' like the bleak camp at Minidoka, Idaho.[19] The term 'concentration camp' had been quietly dropped. Taking little more than they could carry, they lost homes and property worth $400 million.[20] A riot in one camp was quelled by soldiers who killed two and wounded many more. When a doctor revealed protesters had been shot in the back he was sacked.[21]

Internment found critics in unexpected quarters. The director of the War Relocation Authority was dismayed by the policy he had to implement. He believed that it 'added weight to the contention of the enemy that we are fighting a race war; that this nation preaches democracy and practices racial discrimination'.[22] The victims of Order 9066 also pointed out the hypocrisy of the government's stance: 'Although we have yellow skins, we too are Americans. [So] how can we say to the white American buddies in the armed forces that we are fighting for the perpetuation of democracy, especially when our fathers, mothers and families are in concentration camps, even though they are not charged with any crime?'[23]

The difference between the way the USA fought its war in Europe and Asia also showed the influence of race. One veteran remembered how his drill instructor declared: 'You're not going to Europe, you're going to the Pacific. Don't hesitate to fight the Japs dirty'.[24] A war correspondent recalled: 'We shot prisoners in cold blood, wiped out hospitals, strafed lifeboats ... finished off the enemy wounded.'[25] Sometimes the purpose was merely to extract their gold teeth.[26] When the same veteran asked about a shooting he heard, he was told: 'It was just an old gook woman. She wanted to be put out of her misery and join her ancestors, I guess. So I obliged her.'[27]

When Britain's Bomber Command asked the Eighth US Air Force to participate in 'Operation Thunderclap' which aimed to kill some 275,000 Berliners, America's General Cabell protested that such: 'baby killing schemes [would] be a blot on the history of the Air Forces and of the US'.[28] This did not prevent the USA from participating in the bombing of Dresden but the reasons were strategic. Like the British, Senior US commanders were aware that their air forces 'are the blue chips with which we will approach the post-war treaty table' and that it was important to ensure 'Russian knowledge of their strength'.[29]

In war with Japan the racial overtones were more prominent. 'Baby killing schemes' were routine US policy in the Asian theatre, and those who said these were 'un-American' were denounced because, as the *Weekly Intelligence Review* suggested in tones reminiscent of Stanley Baldwin: 'We intend to seek out and destroy the enemy wherever he or she is, in the greatest possible numbers, in the shortest possible time. For us, THERE ARE NO CIVILIANS IN JAPAN.'[30]

An example of what this meant in practice was the raid on Tokyo, 10 March 1945. It killed 100,000. Air Chief Curtis LeMay called it 'the greatest single disaster incurred by any enemy in military history … There were more casualties than in any other military action in the history of the world'.[31] US Atomic energy Commission chair, David Lilienthal summed up how the war developed against Japan:

> Then we burned Tokyo, not just military targets, but set out to wipe out the place, indiscriminately. The atomic bomb is the last word in this direction. All ethical limitations of warfare are gone, not because the *means* of destruction are more cruel or painful or otherwise hideous in their effect upon combatants, but because there are no individual combatants. The fences are gone. And it was we, the civilized, who have pushed standardless conduct to its ultimate.[32]

This is a valid judgement on Hiroshima and Nagasaki. Although the US was fully aware that Japan was suing for peace,[33] the Secretary of State – Stimson – wanted the atom bomb deployed and 'the most desirable target would be a vital war plant employing a large number of workers and closely surrounded by workers' houses'. One historian adds: 'Stripped of polite euphemisms, that meant massively killing workers and their families, the residents of those houses.'[34]

Harry Truman, Roosevelt's successor, realised the atomic bomb was 'far worse than gas or biological warfare because it affects the civilian population and murders them by the wholesale'.[35] Nuclear bombs killed around 200,000 in the short term, and wiped out the very medical services which might have helped civilian casualties. In Hiroshima:

> Of a hundred and fifty doctors in the city, sixty-five were already dead and most of the rest were wounded. Of 1,780 nurses, 1,654 were dead or too badly hurt to work. In the biggest hospital, that of the Red Cross, only six doctors out of thirty were able to function, and only ten nurses out of more than two hundred.[36]

And the effect of the bomb on people virtually defies description:

> The sight of them was almost unbearable. Their faces and hands were burnt and swollen; and great sheets of skin had peeled away from their tissues to hang down like rags on a scarecrow ... And they had no faces! Their eyes, noses and mouths had been burned away, and it looked like their ears had melted off.[37]

THE JEWS

The ending of the Holocaust is perhaps the most potent argument for the Second World War being a 'good war'. So what was Allied attitude to the plight of the Jews? When Hitler annexed Austria in 1938 London slapped on visa restrictions to make it difficult for Jews to escape.[38] By the outbreak of war only 70,000 of the 600,000 Jews who sought asylum had been accepted.[39] After 1939 the door snapped shut, because anyone coming from Axis territory was now branded an enemy alien. Britain's Foreign Secretary vetoed the rescue of 70,000 Romanian Jews (fully funded by the American Jewish community) because: 'If we do that, then the Jews of the world will be wanting us to make similar offers in Poland and Germany. Hitler might well take us up ... .'[40]

'Amazing, most amazing position', exclaimed one American official,[41] and this shows that the USA had a better approach. In January 1944 it set up a War Refugee Board which saved up to 250,000 Jewish lives.[42] However, before getting carried away it is important to note that the Government provided a mere 9 per cent of its funding. The rest came from private sources.[43] Moreover, as Wyman makes clear in his excellent book *The Abandonment of the Jews*, 1944 was very late, and the road to the establishment of the Board had been a rocky one. As early as 1941 the US authorities knew about the extermination taking place in Europe. Indeed, in July 1942 a 20,000 strong assembly in New York protesting at the Holocaust received messages of sympathy from both Roosevelt and Churchill.[44]

Yet Roosevelt appointed Breckinridge Long, who Eleanor Roosevelt described as 'a fascist',[45] to oversee immigration rules. His policy was to 'postpone and postpone and postpone the granting of visas' and thus 'delay and effectively stop [immigration] for a temporary period of indefinite length ...'[46] To assist in this process the USA visa application form was four feet long and:

> had to be filled out on both sides by one of the refugee's sponsors (or a refugee-aid agency), sworn under penalty of perjury, and submitted in six copies. It required detailed information not only about the refugee but also about the two American sponsors who were needed to testify that he would present no danger to the United States. Each sponsor had to list his own residences and employers for the preceding two years and submit character references from two reputable American citizens whose own past activities could be readily checked.[47]

Then a cruel Catch-22 was introduced. There were no consuls to issue visas in Axis-controlled Europe, but those who escaped from there to places such as Spain and Portugal were deemed to be 'not in acute danger' and therefore refused visas.

Such actions led a prominent Jewish Socialist member of the Polish National Council to commit suicide. He explained his decision thus:

> The responsibility for this crime of murdering the entire Jewish population of Poland falls in the first instance on the perpetrators, but ... by the passive observation of the murder of defenseless millions and of the maltreatment of children, women and old men, [the Allied states] have become the criminals' accomplices ... As I was unable to do anything during my life, perhaps by my death I shall contribute to breaking down that indifference.[48]

The welcome establishment of the War Refugee Board close to the end of the war pales in significance when set against the USA's refusal to stop Auschwitz operating. Detailed information about this death camp came from two escapees, Vrba and Wetzler, in early 1944. Wyman shows that up to 437,000 lives could have been saved if Auschwitz's railways lines and crematoria had been bombed,[49] but the War Department declared this 'impracticable.'[50] In fact, between July and October 1944, 'a total of 2,700 bombers travelled along or within easy reach of both rail lines on the way to targets in the Blechammer-Auschwitz region',[51] and on several occasions the camp actually shook from attacks at nearby installations.

Wyman's verdict has been hotly debated.[52] The counter-argument, that the Western Allies did not wish to be distracted from an exclusive focus on defeating Germany, falls when set against their costly efforts to evacuate Spanish children during the civil war or supply the Warsaw Rising. 'Humanitarian acts' seem to have been carried out only when politically expedient. One convinced 'Rooseveltian' defends his hero by emphasising the President's 'sincere belief that it was essential to put all of America's resources and his own influence into winning the war'.[53] The question is: which war was he trying to win?

The people's war did not focus on gaining political advantage but common decency and protection of human life. Arguments that nothing could be done to save Jews, or that this was a diversion, are disproved by the case of Denmark. Though under German occupation, only 474 of its population of 7,000 Jews fell into Nazi hands[54] because large numbers of citizens hid them when the round ups began.[55] The resistance then organised a flotilla of small ships to smuggle them across the Oresund to neutral Sweden.[56] In Bulgaria significant sections of society 'united in the singular determination to protect Bulgarian Jewry from the pro-Hitler Fascist majority in parliament'. As a result 'the cattle cars ... remained empty. Bulgarian Jews fought alongside their non-Jewish compatriots in a mighty partisan movement.'[57]

This rescue of Jews was not pointless. As one participant argues, many historians 'make a mistake [when] they try to disconnect the rescue of the Jews from the rest of the resistance. It all belongs together.'[58] Many who escaped would return later to fight.[59] An estimated 1.5 million Jewish women and men were involved in combat against the Axis, the US and Russian armed forces having half a million each.[60] In Eastern Europe there were Jewish underground organisations in seven major ghettos and 45 minor ghettos. Uprisings occurred in five concentration camps and eighteen forced-labour camps.[61] Against incredible odds there were armed rebellions in Auschwitz, Treblinka and Sobibor death camps.

Even Jewish resistance had a two-war aspect to it. In many instances established Jewish organisations tried to limit the inroads of Nazism through collaboration. Tzur shows that the Jewish population was divided like others: '[Resistance] could develop only from an active ideology which presented its holders in opposition to the existing circumstances and believed in the possibility of changing the cultural and political ecology. Therefore the resisters usually had a previous history as members of anti-establishment groups.'[62]

An opposite example occurred at the Vilna ghetto, in 'one of the most tragic chapters in the annals of the Holocaust'.[63] The head of the Jewish organisation betrayed the leader of the ghetto's armed resistance group to the Gestapo, just after 33,500 of its 57,000 inhabitants had been buried in pits nearby.[64]

'DOUBLE VICTORY' – BLACK AMERICANS AND THE WAR

In the USA the black population were conscious of the two wars and said so. When Roosevelt announced the USA was defending 'freedom and democracy' Afro-Americans, who made up one-eighth of its population, could not but be aware that in 12 southern states, only 2 per cent of voting-age blacks were entitled to vote, or that the median income of blacks was just 40 per cent that of whites.[65] They may well have remembered the President's response to dozens of lynchings in 1933. When asked by the leader of the National Association for the Advancement of Colored People (NAACP) to back an anti-lynching Bill he said that racist white southern Democrats 'occupy strategic places on most of the Senate and House committees', and so, 'I just can't take that risk'.[66] His future successor, Truman, said in 1940: 'I wish to make it clear that I am not appealing for social equality for the Negro. The Negro himself knows better than that ...'.[67]

Cracks in the edifice of racism appeared when the US armed services expanded from a few hundred thousand to over 14 million. The state now had no choice but to appeal to the country's nine million blacks. In 1940 the Selective Service and Training Act opened the forces to 'any person, regardless of race or color' and promised 'there shall be no discrimination ...'.[68] Yet the Services remained thoroughly segregated. As Roosevelt put it: 'The policy of the War Department is not to intermingle colored and white enlisted personnel in the same regimental organization.'[69] Presumably 'no discrimination' only applied within separate black and white sections, not between them.

The justification given by the Secretary for War was that blacks were 'basically agriculturalists'.[70] Consequently, 'Negro units have ... been unable to master the techniques of modern weapons.'[71] In the Navy blacks could aspire only to be messmen and cooks because, according to the Secretary of the Navy: 'it would be a waste of time and effort [to train those who] by reason of their race and color could not properly and efficiently fill the higher ratings.' Admiral Nimitz warned desegregation was 'the Soviet way, not the American way'.[72] In the army 95 per cent of black soldiers were restricted to service roles,[73] because, as General Marshall put it, integration would have meant 'settlement of vexing racial problems [that] cannot be permitted to complicate the tremendous task of the War Department and thereby jeopardize discipline and morale'.[74] As the morale of racists took priority whites could command blacks, blacks could never command whites. So in 1940 there were only two black army officers.[75]

Segregation even applied to blood donations. Protesters called this 'abhorrent to the principles for which this war is being fought' and a 'Hitler-like policy'.[76] But there were many other outrages. This was the experience of one black soldier: 'I saw German prisoners free to move around the camp, unlike black soldiers, who were restricted. The Germans walked right into the doggone places like any white American. We were wearin' the same uniform, but we were excluded.'[77] In town German POWs sat at the front of buses while blacks were relegated to the back.[78] He concluded the USA was fielding 'two armies, one black, one white'.[79] When proposals emerged for segregated bomb shelters in Washington DC, one paper wryly commented: 'Wouldn't it be just like Hitler to make American whites choose a "fate worse than death" – running into a Negro bomb shelter?'[80]

Some radical blacks responded to the situation by rejecting participation in the war altogether:

Why should I shed my blood for Roosevelt's America ... for the whole Jim Crow Negro-hating South, for the low-paid, dirty jobs for which Negroes have to fight, for the few dollars of relief and the insults, discrimination, police brutality and perpetual poverty to which Negroes are condemned even in the more liberal North?[81]

Answering talk of 'saving democracy', one black newspaper wrote, 'We cannot save what DOES NOT EXIST'.[82] The Second World War was a 'white man's war' to a significant minority.[83] Thirty-eight per cent of black people believed it was more important to 'make democracy work at home' than beat the Germans and Japanese.[84] An apocryphal epitaph summed up the bitterness felt: 'Here lies a black man killed fighting a yellow man for the protection of a white man.'[85]

For the majority, however, the Second World War embodied two separate wars. This was made explicit by *The Pittsburgh Courier*, the largest black circulation weekly, in its popular 'Double V' campaign: 'The "Double V" stands for victory against the enemies abroad and for victory against the forces at home who would deny the Negro full and free participation in every phase of national life. Therefore the Negro is fighting on two fronts.'

There were contradictions and differences within the campaign, however. One *Courier* article claimed that 'Double V is a victory slogan adopted by Negro America as an expression of its traditional patriotism to the ideals ... expressed by President Roosevelt ...'.[86] However, other articles pointed out that under his Presidency 'lynchings, "Jim Crow" laws, discrimination in employment and training, denial of suffrage' continued. With an 'army and navy steeped in prejudice ... [O]ur country still insists on making itself vulnerable to Axis propagandists and their slimy effective methods ... If we can't exercise democracy at home, how can we carry the torch effectively to those who need our assistance and who in turn must aid us?'[87] A black soldier put it still more succinctly. It was a matter of 'Lynching versus Morale'.[88]

The clash between the two wars emerged in several areas of society. On one side corporate America profited as never before. There was burgeoning growth in defence industries which saw profits rise 250 per cent and prices by 45 per cent above pre-war levels. However, wages were frozen at 15 per cent above the 1941 level.[89] Discrimination against African American employment in defence was staggering. Despite labour shortages, in 1941 over half of new defence jobs were formally closed to blacks, while 90 per cent of those who did find work were in low paid service or unskilled employment. For whites the equivalent figure was just 5 per cent.[90]

In January of that year A. Philip Randolph, the socialist leader of the Brotherhood of Sleeping Car Porters Union, declared blacks would 'exact their rights in National Defense employment and the armed forces of the country'.[91] His 'March On Washington

Movement' (MOWM) has been described as 'African America's first large-scale demonstration aimed at federal officials';[92] 'one of the most promising [black movements] in all American history'; and the 'first large black organization in which trade unionists played the leading role'.[93]

Randolph himself argued that: 'The whole National Defense set-up reeks and stinks with race prejudice, hatred and discrimination ...' Promises had been made but: 'it all ends there. Nothing is actually done to stop discrimination ...' So blacks should not politely beg, but act: 'Power and pressure do not reside in the few, the intelligentsia, they lie in and flow from the masses. .... On to Washington ... Let them swarm from every hamlet, village and town ... Let them come in automobiles, buses, trains, trucks and on foot. Let them come though the winds blow... .'[94] Soon the original prediction of 10,000 marchers grew to 100,000.

In reply Roosevelt accused the organisers of aiding the Axis:

> Today's threat to our national security is not a matter of military weapons alone ... The method is simple. It is first, a dissemination of discord. A group – not too large – a group that may be sectional or racial or political – is encouraged to exploit its prejudices through false slogans and emotional appeals ... As a result of these techniques, armament programs may be dangerously delayed. Singleness of national purpose may be undermined ... .[95]

Nevertheless, Roosevelt shifted. He set up a Fair Employment Practice Committee (FEPC) to 'investigate complaints' of discrimination and 'redress grievances,' and the march was cancelled. The FEPC was lauded as 'the most important effort in the history of this country to eliminate discrimination in employment,'[96] but the omens were worrying. Mark Ethridge, appointed the Committee's chair, found there was no power, 'not even in all the mechanized armies of the earth, Allied and Axis – which could now force the Southern white people to the abandonment of the principle of social segregation ... .'[97] A disillusioned Randolph realised the FEPC was facing a situation that was 'of the same cloth as Hitler's Nazism, Mussolini's fascism and Hirohito's militaryism'.[98] Once the threat of a march had disappeared Roosevelt moved to emasculate the FEPC, and Ethridge resigned in disgust.

The clash between people's war and imperialist war in the USA could also take the form of bullets, knives and stones. There was an enormous expansion of non-white employment, due less to the FEPC than sheer necessity. For example, in 1941 there were virtually no Mexican Americans in the Los Angeles shipyards. Three years later there were 17,000.[99] Nationally during the same period a million people moved home.[100] In San Francisco the black population rose at 20 times the rate of the whites.[101] All this put pressure on housing, and the tension that caused generated 242 racial battles in 47 cities during 1943 alone.[102]

The most dramatic episode was in the engineering metropolis of Detroit. By the middle of the war blacks and southern whites were arriving at a rate of 1,400 a week.[103] Whites rioted when a black housing project named after Sojourner Truth, the ex-slave Civil War heroine, was opened. Local police stood back because, as their chief commented: 'My men are naturally in sympathy with the white mob.'[104] As a result 33 of the 38 people hospitalised were black. Yet of the 104 arrests 101 were blacks.[105] This was but a prelude to an even bigger clash in 1943. There were attempts to overcome divisions and in April 10,000 black and white workers marched together against discrimination.[106] Alas, racism was not so easily overcome. Two months later fighting between black and white youths spread to three quarters of the city. Once more, the state was not a neutral bystander to ethnic conflict. 34 people died, 25 of them black. Eighty-five per cent of the 1,500 arrests made were of blacks, and 17 blacks were shot dead by the police.[107]

Can it be argued that these events owed more to a split among the masses than a division between an imperialist-minded Government and the majority of people? It is true that racism infected the white working class. There were numerous strikes to exclude black labour, for example.[108] However, even these strikes showed some social differentiation. There was a clear difference between the American Federation of Labor (AFL) with its origins in the more privileged craft elite of workers, and the Congress of Industrial Organizations (CIO) which was more broadly based. While several AFL unions officially banned blacks, the CIO welcomed them,[109] and set up over 85 anti-discrimination committees to actively oppose racism.[110] In 1943 a delegate at the Michigan state CIO convention pinpointed the origins of the problem: 'Divide the common people and rule has been the economic keystone of those who control the economic destiny of America.'[111]

The rot came from the top. The attitudes expressed by politicians, businessmen, and chiefs of the armed services found their way into civil society. In housing, for example, the National Association of Real Estate Boards bracketed blacks with bootleggers, madams and gangsters, and advised its estate agents to avoid selling to African Americans 'no matter what the motive or character of the would-be purchaser, if the deal would instigate a form of blight ...'.[112] Randolph summarised the way the administration fuelled ethnic conflict: 'the official jim crow of the Negro by the Federal Government itself in the armed forces, the Government departments and defense industries, is a major cause of the wave of race riots sweeping the country'.[113] On occasion the Government might quell the rioting in the interests of war production, but this did not undo the way its policies generated the conditions for such conflicts to erupt.

The scale and location of the Detroit confrontation, and that of Harlem New York which followed,[114] showed the continuing racism of the state, but also the readiness of blacks to fight back. These events had occurred in the North. Yet the 'other war' erupted in the South, too. Against the background of an increase in lynchings[115] came the resistance of black soldiers. They were predominantly transfers from northern cities and were unaccustomed to, and refused to accept, Jim Crow. In total there were over 200 confrontations between black soldiers and the military and civilian authorities, of which two thirds occurred in the South.[116] This followed the mushrooming of black community groups such as the NAACP[117] (which in the 1960s came to be seen as moderate in comparison with the black power movement, but often represented the leading edge of agitation in the Second World War).

In addition there was self-organisation. A black Soldier's Council was formed in the biggest army camp, Fort Bragg,[118] following a fight during which a black soldier and a white military policeman died.[119] A detailed study of a black GI 'insurrection' at Camp Stewart, Georgia, shows how a new militancy was arising.[120] The conditions in Camp Stewart were described in this letter to the head of the NAACP: 'Please for God Sake help us. These old southern officers over us have us quarantined like slaves come down and see ... They really hate colored. Please appeal to the war dept about our treatment at once. We are no slaves.'[121]

Numerous letters from this Camp referred to physical isolation, 'unspeakable' sanitary conditions, white officers kicking black soldiers, and lack of medical care. It was claimed 'at least 3 men die every month as a result of race riots ... [and] at least 2 men die every month as a result of over-exertion.'[122]

After reports of violence against a black woman by white soldiers a column of a hundred blacks in 'military formation' armed with rifles, bayonets and clubs formed up and called others to join them.[123] Military police then began shooting and the camp was 'engulfed by the tumult of battle'.[124] Eventually, after some six thousand rounds of .30 calibre ammunition had been fired, one military policeman lay dead.[125] The battle at Camp Stewart was just one example of a mass of racial conflicts both in the US and abroad.

The outcome of the Second World War for the USA was double-edged. The state emerged as a super-power. If it was not possible to talk about a victory for the peoples at home, at least the front for justice and democracy had advanced. From 1943 white and blacks in the military were allowed to use the same recreational facilities, though at different times.[126] In 1944 some black platoons were assigned to white companies,[127] and by 1948 the armed forces were officially desegregated.[128] Despite all the obstacles, the people's war had unleashed forces that could not be stopped. Led by figures such as Martin Luther King the campaign for black equality would soon rekindle, and it was not long before new forces round Malcolm X and the Black Panthers would take up arms to advance it further.

Part III

Germany, Austria and Italy – Under the Axis

In Axis countries the people's war was fought in darkness behind the doors of the torture chamber. As well as facing the wrath of their own governments, these anti-fascist movements had the added political obstacle of defying their own nation's war effort, and the lack of a sympathetic response from the Allies.

9
Germany – Conservatives and Antifa

Three million Germans became political prisoners during Hitler's reign, and many tens of thousands died. As one writer puts it, 'These numbers reveal the potential for popular resistance in German society – and what happened to it.'[1]

Some establishment figures, who shared a common class and political position to Allied governments, took the road of resistance, but the sort of problems they faced were revealed during the Czechoslovak crisis of 1938. Fearing the Führer would start an unwinnable global war, influential conservative conspirators including the Army's Commander-in-Chief plotted to arrest him. They were confident there could be 'no possibility of a hitch' to their plan just so long as Britain and France were willing to stand up to Hitler.[2] These two countries were duly informed of the conspiracy.

Alas, neither was in a mood to have the German Chancellor deposed. Sir Neville Henderson, Britain's ambassador in Berlin, wrote that Hitler had 'achieved gigantic progress in the military, industrial, and moral reorganisation of Germany'.[3] He regarded Czech objections to Hitler's aggression as being on 'uncertain moral ground'[4] because the Nazis were merely 'consummating *at long last* the unity of Greater Germany'.[5] Above all, Henderson wanted a strong Germany to hold back communism: 'Moscow's chief aim was to embroil Germany and the Western Powers in a common ruin and to emerge as the *tertius gaudens* [the third one wins] of the conflict between them.'[6] So the pleas of the plotters were ignored and Czechoslovakia was sacrificed.

Once the war began, the Allies adopted the opposite policy: 'unconditional surrender'. This was equally fatal to the conservative resistance. Any attempt by them to encourage German peace feelers would, in Churchill's words, be met with 'absolute silence'.[7] This stance paralysed the conservative opposition because, without a prior agreement with the West, toppling Hitler might result in a Soviet takeover, something they abhorred even more than Nazism.

Allied tactics undermined opposition amongst ordinary Germans too. Instead of engaging with the German people in a joint struggle against Nazism, Britain and the USA gave them firestorms accompanied with leaflets saying: 'Our bombs fall on your homes and on you ... You can't stop us, and you know it. You have no hope.'[8] The Red Army reinforced that message. Russian soldiers fighting the 'Great Patriotic War' were encouraged into intense hatred of enemy civilians. Reports reached Stalin that 'all German women in East Prussia who stayed behind were raped by Red Army soldiers'.[9] The bitter choice for German women was expressed in this joke: 'Better a Russki on the belly, than a Yank [bombing you] on the head!'[10] In sum, Allied methods produced sullen co-operation with Hitler's regime. He thus avoided the revolution that befell the Kaiser in 1918. Nevertheless Nazism was resisted – through both imperialist and people's war forms.

THE GERMAN RESISTANCE

Most histories give pride of place to Conservatives. Gördeler, Mayor of Leipzig and Reich Price Commissioner, led an elite grouping which hoped to replace Hitler with himself as Chancellor. Gördeler's supporters had the best opportunity to assassinate the Führer because they mixed with top Nazis. Stauffenberg's bomb of 20 July 1944 came within inches of success. Tragically, Hitler survived, Operation Valkyrie failed, and the plotters paid with their lives.

Their rejection of Nazism was not based on opposition to German imperialism, but a disagreement over how best to maintain it. Like Ambassador Henderson, Hassell (Gördeler's 'shadow' Foreign Minister), argued for 'a healthy, vigorous Germany as an indispensable factor ... in face of Bolshevist Russia'.[11] Gördeler himself intended to retain Austria and part of Czechoslovakia for Germany after the war.[12]

Allied capitulation at Munich may have stymied their 1938 plot, but the Conservatives were galvanised into a new conspiracy by the Hitler–Stalin Pact which, they feared, gave too much influence to Moscow.[13] But once the Second World War began, action against it was again delayed, because the Wehrmacht looked like succeeding. They acted in the summer of 1944 because, as Mommsen puts it, 'the generals of the Opposition, with but few exceptions, only made up their minds to unconditional action when the Bolshevist danger threatened to become a military reality'.[14]

On the domestic front the conservative resistance preferred authoritarian rule or a monarchy to democracy.[15] They judged it expedient to 'carry over, for permanent retention in the reconstructed state, an appreciable amount of what had been achieved by National Socialism'.[16] Indeed, Mommsen believes 'leading generals in the military opposition were also deeply involved in the war crimes of the Third Reich'.[17] Gördeler rejected 'uncontrolled overdemocratic parliamentarianism',[18] concluding an elected chamber should have only advisory functions, and no independent legislative rights.

Only the tiny Kreisau circle, whose members included aristocrats, trade union leaders and socialists, went beyond such reactionary politics; but it was a discussion group. When it was caught up in the repression of the July 1944 bomb plot, its key figure, von Moltke, protested that: 'We only thought ... We are on the outside of each practical action; we get hanged because we have thought together.'[19]

If the conservative resistance was galvanised by fear of defeat and a concern to salvage German imperialism from the disaster Hitler was leading it to, workers' opposition was rooted in fundamental opposition to Nazi dictatorship, war and racism. The communist youth wing warned that young workers were 'being trained to be cannon fodder' and to avert war it was necessary to 'bring fascism to ruin'.[20] The Party called for 'solidarity through sympathy and help for our Jewish comrades',[21] while the socialists demanded the 'overthrow [of] all supporters of despotism and all violent organisations that oppose freedom ...'.[22]

Whereas many of the conservative opposition had been Nazis but broke away over the best policy for German capitalism, the working class resisted the pull of Hitler from the start. This was shown by the Nazi Party's social composition. Labour was under-represented in membership (relative to the overall population) by almost half; the lower middle class was over-represented by one-third; while there was a fourfold over-representation of the elite.[23]

Before Hitler's accession as Chancellor, the Communist Party (KPD) fought Nazis valiantly on the streets. In Prussia alone, during June/July 1932, 82 died in political clashes, the majority being Nazis (38) or communists (30).[24] Alas, Moscow's insistence that the German socialists (SPD) were 'social fascists' and worse than Nazis, produced disastrous divisions in the working class.[25] These were compounded by the SPD's equally false belief that Hitler would be constrained by the democratic constitution of Weimar Germany – 'Our foes will perish through our legality'.[26] These follies fatally undermined the left and made it possible for the German elite, centred on President Hindenburg, to appoint Hitler as Chancellor.

Even after Hitler's accession to power, and wave upon wave of murderous repression, working-class opposition continued.

Although Göbbels' government-controlled media could successfully peddle lies concerning issues of which the population had no direct knowledge, the Nazis fared badly in 1934's government sponsored shop stewards' elections, because the candidates were known personally to voters. The one-party state barred alternative platforms, but 'no' votes and abstentions combined comprised three quarters of the final result.[27] No further elections were held.

Workers tried various methods to withstand the Nazi onslaught. Lacking direct access to Hitler's circle, workers' resistance could not easily mount assassination plots, though heroic individuals attempted this. The SPD hoped to ride out the storm by remaining passive. Although extremely reckless, to its credit the KPD called for 'an unbroken chain of mass resistance and mass struggle ...'.[28] In June 1935 the Berlin KPD alone distributed 62,000 copies of its literature. The SPD's illegal newspaper had a national circulation of 250,000.[29] Sometimes more could be done. Despite the dangers, occasional strikes and acts of sabotage of military production also occurred.[30] Even in concentration camps the left mounted struggles for physical and moral survival. At Berlin's Sachsenhausen camp a group of communists, socialists and non-party prisoners, organised equitable distribution of food and clothes, political education, morale-building cultural work, and even a demonstration of defiance.[31]

But by 1939 mass popular resistance had been smashed. This did not mean working class acceptance of Hitlerism. A report smuggled out and published by the Socialists estimated that: 'Ninety percent of the workers beyond all doubt are convinced anti-Nazis [but there is] no active attitude against the ruling conditions.'[32] Small groups composed of activists from a variety of backgrounds, such as the Red Orchestra (a network spying for Russia), the White Rose (students), and Edelweiss Pirates (youth) continued to splutter into life only to be snuffed out. The 'other war' had been reduced to an occasional skirmish. Nevertheless, as Peukert has argued:

Given the twofold trauma of 1933 – defeat without struggle, and the terror-induced split between the activists and the politically passive proletarian community – the sheer quantity of political opposition, the commitment and self-sacrifice of those involved, and the stubborn determination with which they persisted in secret operations, despite setbacks at the hands of the Gestapo, are certainly remarkable accomplishments. They constitute an immense and historic achievement, quite irrespective of the total impact of the working-class resistance on the Third Reich.[33]

A comparison in size of the conservative and communist resistance is instructive. The former numbered around 200 activists (though in the repression following the July 1944 plot the regime executed some 5,000 opponents).[34] By the end of the Second World War, of the KPD alone, 300,000 members had been incarcerated, and at least 20,000 killed.[35]

As Peukert suggests above, it cannot be said mass resistance was decisive, but it was significant. The war which ultimately destroyed Nazism partly came about because it 'sought to resolve its social antagonisms through dynamic territorial expansion. So Germany was inevitably drawn into a conflict with other Great Powers'.[36] Equally, as Aly has shown, fearing a repeat of the revolution that ended the First World War the Nazis avoided antagonising German workers through lower living standards, and this significantly reduced the Nazi war machine's effectiveness.[37] Churchill and Roosevelt demanded levels of self-sacrifice from their populations that Hitler dared not request.

AFTER THE WAR

Victory in Europe day was 8 May 1945 and the fatal blow was delivered by Allied imperialism. But the motive was not to free the German population. A US spokesperson explained: 'Our aim in occupying Germany is not to liberate it, but to treat it as a defeated enemy state.'[38] Russia agreed and carried out the violent 'ethnic cleansing' of eleven million Germans from Eastern Europe.[39] Furthermore, Stalin saw no reason to object 'if a soldier who has crossed thousands of kilometres through blood and fire and death has fun with a women or takes some trifle'.[40] Though notorious for mass rape, the Red Army was not the only occupying army to do this.[41]

Rather than the welfare of the German population, many of whom were victims of Nazism, the victors were interested in who would gain the greatest share of the spoils. Morgenthau, US Treasury Secretary, wanted to de-industrialise Germany and break it into several small states,[42] but the State Department, mindful of the way the First World War ended in a wave of European revolutions, regarded this as 'a plan of blind vengeance' that would open the door to communism, and close it to American plans for economic reconstruction.[43]

Churchill agreed that 'inflicting severities upon Germany [might allow] the Russians in a very short time to advance, if they chose, to the waters of the North Sea and the Atlantic'.[44] For this reason Admiral Dönitz, Hitler's designated successor, was allowed to continue running government and to issue orders. Churchill even retained Luftwaffe planes and a force of some 700,000 soldiers as insurance against 'Russian armies should they decide to advance farther than is agreed'.[45] It was only the bizarre alliance of Russian and *Daily Mail* protests that put a stop to this outrage, Dönitz finally being arrested two weeks after VE Day.[46]

Imperialist considerations also shaped the treatment of Hitler's henchmen. In West Germany the USA wanted Nazis to be brought to justice without destroying Germany's social structure, lest Russia take advantage of the disarray.[47] This was not easy because, contrary to conventional wisdom, Nazism was not some alien contagion, the result of a charismatic leader or collective madness. Although the Nazi Party started as a collection of counter-revolutionary cranks outside the mainstream, almost from the very beginning it garnered support from significant figures, such as the First World War commander Ludendorff. When the standing of the conventional middle class parties was destroyed first by the hyper-inflation of 1923 and then the 1929 Wall Street Crash millions voted for the Nazis. Now, with the economy spiralling downwards, the establishment realised that however unsavoury rabble-rousing individuals like Hitler might appear, the alternative to Nazism was social breakdown and civil war. So they backed his appointment as Chancellor in 1933. Hitler showed his appreciation a year later in the 'Night of the Long Knives', during which he massacred those of his own supporters gullible enough to believe that Nazism was some radical alternative to capitalism.

By the Second World War the leading Nazis were thoroughly integrated into the social structure and its elite. This posed a problem for the Western Allies. Cutting away much of the summit of society in their sector might release radical forces from below and weaken authority. In East Germany the Russians had no such qualms and took a different approach. They would expunge Nazism, not in order to hand control to ordinary Germans, but to Moscow.

Despite their different approaches, the Allied military authorities in both sectors were therefore hostile to the spontaneous mass movement of anti-fascist committees (Antifas) that emerged as the Third Reich disintegrated. These committees represented the long repressed people's war against fascism. One of their first aims was to forestall Hitler's 'Nero Order', the suicidal self-destruction of Germany's infrastructure. In Leipzig Antifa leaflets urged soldiers to desert, while in Stuttgart pro-war officers were challenged. Such actions were still dangerous. In Dachau the SS repulsed the committee when it stormed the Town Hall. The same thing happened in an assault on Dusseldorf's police HQ. But in places such as Mulheim and Solingen Antifas were in control when Allied soldiers arrived, so they marched in unopposed.[48]

The scale of the movement was impressive, with over 120 committees established nationwide. The Leipzig Antifa claimed 150,000 adherents.[49] Many of these organisations broke through entrenched social barriers to include foreign slave labourers and establish working class unity across political parties and trade unions. Their functions ranged from creating local democracy, to restoring basic services like food supply.[50] An official US report shows the Allies had a clear understanding of what the Antifas stood for:

> Denunciation of Nazis, efforts to prevent an illegal Nazi underground movement, denazification of civil authorities and private industry, improvement of housing and food supply provision – these are the central questions which preoccupy the newly created organizations ... .'[51]

The fact that so many committees adopted similar names and policies poses the question of whether there was a centralised organisation at work.[52]

Communists were prominent in nearly every Antifa[53] despite the opposition of Moscow.[54] Walter Ulbricht, the KPD leader, criticised the 'spontaneous creation of KPD bureaus, people's committees, and Free Germany committees',[55] but he could do little as the KPD central apparatus had no communication link with the rank and file.[56] Once communications were restored he could report: 'We have shut these [Antifas] down and told the comrades that all activities must be channelled through the state apparatus.'[57]

The Western Allies were equally disconcerted by the Antifas self-proclaimed 'ruthless struggle against all remnants of Hitler's party in the state apparatus, the local authorities and public life'.[58] The US authorities expelled the Leipzig committee from its offices, ordered the removal of all leaflets and posters from the streets, and then banned it. Any further use of the name 'Free Germany National Committee' would be punished severely.[59] The military government stopped Solingen's workplace councils purging Nazi activists and then abolished them.[60] Brunswick's Nazis had been arrested by the

Antifa, but were liberated by Allied command.[61] When Frankfurt Antifa housed people made homeless by bombing in apartments abandoned by fleeing Nazis, the authorities evicted them.[62] A GI described his experience of the parallel wars in Germany:

> The crime of it all is that we would take a little town, arrest the mayor and the other big shots, and put the anti-fascist in charge of the town. We'd double back to that town three days later, the Americans had freed all the officials and put 'em back in power. And they threw this other guy aside. Invariably it happened.[63]

It is important to realise that the Allied Military Government did not oppose the Antifas out of tenderness towards Nazism. But there was a greater enemy, as this German industrialist explained: 'Frankly, we are expecting a revolution ... Not without reason has the Military Government imposed curfews and banned assemblies. It has prevented a growing threat coming from that direction'.[64] Hitler's supporters were to be punished as rival imperialists, rather than for their role in German society. There could be no people's war against Nazism in conquered Germany.

So denazification would be on imperialist terms, and not shaped by the people. In Soviet-controlled East Germany half a million cases (or 3 per cent of the population) were investigated.[65] Moscow was keen to replace the former German establishment with its own placemen, and therefore the process was thorough. During the 1945–65 period over 16,000 people were tried, almost 13,000 found guilty, and 118 sentenced to death.[66]

In the Western zone there were also mass arrests, with 100,000 Nazis interned in the US sector alone.[67] However, when the Cold War began, Britain, France and the USA focused on the new enemy and forgave the old one. Suddenly the brakes were applied to denazification. That meant:

> almost every case of even major offenders [was] downgraded to the category of followership, which in turn, rendered the offender eligible for amnesty. This meant that even a majority of those who had belonged to groups defined as criminal organizations (SS, Gestapo, and others) by the Nuernberg Tribunal were exonerated ... .[68]

The impact of this at local level was illustrated when Sinti witnesses (Gypsies known by their German name of 'Zigeuner') described the crimes of a brutal Nazi guard called Himmelheber to a German court. Despite hundreds of thousands of Sinti and Roma perishing during the Holocaust, Himmelheber was acquitted on appeal because it was 'commonly known that accounts of "Zigeuner" are not reliable'. Racist attitudes continued and in 1951 a senior policemen still described Sinti and Roma as 'genetically criminals and anti-social persons'.[69]

In the British zone 90 per cent of Nazi internees were cleared.[70] In West Germany, with a population three times that of the East, just 12,500 were tried, 5,000 convicted and 9 faced death.[71] Such leniency contrasted with Nazi military courts which had executed 26,000; but no judge or prosecutor from that time was even tried.[72] As one historian has put it:

> The tribunals soon came to be likened to laundries: one entered wearing a brown shirt and left with a clean starched white shirt instead. Denazification had finally become, not the cleansing of Germany's economy, administration and society of Nazis, but rather the cleansing and rehabilitation of individuals.[73]

Conforming to the political needs of the imperialist powers, the 'small fry' were punished while the chief culprits, who belonged to the capitalist establishment, escaped.[74] Thus in West Germany giant businesses such as IG Farben (producers of the gas used at Auschwitz) and the big banks emerged virtually unscathed from decartelisation proceedings, which were scaled down in 1947.[75]

Before and during the Second World War ordinary Germans suffered the vicious repression of Nazism. Then the Allies imposed collective punishment in the form of area bombing and condoning of mass rape. When the opportunity finally came to distinguish between those who had been part of the Third Reich, and those who had been its victims, the Allies showed no interest. Gestapo repression had given little space for the development of people's war. As a consequence, when 1945 saw a welcome end to the abomination of Nazism, on both sides of a divided Germany the popular resistance that finally emerged in the form of an Antifa movement stood little chance against the combined weight of the Allied conquerors.

10
Austria – Resistance and Ruling-Class Capitulation

Even before Spain, Austria witnessed the first skirmishes of the people's war when in 1934 the working class in Vienna rebelled against fascist dictatorship. The background to this event was the collapse of the Austrian Empire after the First World War and the Wall Street crash. The ruling class was bitterly divided over how to cope. One wing favoured *Anschluss* – caving into Hitler's demands for a merger. Another believed independence could still be viable if it leaned on Mussolini's Italy as a counter-weight to German influence.[1] The latter faction, the Austrofascists, adopted Italian methods, suspended Parliament and outlawed strikes.

So sharp was the conflict between the two wings that pro-Nazis murdered the Austrofascist Chancellor, Dolfuss, and attempted to seize power. Though they failed, Dolfuss' successor, Schuschnigg, was in a precarious position. Despite their differences, however, both sides agreed that the weakness of Austrian capitalism required an intensified exploitation of labour through dictatorship.

Resistance began on 12 February 1934, when Vienna's workers took to the barricades. Their slogan was: 'Strike fascism down, before it crushes you ... Workers, arm yourselves.'[2] Four days of fighting followed during which the army bombed council housing estates and eventually quelled the opposition. A participant drew up the balance sheet: 'Despite its defeat, the February struggle had great historical significance well beyond the borders of Austria. The German working class had capitulated to Hitler without a struggle. Now, for the first time, workers were mounting resistance to fascism weapons in hand. They lit a beacon!'[3]

And in spite of the repression it burned on. For example, the August–September 1937 edition of the illegal union paper *Gewerkschaft* (Union) reported strikes at Austro-Fiat, a wagon works, a steel plant, glass factory, textile mill and 12 other establishments.[4]

Austrofascism was fatally undermined when Italy joined the Rome–Berlin Axis and gave Hitler *carte blanche* to take over. In

1938 Hitler made his move. He summoned Schuschnigg to his mountain retreat in Berchtesgaden and demanded annexation. The stakes were high. As a conservative historian has suggested, even '24 hours of resistance, the launching of a general strike, and spontaneous mass demonstrations could have generated a common defensive struggle ...'.[5] Workers' representatives were calling for exactly that. Ten days before the *Anschluss* they took a considerable risk and emerged from the underground to beg Schuschnigg to mobilise popular resistance to Nazism.[6] All they asked was that left-wing political prisoners be freed and anti-union laws lifted. Schuschnigg, however, recalled a fateful point Hitler made at their meeting in Berchtesgaden. Referring to the Spanish revolution, the Führer asked him: 'Do you want to make another Spain of Austria?'[7] Schuschnigg did not, and refused to co-operate with the workers' leaders, saying this would be equivalent to 'conspiring with Bolsheviks'.[8] This left his regime isolated and unable to defend itself.

On 12 March 1938 Hitler's forces flooded across the border. One left activist saw workers with 'weapons in hand' ready to fight 'to the death' for Austrian independence. They were met by police who taunted them: 'Why are you still demonstrating? Schuschnigg has already abdicated.'[9] This finally destroyed any hope of a united resistance. The depth of capitulation was illustrated by the fact that unlike every other country occupied by Germany, Austria had no government in exile.[10] Even Karl Renner, the Socialist Party leader, advocated a 'yes' vote in the referendum Hitler held on annexation, to the disgust of many of his comrades.

A 'people's war' against Nazism developed nonetheless, though it was conducted by a small minority for the benefit of the masses, rather than by the people themselves. Following Renner's treachery the once solid and influential Socialist Party split.[11] The breakaway Revolutionary Socialists grouped around the veteran Otto Bauer attracted some members, but most went to the Austrian Communist Party (KPÖ). Indeed six out of seven communist resisters were former socialists and they constituted 75 per cent of those tried for political opposition.[12] As one historian puts it: 'on the basis of a large sample of active members of all types of underground resistance groups ... almost every Austrian actively resisting the Nazis was affiliated to the KPÖ.'[13] What was left of the remaining opposition was generally Catholic orientated.[14] Indeed, the only large demonstration against Nazism after *Anschluss* was in October 1938 under the slogan 'Our Führer is Christ' (rather than Hitler).[15]

In spite of great heroism, Austrian resistance remained splintered and weak. An example of this was the O5 organisation which made contact with the Allies towards the end of the war. Like the conservative opposition in Germany, its track record was not promising. There were many Austrofascists and monarchists in its ranks who outmanoeuvred those members who were on the left. Only partisans in Carinthia Province (who consisted mainly of Slovenians aided by Tito's forces in Yugoslavia), and the working class resistance, gave the Nazis any real problems.

The opponents of Nazism had to deal with the additional handicap of Allied policy. In 1943 the Foreign Ministers of the USA, Russia and Britain issued this joint declaration: 'Austria was the first free land to fall victim to Hitler's aggression.'[16] Perhaps they hoped to encourage an Austrian breakaway from Germany, but their position had dire long-term consequences. As one commentator has put it: 'You gave us a historical out, and we grabbed it.'[17] Granting *all* Austrians victim status meant, when the war ended, that former Austrofascists or Nazis were accorded equal status to anti-fascist resisters, in a situation where the former greatly outnumbered the latter. Post-war denazification investigators calculated that there were 100,000 Nazi members in Austria before the *Anschluss*, and 700,000 by 1945.[18] Over the same period 5,000 Austrian resistance fighters had been killed and 100,000 arrested.[19]

Even before 1949, when ex-Nazi Party members were permitted to vote and became an important electoral factor, prominent politicians were using the Allies' 'victim theory' to whitewash fascist crimes. In 1945 the country's Foreign Minister exonerated local Nazis by insisting: 'The persecution [of Jews] was ordered by the German Reich authorities and carried out by them.'[20] Renner, now elevated to Chancellor by the Russians, described Austrian anti-semitism as 'never very aggressive'.[21] Those who, in 1938, had been forced to clean Vienna's pavements with toothbrushes under a hail of abuse from passers-by might have disagreed; but the 70,000 Austrian Jews who perished in gas chambers could not object. With such politicians in charge, it was small wonder that in 1946 an opinion poll recorded 46 per cent of Austrians opposed to the return of the tiny remnant of the Jewish population that had survived.[22] There was a certain cold logic to this. Many pro-Nazi Austrians had profited from 'Aryanisation' of Jewish homes and property.

The disbanding of the Wehrmacht saw many thousands of Hitler's soldiers being welcomed home to Austria as tragic victims, while resisters received little recognition, and often found it extremely difficult even to return. An oral history of Austrian resisters records numerous examples of the US, for example, delaying travel home (because they were so frequently communists).[23] Once back they had pariah status. A telling example of this was during the dedication of a 'monument to the fallen', an event addressed by the highest officer in the Army. He refused to allow the memory of resistance fighters to be associated with the ceremony, because 'such people died as oath breakers and do not belong at this monument'.[24]

Denazification was less than thorough in Austria. In the amnesty of 1948 90 per cent of those under investigation escaped punishment.[25] Post-war Austria never underwent the re-education process that occurred in Germany, and the outcome has been shocking. In 1983 a man implicated in the killing of some 10,000 civilians in the Ukraine was only blocked from becoming President of the Parliament by a petition campaign. Worse still, Kurt Waldheim, known to have been charged of war crimes by the Yugoslavs, and on the US list of suspected war criminals, was elected President in 1986.[26]

Testimonies by two Austrian resisters show how anti-fascists viewed the 'victory' of the Second World War. The first is from Josef Hindels, a prominent trade union leader who found exile in Sweden:

> Despite the great, great joy I felt at the defeat of Hitler and liberation, I had many grounds to be depressed … I had hoped to return home immediately. But right through 1945 I failed, despite great efforts to get the necessary permission to return the Austria. It was only in 1946, and even then required the strenuous intervention of Kreisky [a future Chancellor] to obtain permission for me. That was the first disappointment. The second was that a provisional government was created in Austria with Karl Renner at its head. I had considered that utterly impossible … To me Renner was the man who, in 1938, had welcomed the annexation of Austria by Hitler's Germany. Ever since then I had considered him to be politically dead.[27]

The second comes from Bruno Furch who was released from a concentration camp in 1945:

> A damned, truly vile game began to be played by the two main parties in Austria [the Socialist and People's Parties]. I say it quite bluntly. They used the legacy of Nazi rule and fascism in their heads and their hearts for the purposes of fighting the Cold War in the West. The game was to use the fundamental

legacy of anti-Communism and anti-Sovietism for their own anti-Communist ends, by keeping it alive, if not in power. It was not merely to court the votes of 600,000 Nazi Party members – because that only happened in 1949 during the next election. No, it had already begun in 1945. So it was not only about votes but about harnessing this force from the very beginning.

In one of the housing estates we had a young Jewish comrade who in 1946 returned from exile in England to his home. But he committed suicide. What happened was he had fallen in love with the daughter of a high up socialist official... Her parents were against the relationship and against any marriage because he was Jewish. The young man simply could not cope with the idea that after the victory over Hitler, that anti-Semitism of this sort could still exist in the higher ranks of the re-born Socialist Party.[28]

It is difficult to imagine a wider gulf between the goals of imperialism and of anti-fascism. The readiness of the Allies to collaborate with both the pre-*Anschluss* Austrofascists, and former Nazis in the Cold War era, would poison post-war Austrian politics for decades.

11
Italy – The Working Class and the Two Wars

A feature distinguishing people's war from conventional war was the way it combined social aspirations for equality and emancipation with political goals, such as national independence and democracy. These former aspects were marked in Italy where overt working class struggle was more prominent than elsewhere.[1] One reason was that fascism originated here, so rather than resistance developing in sharp reaction to foreign invasion, it matured over decades under a hated social system that was closely associated with capitalism from its inception in 1922.[2] Business and finance supplied 74 per cent of fascist party funding[3] and in return Mussolini smashed the unions, and imposed draconian wage cuts in 1927, 1930 and 1934.[4]

His regime was less repressive than Hitler's, but it still condemned 17,000 political opponents to internal exile, 60,000 to special surveillance and control, and imposed 28,000 years of penal servitude between 1926 and 1943.[5] Workers made up 85 per cent of those convicted.[6] The Socialist leader Matteotti was murdered, while Gramsci, the founder of the Italian Communist Party (PCI), languished in jail, only being released to die. It has been argued that an 'indefatigable subversiveness' survived within popular culture, but before the Second World War this did not translate into active resistance.[7]

The war changed everything. Italy's entry was not smooth. Spriano tells us that Mussolini's doubts about the ability of his country to withstand a major conflict were pushed aside by the establishment. After witnessing the success of *Blitzkrieg* it was anxious to 'arrive in time to seize an easy and crushing victory'.[8] War brought the ruling class tangible benefits. By 1942 engineers hours had risen to 60 per week[9] and Fiat's share price had soared by 62 per cent. Its director revelled in 'the formidable Japanese conquests in the Pacific and the absorption of the rich territories of Russia into the European Axis economy', as they promised 'expanded production and vaster markets'.[10] Italy's rapacious plans were ultimately frustrated by the Allies, as was the case with Germany and Japan. However, it took

till 1945 and required overwhelming force to obliterate the latter.
Mussolini's rule crumbled two years earlier. Why was it so fragile?

It was partly due to Italy's GNP which was a third of Germany's.
This made the army more vulnerable to defeat in an inter-imperialist
conflict. Even more significant was the fact that the regime was
destroyed from within by people's war. Between 1938 and 1945
the cost of living increased 20 times over. With grossly inadequate
rationing on the one side, and astronomical black market prices[11] on
the other, it was no surprise that many of Turin's 150,000 thousand
strong labour force lost 10 to15 kilograms in weight.[12] Gradually
the gulf between the repression-hardened minority of politically-
motivated resisters and the masses began narrowing.[13]

This became clear when strikes swept across the northern
industrial belt in the spring of 1943. Their epicentre was Turin
where flourishing war production in vast factories generated a
sense of collective power. At the same time Allied bombing had
flattened 25,000 homes but the state provided no air-raid shelters.[14]
Confidence combined with desperation to generate strike action
even though this was a perilous step to take under fascism, especially
during wartime.[15] A leaflet of January 1943 illustrates the mood:

> For food and liberty!
> Down with the 12-hour day and the damned war!
> We demand that Mussolini be chased from power!
> We are struggling for peace and our country's independence!
> For a pay rise that is actually paid out!
> Action, strike, struggle – these are the only weapons we have to
> save ourselves
> Strike, strike, strike![16]

Such appeals fell on fertile ground. During winter 1942/3
stoppages increased from two to five per month.[17] Then, on 5
March, 21,000 workers at Fiat Mirafiori responded to the call of the
80-strong communist cell and struck, despite the signal for action
– the factory siren – being silenced by management.[18] Walkouts
spread through Turin and beyond. By 15 March the movement
encompassed 100,000 women and men[19] and at the end of the
month every factory in Piedmont had shut.[20]

Mussolini was shocked that 'the population was so hostile and
averse to fascism' and offered major concessions.[21] He realised
that: 'This decidedly nasty and extremely deplorable episode has
suddenly thrown us back 20 years.'[22] Hitler, who just a month before

had lost the key battle of Stalingrad, understood the implications too. He found it 'unthinkable that so many people can strike, and no-one dares intervene ... I am convinced that in the circumstances anyone who shows the minimum weakness is doomed.'[23] His words were prophetic.

The Turin strike was the first successful mass walkout in two decades, and arguably the most important of the global war. The shock it administered fascism was supplemented by an Anglo-American landing in Sicily (on 10 July 1943). Then the establishment panicked. It had wallowed in the benefits of fascism for 20 years, but now that association was a liability provoking revolution and/or the wrath of the advancing Allies. To gain some room for manoeuvre Italy's government asked the Germans to accept its withdrawal from war in return for ceding its Balkan conquests, but they refused.[24] Grasping for another way out the government decided to publicly ditch Mussolini and secretly conclude an armistice with the Allies. The Fascist Grand Council itself voted 19 to 7 to depose and arrest the Duce.

The ruling class hoped the change would be no more than cosmetic. Pirelli, the industrial magnate, began discussions with the Allies[25] on the basis that 'the monarchy, the crown, the church, the army and the leaders of the economy' would remain at the helm.[26] There was a slight presentational difficulty. It was this very monarch King Vittorio Emanuele III who made Mussolini dictator in 1922. The Duce had touted the myth that he came to power in a daring seizure of power during which 3,000 martyrs had died – the March on Rome.[27] But the claim was fake. As one writer put it: 'Only when all was over did there begin the spectacle which has been called the March on Rome.'[28] Some advisors had begged the King to invoke state power to counter Mussolini's antics but he openly boasted about his refusal: 'I desire that all Italians know that I signed no decree for a state of siege.'[29] This decision paid off. With Mussolini as his PM, Vittorio Emanuele would add Emperor of Ethiopia and King of Albania to his list of titles. So now, even after Mussolini was formally deposed, the King insisted that 'fascism cannot be dismantled in one go. It needs to be gradually modified in order to remove those aspects which are shown to be harmful to the country'.[30] His new PM was Marshal Badoglio. His anti-fascist credentials were no better. He too had energetically supported Mussolini and earned promotion and the title of Duke of Addis Ababa in the process.

If the Second World War had been an unambiguous battle against fascism, then this supposed metamorphosis of the Italian government would have been recognised for the fraud it was. However, the Allied powers embraced the King and Badoglio with open arms. They had no qualms because, as one writer puts it, 'there was no ideological prejudice against personalities of the Fascist regime'.[31] The Anglo-Americans shared the Italian establishment's fear of revolution and willingly forgave past misdemeanours, just so long as Italy quit the rival imperialist coalition. Indeed, the US had made overtures to the King before and after Italy's entry into the Second World War.[32] Churchill's admiration of the Duce dated from 1927 and was undimmed when, in 1943, he contemptuously dismissed 'the usual arguments against having anything to do with those who had worked with or helped Mussolini'.[33] The King had other surprising friends. When the US expressed doubts about his ability to keep control, Russia granted him full diplomatic recognition. It was the first Allied power to do so.[34]

Demonstrators who ecstatically welcomed the Duce's downfall on 25 July 1943 were unaware of these sordid games. Tearing down the symbols of dictatorship they celebrated the end of fascism and war. Their joy was premature. The government ordered newspapers to 'avoid criticising the men and events of the previous regime [or] the war. Exercise maximum care towards our German ally. Do not call for the freeing of political prisoners ... .'[35] Badoglio, as military governor of Italy, declared: 'it is necessary to act with maximum energy to prevent the current excitement degenerating into a Communist or subversive movement.'[36] Using language reminiscent of Athens, the army and police were instructed to confront the jubilant crowds 'in combat formation, opening fire from a distance, but also using mortars and artillery as though proceeding against enemy troops'.[37] In Reggio Emilia, 11 were machine-gunned at a demonstration for peace and the expulsion of the Wehrmacht. In Bari there were 19 victims.[38] Italy's ruling class was still equivocating over which imperialist camp would best suit its purposes, but it had no doubt who the real enemy was.

In March 1943 Hitler had berated the Italian government for weakness. Five months later Churchill applauded the murderous actions of a supposedly post-fascist regime:

In Turin and Milan there were Communist demonstrations which *had to be put down by armed force*. Twenty years of Fascism has obliterated the middle class. There is nothing between the King, with the Patriots who have rallied round him, who have complete control, and rampant Bolshevism.[39]

The Allied media could not help noticing the hypocrisy of such talk. The BBC scorned the Italian government's 'failure' to remove fascism[40] and America's *Life* magazine warned that:

> The clear tendency within the fascist regime is to free itself from Mussolini and the Germanophiles, but to preserve the system. This is the idea of the big industrialists today ... In other words, a change from pro-German fascism to pro-Ally fascism. The fascist hierarchy are very impressed by the successful *volte face* of Darlan ... .[41]

Government repression was met with strikes demanding peace, pay rises, the removal of fascists, and release of political prisoners.[42] Some soldiers mutinied and refused to shoot. Nazi Germany watched the unfolding situation with alarm, and the eight Wehrmacht divisions stationed in the North got ready to take charge. The PCI understood the danger and in August 1943 called on Italians to: 'Prepare to repel any German intervention with force [and] organise the armed collaboration of the people and army ... .'[43] This ran directly counter to the government's aim of salvaging what remained of fascism.[44]

Badoglio could only have repulsed the German threat by rousing the populace, but instead treated them 'as though proceeding against enemy troops'. Denying a people's war meant Badoglio could only tack ineffectually between the imperialist blocs, hoping one would cancel out the other. Even as he concluded a secret peace treaty with the Anglo-Americans advancing from the South he sought continued German backing in the North, telling Ribbentrop: 'If this government collapses, it will be replaced by one of Bolshevik hue.' The Nazi foreign minister also feared that 'power would go to those with left radical ideas'.[45]

Without a peace deal, and caught in a pincer movement between imperialist armies, the suffering of the Italian people continued. Allied bombs rained down on them, with 220,000 Milanese losing their homes in just five days during August 1943. Meanwhile, the Germans were left free to entrench their positions.[46] The government's double-dealing eventually ran out of time. On 8 September General Eisenhower, weary of Badoglio's procrastination, broadcast news of the armistice the Italian government had negotiated with the Allies.[47] Amazingly, even now Badoglio still tried to sit on the fence. 'We will fight whoever attacks us', he said, without specifying who that might be.[48] Another military order was clearer: 'In no case are you to take the initiative in hostilities against German troops.'[49]

Such hesitancy left Italy's armed forces totally unprepared for the Nazi backlash. The German army attacked, while the King, Badoglio, and all three armed services ministers fled south to safety in the arms of the Allies. Left with no instructions except not to fight[50] the Italian army of one million was eliminated overnight: 615,000 soldiers were deported to concentration camps and 30,000 died.[51] Although the King had finally thrown his lot in with the Allies, his prior actions symbolised the treachery of an entire governing class, and sealed the post-war fate of the monarchy.[52]

Northern Italy was now subject to the full force of German wartime economic policy which consisted of shifting 'responsibility for funding the Nazi war machine to the citizens of conquered lands'.[53] From Italy the Nazis extracted 84 billion lira, out of an annual national income of 130 billion lira.[54] They used Mussolini as an alibi in this enterprise. He was freed in a daring commando raid and installed as head of a puppet regime – the Republic of Salò. Henceforth resisters applied a single term to the enemy: Nazi-Fascist.

After looting the country, the Nazis required: a) its factory production; b) no distractions from the fight against Allied advance in the South; c) manpower for the German war machine. The resistance of the northern workers and peasants deprived them of all three.

The difference between this people's war and imperialist war was eloquently described by Ginzburg of the Action Party, a radical republic grouping:

The formal declaration of hostilities against Germany by the King and Badoglio was a meaningless gesture which did nothing to change the real situation of the time.

The real war against Nazi Germany was declared on 9 September, after the soldiers were officially ordered to abandon their guns. The Italian people seized hold of them and boldly confronted the armour of the German tanks. Thousands of soldiers and civilians headed into the mountains rather than serve the Germans, and equipped themselves for guerrilla struggle following the heroic example of the Russian and Balkan partisans … The Italian war against Nazi Germany was the war of a people who aspired to full political and social liberty ... This war was not declared in an exchange of diplomatic notes but written in the blood of heroes who sacrificed themselves each day, who had an impact on the future, who weighed in the balance of history ... .[55]

A female partisan witnessed the birth of people's war in Turin. At the very moment that the King and Badoglio were scuttling for cover, 'the youth launched an assault on the barracks ... and we held a grand demonstration in front of the Chamber of Labour where the workers demanded arms and waved placards saying "Turn Turin into Stalingrad" ... This was the real army of the working class on the move.'[56]

Fighting both Salò and the Wehrmacht gave mass struggle a dual character. It was a battle for national liberation, and 'a true civil war'[57] for 'class emancipation'.[58] Italian conditions favoured such a development. In France the Nazis had collapsed so suddenly at the end that there was no need for the resistance to consolidate its hold before the Allies arrived. By contrast, it took Anglo-American forces from September 1943 to April 1945 to reach Italy's northern frontier. As one British diplomat wrote ruefully: 'The pace of Allied advance has undoubtedly contributed to the birth of an independent government in the North.'[59]

Italy's people's war, which fused workers' action in industry with armed operations, was far more audacious than anything witnessed in Germany or Austria. Valiani, of the Action Party, explains why:

If the movement took the Germans by surprise they gave in and made concessions ... But if the movement did not spread and remained isolated in a single city the Gestapo could focus its attack, raiding and deporting people to Germany. This included members of the improvised committees with whom they had previously negotiated, as well as political suspects. Paradoxically the degree of daring, the spreading of strikes to the largest number of localities, represented a precautionary approach.[60]

Milan became the headquarters of the Committee for National Liberation (CLN), and emulated Turin by staging a classic strike, this time under a German regime. The demand was for a dramatic pay rise, doubling of rations, provision of oil and sugar, no to sackings, an end to curfew, and exclusion of Nazis from workplaces.[61] The stoppage began on 10 December 1943 and within days the Lombard capital ground to a halt.

While employers like Pirelli conceded 30 per cent pay rises, others proclaimed their willingness to meet demands only if the German commander, General Zimmermann, approved.[62] He ordered a return to work. With the workers unbending the SS began rounding them up. So a new demand was added to the list – freedom for those arrested! Now General Zimmermann promised vague concessions, but the strikers were unimpressed: 'On to complete victory. Your threats do not frighten us. Just give us what we demand and we will return to work!'[63]

Events at the Breda Funk works show the local dimension. After the boss assembled the 6,000-strong workforce to report he would meet their demands in full, and have those arrested released, he asked: 'Will you return tomorrow?' The resounding response was still 'No!' Perplexed the management suggested the workforce might like to elect representatives to meet General Zimmermann. No-one responded.[64] Eventually a delegation did step forward, but on condition that it would only talk to the management, not the Nazis. This was not honoured. When the delegation arrived at the Breda plant the bosses melted away, the Germans appeared, barred the exits and attempted to begin negotiations.

Eventually, to try and end the strike city-wide, the Nazis offered pay rises of 40–50 per cent, along with improved rations. Still the workers held out! Armoured cars toured Milan's factories, and soldiers attempted to compel people to return – to little avail.[65] The strike ended after a week, but those involved made it plain they did this because they chose to, not because of Nazi pressure.

Workplace resistance was but one form of the people's war. Communist-led Patriotic Action Groups (GAP) and Patriotic Action Squads (SAP) operated in the urban setting.[66] In the countryside there were partisan squads. These were headed by seasoned anti-fascists (many of them veterans of the Spanish Civil War), or occasionally soldiers who had reached the mountains under arms before the Germans could capture them.[67] As with the French *maquis*, mass recruitment was stimulated by Nazi-Fascist round-ups and the death penalty for draft dodgers. One young man's diary described the dilemma facing many: 'What am I to do? Present myself? Never! … So here I am, 22, on the run and wondering – will I be shot? Or should I take refuge in the woods?' Despite his mother being taken hostage he chose a life of 'seizing arms, munitions, anything that serves the struggle … .'[68] In Pavia alone 50 per cent of those summoned failed to appear.[69]

The effectiveness of the partisans is attested to by numerous sources. The Allied commander, General Alexander, estimated that six of the Wehrmacht's 25 divisions were diverted to dealing with them.[70] From the opposing side, Kesselring, Germany's plenipotentiary for Italy, complained that once 'unlimited guerrilla warfare' commenced in June 1944 the 200,000 to 300,000[71] partisans 'constituted a real menace to Germany's armed forces and played a vital role in the campaign. Eliminating this threat was of decisive importance to us.' He judged that 'the battle against the regular enemy forces and against the partisan bands had equal importance [so] the very best troops had to be used ...'.[72] The guerrillas' claimed 5,449 surprise actions, 218 pitched battles, 458 locomotives destroyed, 356 bridges blown up and 5,573 operations to sabotage power lines and communications, as well as tens of thousands of enemy soldiers killed.[73]

The guerrilla method of the people's war was quite different from imperialist combat. When Giovanni Pesce, a partisan, went to collect weapons from the royal army, an officer demanded to know his grade. Pesce was scandalised: 'Neither the utter collapse of 8 September, nor the partisan insurrection, had shaken this man's rigid view that there must be a fixed and immutable hierarchy.' Another partisan resented the 'social disparity between officers and troops' that he found and contrasted that with 'our formations that are based on absolute democracy'. Guerrillas found 'the institution of the officers' mess incomprehensible. An officer in the Garibaldini [the communist-led grouping] shares bread, board and heating with the other soldiers.'[74] Incomprehension was mutual. General Cadorna, sent north to command the partisans in the name of the King, was shocked by their political engagement and the 'election of officers by consensus of the base' that occurred in some units.[75]

Money was another bone of contention. To the GAP leader, Cichetti, the very idea of receiving a salary was offensive: 'I detested the idea of being paid to be a partisan. I had not seen a lira for six months, but had always been able to make do, without turning to the laws of the market to survive.'[76] Higher pay for partisan commanders was usually rejected because 'we are in a people's war which is fought by volunteers motivated by high patriotic spirit'.[77]

Unlike professional or conscript armies, where political debate is frowned upon, the partisans were simultaneously a prototype alternative state and militia. In August 1944 a typical agreement between various partisan groups declared:

Far from being a miniature replica of the old military structure, the partisan army is the symbol of an independent movement that owes its being to the will of the people, which is in itself an unequivocal political affirmation. The war against the Nazi-Fascists is only the preliminary step on the road towards our ultimate objective; the radical reconstruction of the political, moral and social life of our country... we are fighting for democracy, freedom in the fullest sense of the word, justice, and the dignity and respect that are due to man.[78]

These principles could be put into practice when Axis forces were expelled from entire districts. Fifteen partisan republics appeared,[79] in places like Carnia (150,000 inhabitants), Montefiorino (50,000) and Ossola (70,000).[80] Their administrations were quite unlike those of Salò, or Badoglio's for that matter.[81] In Varzi, for example, mass assemblies elected a local government purged of fascists using direct democracy. Observers saw 'people of every race ... coming and going on the steps of the town hall. There were peasants who wanted permits, who came to collect their share of requisitioned goods, or to protest against an abuse – bourgeois, partisans working class women, many new faces.'[82] Requisitions were paid for in kind, or with partisan 'money', that could be redeemed after the country was liberated.[83]

This financial arrangement also operated in the Republic of the Val d'Ossola[84] where crime was eliminated, a 'Popular University' frequented by all classes was established, Italy's first female Minister appointed, and trade unions restored.[85] It has been claimed that this area 'was the only substantial part of Hitler's occupied Europe to achieve independence, and obtain recognition from Switzerland'.[86] The partisans expected the republic to receive substantial outside aid because its 'capital', Domodossola, was close to Milan and would be a useful launching pad for any Anglo-American offensive there. But the Allied representative on hand was dismissive: 'You must not pretend to be in charge of military operations, like Alexander and Eisenhower ... .'[87] Another explained that the republic's continued existence made it 'not only a rival to the Italian government in Rome, but also a rival to the Italian Army ...'.[88] A partisan leader lamented that 'the indifference shown by the Allies in regard to the efforts at Domodossola, provoked a wave of bitterness'.[89] Without assistance the republic was finally crushed in six days of savage fighting.

Further evidence of tension between the parallel wars emerged in debate over *attentism*. Opponents stood for an immediate people's war of liberation, supporters wanted to wait for salvation by imperialist armies. Battaglia has paraphrased the arguments. The attentists said: 'It is useless for us to attack the Germans; there aren't enough of us to do any good, and what's more, any attempt we make will simply provoke reprisals: apart from ourselves, the civil population will suffer, and suffer hideously.'

He then lays out the flaws in this logic: 'How could the Resistance increase in strength or extend its scope if it remained completely passive, completely static? Furthermore, what the Attentistes had signally failed to recognize was that, for local, national, sentimental and strictly common-sense reasons, it had become absolutely necessary to fight the Germans.'[90]

A factor impelling independent action was that the Allies denied Italy all rights because it had been an Axis power. Thus Churchill's Foreign Minister was outraged when the Italians replaced Marshal Badoglio: 'A nation which has unconditionally surrendered has no right to present the Allies with a Government chosen by themselves.'[91] Britain was simply not there to free Italy, as Radio London admitted: 'The liberation of the peninsula is not, and cannot be, the ultimate aim of the Allies. It is just a means of defeating Germany ... .'[92]

This attitude led some commentators to quip that Italy was now under two occupations. In the South were the Allies supported by a fascist King; in the North were the Germans supported by Mussolini's Salò Republic.[93] Put like this, attentism amounted to either accepting Nazi-Fascism or Allied imperialist domination through the AMGOT (Allied Military Government of Occupied Territory).

The only alternative was a liberation struggle. One form this took was further mass strikes. In the spring of 1944 half a million downed tools in the largest stoppage of the World War. It was directed almost as much at convincing the Allies that heavy aerial bombing was unnecessary.[94]

Another related issue was 'terrorism'. Should partisans target individual Nazis behind the lines, even if it provoked the Germans to murder hostages or civilians, or wait for the Anglo-Americans? A notorious example of the risks involved in terror actions followed the killing of 32 SS guards in Rome. In revenge the Nazis executed 335 Italian hostages at the Ardeatine caves.[95] For the attentists this horrific collective punishment proved the need to hold back, and some peasants did indeed turn against the partisans for fear their actions could attract reprisals.[96]

The guerrillas were acutely aware of the problem, but had a solution. Valiani, whose Action Party was linked to the Justice and Liberty partisans, explains that urban terrorism aimed to avoid collective punishment and to inspire youth to join the struggle.[97] Whereas Axis troops were under attack at the front, in cities 'terrorism was not directly against enemy soldiers, but against the machinery of police, repression and reprisal. It was adopted, despite the risks, as a method of self-defence.'[98] Successful actions showed the enemy was not invincible. Pavone offers an illustration: when fascist police began an anti-guerrilla operation in one area, the GAP killed 17 of them. As a result 100 out of the remaining 150 deserted their posts, some even joining the partisans.[99]

Demonstrative action was effective as long as it did not substitute for, or become an alternative to, mass actions such as strikes. Partisans dared not become cut off from the wider population on whom they depended for shelter, food, and general support. Awareness of these reciprocal relations helped avoid the pitfalls of terror operations that might have demobilised the masses and left them as passive bystanders. An example of how the link-up could work was given by *Our Struggle* in February 1944. The Germans wished to ship labour and machinery from Italy to assist its war efforts, but the resistance responded: 'Not a machine, not a worker must go to Germany! To achieve this the actions of the mass of workers [will be backed by] armed defence squads (GAP) and partisan formations, [and] will systematically interrupt and destroy communication links with Germany.'[100]

Perhaps the most powerful argument was given by a hostage of the Nazis: 'Don't give up the struggle. Don't let my situation hold you back. If I survive, I survive, but if I must die I will be fulfilling my fate. The important thing is *that you never give in!*'[101] Whatever doubt there might be about using terrorism as a weapon in the people's war arsenal, this pales against the barbarity of indiscriminate bombing so beloved of the Allies.

Regardless of the merits of the debate, attentism suited the Allied imperialist cause. On 10 November 1944 General Alexander, Commander of Allied Forces in Italy, announced that his forces would not advance that winter and that the partisans should stand down, cease offensive operations, return to their homes and await further orders.[102] This declaration had a devastating impact on morale. The guerrillas were battling in deteriorating weather conditions against enormous Nazi-fascist armies who now had *carte blanche* to attack. Longo, the most prominent communist in the resistance, saw Alexander's move 'as an attempt on the part of the Allied·command to eliminate the Italian liberation movement'.[103] In the General's favour it has been argued that the Germans' Gothic Line defences were impregnable and that Allied commanders had 'no political considerations in their minds; they thought solely of the interests of the partisans'.[104] However, Behan finds it strange that Alexander's statement 'was not broadcast in code, as was the norm. Even worse, Resistance leaders were not consulted or informed beforehand...'[105]

To suggest, in a North Italy infested with German and fascist troops, that the partisans cease operations, showed no appreciation of the on-going deportations of labour to Germany, the daily acts of repression against the population, etc. The guerrillas' reply was that 'the partisan war is not, on the part of the Italian people and the patriots who have taken up arms, a mere whim, an idle caprice to be refrained from at will. It arose from the vital necessity of defending our material, moral and social heritage; this is the supreme cause for which we have been fighting and must continue to fight day after day ... The war must go on.'[106] Whether Alexander was motivated by the politicians' distaste for Italian self-liberation or military considerations alone,[107] this episode is a graphic example of the two wars in practice.

Although workers played such a prominent role in Italy, even here the people's war was never a pure class phenomenon. Thus the more astute northern employers realised that bitter disputes with labour invited Nazi intervention, which could lead to their workers (and factories) being shipped to Germany.[108] To forestall this they made concessions and protected 'their' employees.[109] Behan describes the 'ducking and weaving' of Fiat. Even as it produced tanks and V2 rocket parts for Germany it maintained links with US intelligence services, and provided massive funds to the CLN. The resistance leader at Fiat Mirafiori understood how his employers 'had no scruples about facing in several directions at the same time to safeguard their primary interest: profit'.[110]

Similarly, in the interests of national unity, the Italian resistance brought together a multitude of parties representing a constellation of class forces. Thus the day after the 8 September 1943 armistice the five main political parties – Communists, Socialists, Action Party, Christian Democrats and Liberals – formed the Comitato di Liberazione Nazionale Alta Italia (North Italy National Liberation

Committee – CLNAI). Local committees spread quickly. In turn a centralised military structure – the CVL (Corpo Volontari della Libertà (Volunteers for Liberty Corps) – was set up to oversee partisan activity.

The relationship between the summit and the base of this people's war was complex, and the most important and interesting interaction took place within the PCI's sphere of influence. Although the statistics differ, it is clear the PCI was the dominant force. Spriano suggests that between 80 and 90 per cent of political detainees were communist in the early stages.[111] When the mass anti-fascist movement took off, PCI influence persisted. By October 1944 perhaps five-eighths of the partisans were in the communist-controlled Garibaldi Brigades,[112] and 60 per cent of partisans who died were linked to communist formations.[113] Even political rivals admitted to communist numerical preponderance, with Valiani of the Action Party, the second most important grouping, estimating 41 per cent of partisans were in the Garibaldini as opposed to 29 per cent in his Justice and Liberty bands.[114] The pre-war PCI membership of 6,000 had become 1.8 million by its end.[115]

Working class politics therefore set the tone even for political or ideological rivals. Thus Olivelli, leader of the Catholic Green Flame partisans, took it for granted that:

> the age of capitalism that has produced astronomical wealth and led to unspeakable misery, is in its death throes. A soulless regime encouraged the spread of a poverty that was beyond belief, sabotaged the productive efforts of the people, and deliberately provoked man's inhumanity to man; it exalted the cult of might and violence, manifested itself in tyranny and oppression, and burnt itself out in the flames of war. From the final convulsions of this age a new era is being born, the era of the working classes, infinitely more just, more fraternal, more Christian.[116]

The PCI's working-class base encouraged it to reflect the need of the people's war, but its leadership felt other pressures. Since 1926 fascist repression had driven this group into exile (in France and Russia). It was so cut off from its membership that, according to one scholar: 'In most of the towns and villages none of [the rank and file] had any contact with the party apparatus for years... .'[117] The top leadership, headed by Palmiro Togliatti, was shaped instead by Stalinism. Togliatti sought to control and channel the spontaneous aspects of struggle into ever more centralised structures – the CLNs, the CLNAI and the CVL. Such a development was partly driven by the exigencies of war, which required increasing co-ordination as the scale of the fighting grew. It also reflected the PCI leadership's programme. The democratic base and the centralist needs of armed struggle were not inherently antagonistic. Each could strengthen the other. However, the people's war did come into conflict with centralism, because that was driven by Togliatti's pursuit of Russian foreign policy aims.

The most dramatic expression of this occurred in March 1944 when Togliatti joined Badoglio's cabinet. This so-called 'Salerno turn' was totally unexpected. Two months before, a PCI conference in Bari had strongly criticised Badoglio,[118] and the PCI newspaper, Unità, ridiculed the idea that the southern regime could fight Nazism: 'How could this government that is terrified of the people, lead a people's war.'[119] During fascism the PCI had suffered terribly from the likes of Badoglio and the King, yet now Togliatti wrote: 'The working class must abandon the position of opposition and criticism which it occupied in the past … .'[120] Not without reason has Broué suggested that the Salerno turn represented 'a Stalinist apparatus brought into Italy from outside, struggling to impose itself from above upon the real party, the true party … .'[121]

Togliatti's policy conformed to the decisions made at the Yalta conference of February 1945[122] when Stalin, Churchill and Roosevelt divided Europe into spheres of influence. Since Italy fell into the Anglo-American sphere, the resistance must be sacrificed to honour a deal giving Russia dominance in Eastern Europe. The Salerno turn transformed the PCI's role in the resistance. Class struggle was now to be replaced by 'national unity' with the bosses, the monarchy, ex-fascists, and anyone not overtly in the Nazi camp. The May 1944 edition of the PCI's guerrilla newspaper, Il Combattente, insisted that 'every disagreement about the regime we want in our country, every legitimate reform, if it is not urgent, must take second place, be set aside, be delayed until after the victory'[123] What a contrast to its words six months before: 'The struggle of peasants and workers for their immediate demands is sacrosanct, unavoidable [and] must be linked to the armed struggle without which both would sooner or later suffocate.'[124]

Some rank and file activists saw Togliatti's move as 'an act of betrayal'.[125] It 'caused perplexity, especially among those who were in jail for years'.[126] Even prominent individuals such as Amendola admitted: 'as the Central Committee carried out its political activity along the lines of national unity, nearly all the groups with which it was in contact ... tended not to understand or approve.'[127] Scoccimarro, found Togliatti's views 'absolutely inopportunune, and it is to be hoped they are not repeated'.[128]

The staunchly republican Action Party, which had been more middle class, white collar, and moderate than the PCI,[129] was now to its left. Valiani initially thought news reports of the Salerno turn were a forgery, and noted the glee with which Mussolini's Republic of Salò described the PCI as selling out to royalty.[130] The Action Party warned Togliatti that he threatened to split the anti-fascist movement.

One consequence of the Salerno turn was the growth of revolutionary movements outside the PCI advocating 'the class struggle transposed on to an international plane'.[131] By June 1944 the Stella Rossa (Red Star) group, which accused the PCI of betraying the working class and joining the bourgeoisie, had as many members as the PCI in the key industrial city of Turin.[132] Bandiera Rossa (Red Flag) had more fighters in Rome than the PCI. This movement thought the PCI had forfeited its right to call itself communist.[133]

However, Togliatti held a trump card: his association with the USSR and its Red Army, which at that very moment was hurling back the Nazis on the Eastern Front. As Russian forces approached Flossenburg concentration camp a captured Garibaldini inmate described how he 'heard a roar ... Those cannons were the voice of Stalin'.[134] Another prisoner, though an Action Party member, expressed disappointment at being liberated by US soldiers rather than the Red Army. Togliatti's Salerno turn drew legitimacy from the myth that Russia represented 'actually existing socialism', or as street graffiti expressed it, the USSR 'truly relied on the poor, the humble, the proletarians and workers ...'.[135] Before Togliatti's somersault 'the bosses' were described as 'vampires who feed on labour, these profiteers from war and German occupation ...'.[136] Now, wielding Soviet authority, the PCI leadership demanded its Italian followers unite with 'industrialists, intellectuals, priests, ex-fascists ... no-one is excluded'.[137] Therefore, those who raised clenched fists or wore symbols like the hammer and sickle must be dealt with 'severely and made to tow the party line'.[138]

In return for financial support the resistance also accepted the 'Rome Protocols' which stated: 'As the enemy withdraws, all components [of the partisans] will come under direct command of the [Allied] Commander-in-Chief ... and will obey any order issued by him or by Allied Military Government on his behalf, including such orders to disband and surrender their arms, when required to do so.'[139]

There were limits to how far the PCI leadership could move rightwards, because it still had to placate its membership, compete with rival political groupings, and retain bargaining strength in the post-war era. Card-carrying Communist Party members were a minority and partisans were not automatons. Lines of communication and command were tenuous; and formal hierarchical structures rarely corresponded to the anarchic conditions of combat on the ground. So the PCI did not entirely abandon radical language. Squaring the circle, Togliatti still called for an 'insurrection', but it would not be 'socialist or communist but for national liberation to destroy fascism'.[140] Equally, the PCI rejected attentism and Allied efforts to marginalise the partisans'. It encouraged the establishment of CLNs in every village, district and factory.[141] This institutionalisation of the movement was simultaneously a means of defying the AMGOT and royal government, a means of exerting control from above, and a method of organising a more efficient struggle from below. Nevertheless, a tense relationship between people's war and the imperialist war currents within the resistance movement persisted.

By April 1945 the Allied offensive seemed poised to finally break into the North. At that moment the CLNAI issued Directive No. 16, its call to 'national insurrection'. Sounding a note of realism it cautioned that 'the Allies may decide, for one reason or another, to withhold their support, instead of making the contribution for which we have asked'. Nevertheless, 'Partisan formations will attack and eliminate Nazi-Fascist headquarters and effect the liberation of cities, towns and villages ... [We] will proclaim a general strike ... the culmination of the people's long campaign for freedom and the expression of their unshakable determination.'[142]

During the month that the final liberation of Italy took to complete, the two types of war complemented each other, with the Allied armies attacking at the front while partisans struck from the rear. Immense general strikes shook the northern industrial cities and thwarted German plans for a 'scorched earth' policy of destroying the North's infrastructure. Yet the distinction between the parallel wars did not disappear. A good example was the liberation of Genoa, whose story has been told by Basil Davidson, a British Liaison Officer working with the partisans.

Genoa was a port city that, along with Milan and Turin, formed the 'industrial triangle' powering Italian economic development.

In April 1945 there were *over* 15,000 strongly armed Germans in occupation.[143] In a move similar to von Choltitz's in Paris, General Meinhold offered to declare Genoa an open city if the partisans allowed the Wehrmacht to retreat unhindered. On 23 April the CLN decided to prevent Meinhold's forces fighting elsewhere, by making an immediate stand. At this time the partisans numbered some 6,000. Lacking adequate supplies from the Allies, most were minimally armed.[144] Nevertheless they fought the Nazis to a standstill and on 25 April 9,000 Germans surrendered unconditionally. Two days later, a 7,000-strong section tried to break out, but eventually surrendered to a force of just 300 SAP fighters.[145]

The CLN had liberated Genoa. At that very moment the US Army appeared in the shape of General Almond. Not speaking Italian he could only address the CLN leadership via the intermediary of Davidson:

> 'Tell them,' General Almond said, 'that my troops have liberated their city, and they are free men.'
> A silence followed: which continued.
> The general looked at me with some surprise: couldn't I speak the language?[146]

Davidson, who had fought alongside the partisans and knew what they had achieved, dared not translate Almond's words. He continues:

> Then Providence intervened … There came, from outside that room, the sudden din of shouts and uproar. We rushed through the floor-to-ceiling windows to a balcony giving on that street of arcades.
> Looking down, we saw far up that street the dense fore-ranks of a crowd of advancing men, and then we saw it was a column, a column of German prisoners a dozen or more abreast, hundreds of them, thousands of them, marching down that street unarmed but with armed partisans on either side. Then we went back into the salon and General Almond gave me a measuring glance and said, 'All right'.[147]

The example of Genoa was repeated in various ways across the whole of northern Italy. Despite General Alexander's unfortunate statement and the withholding of substantial supplies of weapons to all but the attentists, the resistance had played a significant part in the liberation.

The irony was that it would be disarmed, not by the Germans, but from within. The working class had often been the spearhead of the movement, but the party to which it was loyal accepted a return to capitalist normality. General Almond had no option but to acknowledge the work of the CLN on the day Genoa was freed, but immediately afterwards Davidson received new words to translate from a British brigadier: 'Tell them, will you please, that the committee, this committee, is dissolved as from tomorrow. All their functions cease. All their responsibilities are assumed by AMGOT.'[148] But the Anglo-Americans lacked the ability to enforce their demands, as Davidson explains:

> Those severe Ligurians listened in silence. ... they had reckoned with its coming. That was one large reason why they had launched an insurrection and carried it through. And they were right. What the CLN had foreseen, this CLN as well as other CLNs held good. AMGOT officers might have all the force of the Allied armies at their call, but it proved beyond all practical powers of AMGOT to remove the democratic nominees now placed in positions of responsibility.[149]

The Anglo-Americans could not do it, but as Davidson explains, the political leaders could. They had made commitments and these 'had to be carried through. The democratic nominees were not eliminated; but they had to assist in the elimination of their movement. The CLNs were set aside and left to vanish in futility.'[150] If imperialism robbed Italy's resistance of the opportunity to transform the fundamental structure of society, its achievement was still undeniable, and utterly different to the work of both Axis and Allied rulers. Despite the efforts of the AMGOT, the Italian capitalists, and the ex-fascists, the people's war left an indelible mark on subsequent Italian politics, even if this was mainly reflected through the strengthened position of the PCI that had betrayed it.

Part IV

India, Indonesia and Vietnam – Different Enemies

Anti-colonial movements in Asia are rarely treated as part of the Second World War resistance. However, uncritically accepting the subordinate status accorded by European imperialists, or seeing the struggle for freedom as uniquely Western, is conceited if not downright racist. Although they directed fire as much against their European masters as against Japan, the Axis power in the region, these movements differed from their equivalents in Europe in form, but not in substance.

12
India – From Famine to Independence

On 3 September 1939 Indians woke to discover they were at war. London did not bother to ask them for approval, unlike Dominions such as Canada or Australia.[1] When Churchill told the Commons that 'India has a great part to play in the world's struggle for freedom',[2] that did not include independence for India's 400 million, a population that exceeded the maximum number conquered by the Third Reich.[3]

One consequence of the 'struggle for freedom' was the Bengal famine of 1943. The Viceroy called it 'one of the greatest disasters that has befallen any people under British rule'.[4] It consumed between 1.5 and 3.5 million lives[5] despite civil servants describing the preceding harvest as 'a good one'.[6] Government intelligence reports recounted:

> the daily removal of corpses from streets and houses. In Dacca, the poor are living on what rice water then can get, since even the rich are unable to obtain rice. Cholera, smallpox and starvation are causing hundreds of deaths daily in the surrounding villages ... Suicides and child-selling have been reported.[7]

This continued an appalling record – 12 major famines since colonisation began.[8] In the 1860s an Indian economist had discovered the basic cause: a sum greater than the sub-continent's land value was drained off annually to support British occupation and profits.[9] Another contributory factor was the custom of making impoverished India pay for Britain's Asian adventures, as in the case of the two Afghan conflicts in the late nineteenth century.[10]

The 1943 famine was directly connected to India's involvement in the Second World War, because after it began eleven times the usual number of soldiers were maintained at the country's expense.[11] A full year before the tragedy struck, officials had warned London of the likely consequences. To pay for the troops the money supply would have to expand exponentially[12] and 'an inflationary position would result. There would be the danger of a flight from currency into goods, which would result in hoarding. This in turn might give rise to famines and riots'.[13] That prediction was borne out when the cost of rice increased tenfold between May and October 1943.[14]

London's resistance to rationing, and its shameful response to the Japanese conquest of neighbouring Malaya and Burma worsened the situation. In the words of the Indian National Congress:

> Officials whose business it was to protect lives of people in their areas utterly failed to discharge responsibility and, running away from post of duty, sought safety for themselves leaving vast majority of people wholly unprovided for. Such arrangements for evacuees as were made were principally for the European populations and at every step racial discrimination was in evidence.[15]

Loss of Burma severed an important source of rice, but instead of locating alternative providers, a scorched earth policy was instituted in Bengal, the border region. Bridges and local boats were destroyed even though, as Congress warned, 'life is impossible without them ...'.[16] Now it was difficult to transport the local harvest to market.

The Secretary for India was Leo Amery, who has been described as a 'passionate advocate of British imperialism [and] right-wing politics'.[17] His reaction to the first reports of starvation was expressed in a letter to the retiring Viceroy, Lord Linlithgow. Amery welcomed this distraction from the movement for independence. The public were 'now absorbed in questions of food and cost-of-living' which might 'infuse a tinge of realism into politics ...'.[18]

However, when the seriousness of the crisis became clear Amery also backed urgent food imports. The minimum necessary was calculated as the equivalent of one million tons of grain over the year.[19] Was it pure coincidence that this was *exactly the same amount* as the army's annual consumption in India?[20] Amery's appeals fell on deaf ears. London insisted that 'Defence Services demand must be first charge on indigenous or imported grain'.[21]

The wording of the War Cabinet's response to Amery's frantic appeals was shocking:

> After the requirements of Ceylon and the Middle East had been met, it would be extremely difficult to find further ships which could be sent to Australia to fetch grain [for India]. If however the War Cabinet decided that some action should be taken ... arrangements should now be made to import not more than

50,000 tons as a token shipment. This should, however, not be earmarked for India but should be ordered to Colombo to await instructions there.[22]

Those who dared accuse the Government of wishing 'deliberately to starve the people by acquiring the whole crop for the Army' would be pursued and prosecuted.[23]

Field Marshall Wavell, who replaced Linlithgow as Viceroy, was also exasperated: 'It is scandalous that we are making no progress about food imports after about six months' discussion ... .'[24] He pointed out the 'very different attitude towards feeding a starving population when there is starvation in Europe'.[25]

Churchill was unabashed. British rule would be seen as a 'Golden Age as time passes'[26] and sending food amounted to 'appeasement' of the Congress Party.[27] The official record notes that the Canadian PM had 100,000 tons of grain loaded on a ship bound for India, but was 'dissuaded by a strong personal appeal from Winston' from sending it.[28] When the British military commander in the South East Asia offered to use 10 per cent of his shipping capacity to assist Bengal, Churchill cut his allocation by 10 per cent.[29] Finally, no help would come from Britain itself because, said Churchill, to divert ships to India might affect 'imports of food into this country'.[30]

Underlying this was deep-seated racism. Amery, for example, thought the country needed 'an increasing infusion of stronger nordic blood, whether by settlement or intermarriage or otherwise ... and so breed a more virile type of native ruler.'[31] Yet the Secretary for India's prejudice was nothing compared to the PM's. The latter complained Indians were 'breeding like rabbits' and said: 'I hate Indians. They are a beastly people with a beastly religion.' Amery told him to his face that he took a 'Hitler-like attitude'.[32]

Imperialist war was disastrous for India, and clearly had nothing to do with publicly stated humanitarian aims. In the words of Jawaharlal Nehru, a leading member of the Indian National Congress, London was simply 'defending the British Empire'.[33] Churchill would not have disagreed, saying: 'I have not become the King's First Minister in order to preside over the liquidation of the British Empire'.[34] That approach was not exclusive to Tories. The Labour Party's attitude was set out during its first administration in 1924. On arriving at his office, the Colonial Minister uttered words bearing an uncanny resemblance to Churchill's: 'I'm here to see that there is no mucking about with the British Empire.'[35] During the

Second World War Labour's line on India remained indistinguishable from the Conservatives.[36]

The irony of Britain's declaration of war on India's behalf was that, if help had been asked for it would have been forthcoming. Politicians such as Nehru had a record of anti-fascism that far surpassed that of the British government. While London appeased in the 1930s, he had visited and expressed support for Spain's International Brigades, Czechoslovakia, and China under Japanese attack.[37] Despite Britain's high-handed action he continued to champion the anti-fascist cause within the Indian National Congress. As a consequence it resolved to avoid 'taking advantage of Britain's difficulties ... In a conflict between democracy and freedom on the one side and Fascism and aggression on the other, our sympathies must inevitably lie on the side of democracy.'[38]

Alas, the willing co-operation of an independence movement was the last thing London wanted. Instead, using the cloak of the Second World War, it instituted the Defence of India Ordinance restricting civil liberties, and attacking the Congress.[39]

Not everyone shared Nehru's approach, however. There were collaborators like Sir Ramaswami Mudaliar who prided himself on 'having laboured hard ... to produce a sense of loyalty' to Britain.[40] He was rewarded with attendance at the British war cabinet (though excluded from discussions on India, of course).[41] Surprisingly, the Indian CP (CPI) was in the same camp. Illegal until 1939, it was the only party which argued the Popular Front line that British 'victory is an end in which every citizen should be interested ...'.[42] At the opposite end of the spectrum was Subhas Bose whose Indian National Army, as we shall see, fought alongside Japanese forces.

Between these extremes sat the Congress and Muslim League, whose rivalry was the product of a classic imperialist manoeuvre of divide and rule: the British Raj had deliberately stoked up communal tensions between the Hindu majority and the 90 million-strong Muslim minority. Nevertheless both organisations saw the war as an opportunity to extract concessions from the colonial masters, although they profoundly differed as to goals. The Muslim League hoped to win British approval for the post-war creation of Pakistan. It therefore stood aloof from Congress campaigns for a unified, independent India.

As the largest anti-colonial organisation, India's Congress Party combined many different social layers behind its nationalist, cross-class programme. It was less communalist than the Muslim League (its wartime President was a Muslim) and wanted freedom in the short-term. Congress understood the duality of the Second World War and in 1941 passed a resolution that expressed solidarity 'with the peoples who are the subject of aggression and who are fighting for their freedom' against the Axis, but affirmed equally that a 'subject India cannot offer voluntary or willing help to an arrogant imperialism which is indistinguishable from fascist authoritarianism'.[43]

In 1942 Churchill despatched Sir Stafford Cripps to solve a public relations problem. The US Senate Foreign Relations Committee wanted India to have autonomy, 'otherwise the United States would be just fighting to preserve the British Empire', and Indians would die so as 'to prolong England's mastery over them'.[44] Accordingly, on 10 March, Roosevelt telegrammed Churchill proposing representative Indian self-government in line 'with the democratic processes of all who are fighting Nazism'. (Incidentally, the President added a revealing secret rider: 'For the love of Heaven don't bring me into this ...'[45]) To appease the US, Cripps was sent off to India the very next day. The PM regarded talks on autonomy as a necessary evil: 'the Cripps mission is indispensable to prove our honesty of purpose ... If it is rejected by the Indian parties for whose benefit it has been devised, our sincerity will be proved to the world.'[46] But when it looked like Cripps's proposals for Dominion status would not be rejected Churchill made him set new terms guaranteed to fail.

Congress was divided about what to do next. Its leader, Mahatma Gandhi, proposed a campaign of non-violent civil disobedience in favour of immediate independence. A debate in Congress's leading body, the Working Committee, shows the complexity of the situation:

Nehru: Japan is an imperialist country. Conquest of India is in their plan. If [Gandhi]'s approach is accepted we become passive partners of the Axis powers.

Achut Patwardhan: The British Government is behaving in a suicidal manner. [Nehru]'s attitude will lead to abject and unconditional co-operation with British machinery ...

Vallabhbhai Patel: ... it was made clear that the door was still open and our sympathies were with allies. It is time the door is finally closed after the repeated insults heaped upon us. I agree with [Gandhi's] draft before us.[47]

Gandhi won the day, and his 'Quit India' resolution was passed on 8 August. It still offered Britain support in a genuine war for democracy and human rights:

> A free India will [throw] all her great resources in the struggle for freedom and against the aggression of Nazism, Fascism and Imperialism ... On the declaration of India's independence, a provisional Government will be formed and free India will become an ally of the United Nations [i.e. the Allies], sharing with them in the trials and tribulations of the joint enterprise of the struggle for freedom ... The freedom of India must be the symbol of and prelude to this freedom of all other Asiatic nations under foreign domination. Burma, Malaya, Indo-China, the Dutch Indies, Iran and Iraq must also attain their complete freedom.[48]

The movement to attain the Quit India resolution was not designed to be provocative. It would be 'on non-violent lines on the widest possible scale, so that the country might utilize all the non-violent strength it has gathered during the last 22 years of peaceful struggle ... non-violence is the basis of this movement'.[49] 'Gandhiji', the prophet of *ahimsa* (non-violence) was officially entrusted with its leadership.

An understanding of the fragile figure of 'the Mahatma' (great soul) is essential here. Gandhi's progressive nationalism marshalled very diverse social classes behind the shared goal of independence. He was the fulcrum upon which balanced peasants and the middle class, rich industrialists, and workers. To exert pressure on Britain vast numbers of poor Indians had to be mobilised; but this risked unleashing a social radicalism that could threaten their rich compatriots, undermining Congress unity. Gandhi found a way out of this conundrum through a policy centred on his own self-sacrifice, and mass *satyagraha* – non-violent civil disobedience (like fasting as a form of protest).

With his individual persona at the centre of affairs he could open the tap of popular action, but close it as soon as militancy became predominant. An example was the campaign against the repressive Rowlatt Act in 1919. When the mass demonstrations he had encouraged were attacked and fought back, Gandhi 'persuaded the mob to disperse, rebuking them severely and threatening to undertake a personal *satyagraha* against them if they did not behave properly'.[50] Although emphasis on a leader's spiritual and moral integrity was unusual, Gandhism was actually a typical example of reformist nationalism that deployed mass activism but feared class struggle and revolution. Opposed to imperialist war, he stopped short of people's war.

Such was the spirit with which Gandhi approached 'Quit India'. When the policy was adopted he said: 'The actual struggle does not commence this moment.' He would now 'wait upon the Viceroy and plead with him ... That process is likely to take two or three weeks'.[51] The British had other ideas, and arrested the entire Congress leadership the following morning. In Nehru's case incarceration lasted 1,040 days.[52] When violent protests erupted to free the leaders Gandhi distanced himself. From jail he condemned the 'sad happenings', 'calamity', and 'deplorable destruction' caused by 'people wild with rage to the point of losing self-control'.[53]

But it was he who was losing control. Caution was giving way to a people's resistance movement for democracy and freedom. The initial phase occurred in urban centres. Strikes broke out in Mumbai, Calcutta and Delhi. By 12 August only 19 of Mumbai's 63 mills were functioning.[54] Workers at Tata Steel's giant Jamshedpur plant declared 'they will not resume work until a national government has been formed', while the three month textile strike in Ahmedabad earned it the nickname of 'the Stalingrad of India'.[55] The middle classes and students also played a prominent role. At Patna crowds were machine-gunned from the air after they seized the city.[56] That was the first of six occasions where the RAF was employed in this way.[57] Such massive repression was supplemented by the arguments of the Indian CP which, like in Britain, promoted maximum production to aid Russia. Together they restored order in the big towns.

A second phase began in late August with 'a veritable peasant rebellion'.[58] The fight was for something wider than independence, as local studies demonstrate. In Satara a parallel government (which lasted till 1946) published a fortnightly newspaper, set up schools, redistributed land, fined moneylenders, and ran a standing army.[59]

During September 1942 2,500 people in Medinipur District gathered to prevent rice stocks being shipped out by millowners. After three demonstrators were killed by police another parallel government was set up, with departments for defence, finance, judiciary, education and so on.[60] Grain exports were banned, fixed prices were imposed on merchants, and some supplies were seized and distributed to the people.[61] How far Medinipur had gone beyond Gandhi's non-violence was indicated by students who shouted: 'We shall cut off (King) George's head, and finish England with fire and the sword.'[62] The aim was to 'loot the Government banks, treasuries and post offices' while 'Police stations and courts too will be razed to the ground'.[63] However, the influence of Gandhism had not entirely disappeared. The Mahatma had issued a mantra in relation to Quit India – 'Do or Die'. The first word is usually emphasised and it is taken as a militant challenge to British rule. However, a local Congress leader, Dr Shivpujan Raj, revealed its other aspect when he remonstrated with the crowd: 'It is not by killing but by dying that we shall attain our goal. The leader of the nation has ordered this. We cannot violate his wishes.' So, casting their weapons aside, demonstrators marched unarmed on government offices. When they arrived seven were shot dead, including Dr Raj. The rest chose to 'do' rather than 'die', and the next day they returned to sack the building, a police station, seed store, and railway station (while still chanting Gandhi's name).[64]

Despite appearances the struggle had effectively renounced Gandhian doctrine and was moving towards people's war under J.P. Narayan, the 'one prominent all-India leader to emerge from the Quit India movement'.[65] In September 1942 British secret reports stated that Narayan's Congress Socialist Party 'holds the field ...'.[66] He gave clear expression to the idea of parallel wars.

In 1939 he wrote: 'There can be no hope that this war which in its origins is a war of imperialist rivalries will, as the war progresses, change automatically its imperialist character into one for democracy and world peace.' This was confirmed to him by the response to the Quit India resolution. India was now under a 'British type of Nazi hell [and] the savage tyrannies of the British fascists ...'.[67] Therefore, a different war was needed:

India's fight for freedom is at once anti-imperialist (and therefore also anti-fascist for Imperialism is the parent of Fascism) and a drive to end the war through the intervention of the common man ... We work for the defeat both of Imperialism and Fascism by the common people of the world and by our struggle we show the way to the ending of wars and the liberation of the black, white and yellow.[68]

Answering British accusations that the movement aided the enemy he asked:

why should the liberation of one-fifth of humanity come in their way? If the [Allies] are truly fighting for the aims they profess, the Indian struggle for freedom should not hinder but help them.

If it hinders them, it is only proof of the fact that the basis of their war is false.[69]

Narayan criticised the official Congress approach which amounted to the Quit India resolution as no more than a bargaining tool with the authorities. There had been a deliberate lack of planning for a mass movement,[70] and now, having 'failed in their obvious duty' they 'turn round and disown the people's travail and suffering ...'.[71] Attempting to plug the gap in leadership Narayan offered detailed advice on how to organise and conduct a guerrilla war against the British, recognising that 'if this does not accord with Gandhiji's principles, that is not my fault'.[72] One outcome was the Azad Dastas who were consciously modelled on 'European guerrillas ... or the Russian partisan'.[73]

Did the Quit India movement amount to a people's war? The colonial authorities noted that key industrial concerns, such as the Tata and Birla empires, backed Quit India to the extent of paying workers to strike, for months in some cases. However, British officials believed that with Japanese invasion a distinct possibility, Indian capitalists were funding 'a war risk insurance policy.'[74] The calculation was that in the event of their victory 'we can expect gratitude and the retention of our factories intact. Should the British win, however, we lose nothing'.[75] This plan evidently succeeded, with one journalist remarking: 'It is bewildering to know how prominent financial magnates with Congress affiliations have secured war contracts from the Supply Department of Delhi'.[76]

More important, as numerous writers have pointed out, Quit India was also 'conspicuously supported by the poor and labour classes, who were the most hard hit by wartime inflation and food shortages'.[77] In Patna an eye-witness described the radicalising effect this had. After a student procession was fired upon:

all signs of British rule disappeared from Patna. No rickshaws or ekkas [horse-drawn carriages] were plied. The students were no longer the leaders, leadership had passed to the rickshaw-pullers, ekka-drivers and other such people whose political knowledge extended only this far – that the British were their enemies.[78]

Quit India amounted to a real war. At the end of August 1942 Viceroy Linlithgow wrote to Churchill:

I am engaged here in meeting by far the most serious rebellion since that of 1857, the gravity and extent of which we have so

far concealed from the world for reasons of military security ...
If we bungle this business we shall damage India irretrievably as
a base for future allied operations ... .[79]

The statistics bore out his assertion. In the first week alone 250
railway stations and 150 police stations were attacked, and 59 trains
derailed.[80] After a year, 945 post offices had been destroyed and 664
bombs planted.[81] The British authorities deployed a mass of armed
police plus 30,000 troops in 112 battalions.[82] They opened fire 538
times; in Mumbai alone over 100 times.[83] The methods used were
shocking. A senior official in the Central Provinces 'boasted at the
club in the evening that he had jolly good fun having shot down
twenty-four niggers himself'.[84] In the village of Chimur all adult
males were arrested, and then, 'the soldiers out-raged the women
to their heart's content...No woman was safe even the pregnant or
the girls of 12 or 13'.[85]

In total there were almost 100,000 arrests and between 4,000 and
10,000 were killed.[86] It was war, but a very asymmetrical one. In
comparison to Indian casualties, just 11 soldiers and 63 policemen
died.[87] This disparity in armed power was duly noted by Subhas
Chandra Bose.

THE INDIAN NATIONAL ARMY (INA)

Bose was a prominent campaigner for independence. Twice elected
as Congress President (1938 and 1939), he had undergone eleven
prison terms. Bose's first response to the Second World War was
similar to Narayan's: 'There could be no question of supporting
either side in the European war, since both were imperialists
fighting for colonial possessions.'[88] In 1940 he organised a massive
demonstration for an immediate independence struggle, calling
on Gandhi 'to come forward and launch his campaign of passive
resistance ... it was high time for India to play her part in the war'.[89]
His argument made an impact. Historians have plausibly argued
that one reason Gandhi launched Quit India was to 'ward off the
evils he apprehended from the growing strength of the revolutionary
ideas [and act as] a safety-valve for youthful energy'.[90]

After being jailed yet again, Bose grew to doubt the potential of
his country's internal forces on their own: 'We do not believe that
India can achieve freedom without use of arms ... We have to fight
the enemy with modern methods and with modern arms.'[91] He
continued: 'it goes without saying that if you could do without any

help it would be the best course for India .... [But] every freedom movement in history has had to seek some help or other from abroad, before it could achieve success.'[92] From whom could such help be obtained?

Bose was not fussy. He escaped from custody and headed for Moscow. When his pleas for Soviet aid against the British were ignored he went to Berlin, saying the Axis powers 'are the best friends we have in the world today'.[93] Hitler was an unlikely partner. Bose himself had been infuriated by Hitler's 1935 speech declaring whites were destined to rule over blacks,[94] and such was the Führer's racism that he lamented Japan's victories at first: 'It means the loss of a whole continent, and that is to be regretted, for it is the white race which is the loser.'[95] It was with Tokyo, at war with the Allies since December 1941, that Bose eventually clinched a deal.

If pragmatic considerations led Bose to this decision, on the basis that 'the enemy of my enemy is my friend', this was not aired. In public he accepted Tokyo's claim of establishing 'a new order in East Asia on the right basis of freedom, justice and reciprocity',[96] despite knowing of the atrocities in China. Bose's ideological statements showed breathtaking opportunism: 'our political philosophy should be a synthesis between National Socialism and Communism ... I see no reason why we cannot work out a synthesis of the two systems that will embody the good points of both.'[97] Consistent in his inconsistency, after backing the Axis powers, in 1945 he turned once more to Stalin the 'one man in Europe who holds in his hands the destinies of the European nations ...'.[98]

Bose's public stance on fascism makes problematic the inclusion of his Indian National Army in a book on war against the Axis. Nonetheless, his assertion that 'every freedom movement in history has had to seek some help from abroad' had some merit. During the First World War, supporters of the 1916 Easter Rising in Dublin sought arms from Imperial Germany. A year later Lenin caused great controversy when he accepted an offer (from the same source) of a sealed train to take him across the war fronts from Zurich to Petrograd (St Petersburg). However, unlike Bose, these revolutionaries refused to pay homage in any way to imperialism.

The INA deserves consideration here because its story was much more than quisling collaboration. The Army existed before Bose's arrival and its soldiers volunteered through the same sense of social and political injustice as resistance movements elsewhere. The INA recruited volunteers from the 60,000 Indian soldiers held as POWs after Japan's conquest of Singapore, an event Churchill called 'the worst disaster and largest capitulation in British history'.[99]

To understand their readiness to sign up it is necessary to look at Britain's Indian regiments. Amery described these as 'a mercenary army',[100] because intense poverty drove many to enlist. Divide and rule was the method used to maintain control. Units were assembled 'from distant parts of the country, preferably speaking different languages, both from each other and from the local population. Where possible, each Indian regiment was further divided into Hindu, Muslim and Sikh companies.'[101] An additional split was created between the so-called 'martial races', from whom recruits were drawn, and the rest.

These tactics began to break down during the Second World War. Recruitment had to go well beyond the 'martial races' and communal differences paled before the gross racism encountered. The income of an ordinary Indian private (a sepoy) was one third of a British soldier's; and despite the army's enormous growth, British officers in the combat sections still outnumbered their Indian equivalents by 12 to 1 and received twice the pay.[102] Only one Indian commanded a Brigade, and none a Division. In the famous post-war show trial of INA soldiers in Delhi a defendant asked, since Indians fought as bravely as the British 'why then there should be so much difference in their pay, allowances, food and living conditions?'[103]

It was ordinary soldiers rather than officers who tended to sign up to the INA.[104] Under post-war British interrogation captured prisoners advanced various reasons for joining. Avoidance of Japanese prison camps (Tokyo offered to free those who joined the INA) and expectation of imminent British defeat played a part. The INA was also 'demonstratively non-communal';[105] the Delhi show trial saw a Hindu, Muslim and Sikh standing side by side in the dock. According to one officer, opposition to imperialism *from any quarter* was the most important motive:

the only solution that we could think of for our country's problems was the formation of a strong and well-disciplined armed body which should fight for the liberation of India from the existing alien rule, should be able and ready to provide protection to their countrymen against any possible molestation by the Japanese, and to resist any attempt by the latter to establish themselves as rulers of the country in place of the British ... .[106]

This independent attitude showed itself in strained relations between the INA and the Japanese. For example, it took five days of hard bargaining to win Captain Mohan Singh, the INA's first commander, to setting it up in the first place. He was suspicious of Japanese intentions[107] and refused to allow the INA to be deployed in Japan's conquest of the Dutch East Indies, insisting it could only fight against Britain.[108] Matters came to a head when Mohan Singh demanded a guarantee from Japan that it had no designs of its own on India. When this was not forthcoming he ordered the dissolution of the INA and was arrested.[109] A Japanese officer explained the root of the disagreement: 'As a colonial people with long history of oppression they have developed some sort of prejudice, and whenever liberation has been proposed they have tried to assert equality with other nations which was beyond their power ... .'[110]

Captain Singh lacked the political stature of Subhas Bose, who was in a better position to win a degree of independence for the INA. On his arrival in 1943 he re-launched the movement, mobilising support from the three million-strong Indian community in Southeast Asia as a counter-weight to Japanese preponderance.[111] Finally, rather than depending on Japanese conquest of India to reach his goal, Bose conceived of the INA acting as a catalyst for a revolution from within:

> [We] are going to organise a fighting force which will be powerful enough to attack the British Army in India. When we do so, revolution will break out not only among the civil population at home, but also among the Indian Army which is now standing under the British flag. When the British Government is thus attacked from both sides, from inside India and from outside it will collapse ... .[112]

Imperialists on either side of the Second World War showed the same contempt for the people's war and so the INA was shabbily treated by Japan. Singh had wanted a force of 200,000, and although Bose scaled this down to 50,000, the Japanese provided only light arms for some 30,000.[113] The Subhas Brigade, for example, had no artillery, mortars or communications equipment, and an inadequate supply of machine-guns.[114] Bose demanded a leading role in the attack on the Raj so that 'the first drop of blood shed on Indian soil should be that of a soldier of the INA'.[115] But one officer described this 'front line role' at the incursion at Imphal as, 'a) road-making or preparing, b) repairing bridges, c) extinguishing jungle fires, d) driving bullock carts carrying rations for Japanese troops'.[116] There were only 8,000 INA soldiers deployed compared to 230,000 Japanese, and when the Japanese offensive stalled INA soldiers were abandoned and left to starve. 6,000 were captured or surrendered to the British.[117]

At the end of the Second World War it appeared as if the people's war had failed. However, this was deceptive. The scale of the Quit India campaign in 1942 convinced Britain that the colony's freedom was inevitable, and the Viceroy advised Churchill to forestall future trouble with Congress: 'it would in fact be wise to start negotiations before the end of the war brought a release of prisoners and unrest ...'.[118] Bose's prediction that the INA could spark a revolt came true, just three months after his death in a plane crash. Protests against the INA trial overcame communal boundaries and in places like Calcutta Bose supporters, Congress, the Muslim League and communists, marched together in massive demonstrations which the authorities barely managed to control. As Sarkar puts it:

> The INA never amounted to very much in sheer military terms ... yet we must not underestimate the impact on the patriotic imagination of an actual army fighting, however, ineffectively, for the country's liberation ... the probable link between the INA experience and the wave of disaffection in the British Indian Army during the winter of 1945–46, which culminated in the great Bombay naval strike of February 1946 was quite possibly the single most decisive reason behind the British decision to make a quick withdrawal.[119]

In Europe and America the wars mostly ran in parallel because they both confronted the same enemy, even if they had very different motives for doing so. They came into various degrees of conflict, but this took time. The geometry of the parallel wars metaphor breaks down as far as India is concerned, because while there was both a people's war and an imperialist war, the two were at loggerheads from the start. Yet the events that shook the sub-continent were just as much the product of the Second World War as those elsewhere, and should be treated as such.

13
Indonesia – Axis and Allies United Against the People

The imperialists officially settled their differences on 'Victory over Japan day', 16 August 1945, but the struggle for Indonesia and its main island, Java, refutes the notion that the Second World War ended on that day. Fighting continued, except this time it was not Japan *versus* the Allies, but a war of both against the people.

Indonesians had ample reason to want freedom. The Netherlands had long exploited the abundant natural resources of coffee and sugar from a country 60 times more extensive and seven times more populous than itself. The entire Javanese economy was remodelled to produce cash crops at the expense of rice cultivation. During the nineteenth century this caused famines and epidemics, but so reliant was Holland on colonial revenue that the authorities' response was not remorse but drastic increases in land tax.[1] Despite rhetoric about reform, by the twentieth century Javanese villages were paying a quarter of their earnings to the colonial power, which contributed to overall income from Indonesia exceeding that of Holland by 30 per cent.[2] Few benefits of 'civilisation' returned east in recompense. For example, between the wars the 70 million population had the services of just 1030 medical doctors.[3] Only one in seven million Indonesians graduated from secondary school.[4] Those profits that did come back to Indonesia largely went to paying the Dutch army[5] to maintain a regime under which advocating a strike attracted a prison sentence of five years.[6]

Despite this background the people's war was slow to arrive in Indonesia. Elsewhere dedicated and visionary individuals or organisations provided the spark, but in Indonesia such leadership was missing. This was partly due to the legacy of colonialism. Nationalism originated as a European idea and was encountered by the miniscule number of educated Indonesians, mainly from the privileged elite, through whom the Dutch ruled. Geography created another obstacle:

[This] sprawling archipelago was divided into 200 or more distinct ethnic groups, ranging from fiercely Muslim Acehnese on the northern tip of Sumatra and the Catholic communities of Flores and Timor to the Hindu Balinese and the animist tribes of the interior of Kalimantan (Borneo) and New Guinea, as well as more recent immigrant communities such as Chinese in western Kalimantan and Europeans in the cities of Java.[7]

For these reasons nationalism had difficulty making headway and had to compete with rival ideologies. After the First World War Sarekat Islam drew on the Muslim sympathies of many, its membership rising from 800,000 in 1916 to two million in 1919. In the mid-1920s it was eclipsed by the Indonesian Communist Party (PKI), the first such party to be established in Asia.[8] However, the PKI suffered rapid decline following abortive risings in Java and Sumatra in 1926 and 1927 during which the Dutch arrested 13,000 communists and shot several.[9]

It took that destruction of its chief competitor to give Indonesian nationalism some traction. Until this moment, its leader, Sukarno had been afraid to appeal to the common people lest their radicalism spill over into support for communism to which he was opposed: 'We nationalists put our emphasis on the national struggle.'[10] With the communists out of the way it was a lot easier to promote cross-class unity: '[Are we] hostile to every well-to-do Indonesian? Not at all ... Do our principles mean that we emphasize the class struggle? By no means!'

Though the oratory of a Sukarno attracted large audiences, organised nationalism remained the affair of a tiny minority. This made Dutch repression relatively easy. Without gainsaying the courage of individual leaders, their collective weakness encouraged them to depend on external assistance. People like Mohammed Hatta and Sutan Sjahrir, who were educated in Holland, hoped national salvation would come through the Dutch social democratic left. By contrast, as early as 1928 Sukarno oriented himself eastwards. He foresaw 'a great struggle in the Pacific, among the imperialist giants, America, Japan and England, who will engage in a struggle for plunder and domination'.[11] This could cause 'hostility between one Asian people and, for example, English imperialism. I would then hope that this Asian people would receive help from other Asian peoples.'[12]

When the Second World War began Hatta and Sjahrir, in similar terms to India's Congress Party, offered to support the Allies if concessions towards autonomy were made. None were forthcoming. The Dutch were 'practising exactly the kind of totalitarianism they criticize' said one nationalist leader.[13] This attitude assisted Tokyo's conquest of South East Asia, which was achieved with remarkable speed and few forces. It took just eight days for Java to fall to the 16th Army in March 1942. As if to confirm Sukarno's predictions jubilation was widespread. One Japanese Admiral encountered 'a frantic atmosphere of welcome [that] ruled the entire region of the East Indies'.[14] Further apparent justification for Sukarno came when Japan proclaimed their Greater East Asia Co-Prosperity Sphere whose peoples, it was claimed, would 'enjoy prosperous coexistence by mutual help and accommodation and, by so doing, to promote the peace and prosperity of the world'.[15] After meeting Japanese officials Sukarno announced: 'Indonesia's independence can only be achieved by cooperation with Dai Nippon [Japan] ... .'[16] Soon he was rallying supporters with the motto: 'We will wipe out America and liquidate England.'[17]

However, 'Co-Prosperity' turned out to have as much practical value as the Allies' much-vaunted Atlantic Charter. The new authorities treated their conquered territory with the familiar mixture of condescension and avarice seen under the Netherlands. On the day the Commander of the 16th Army announced 'the prime objective of the military administration is to let these obedient people bathe in the genuine imperial graces',[18] a more candid spokesman opined that Indonesians had 'been lazy coolies for the Dutch. From now on they must be made diligent workers for Japan and Asia.'[19] Japan set about achieving this through what one writer calls 'exploitation and persuasion'.[20]

'Exploitation' centred on rice, textiles and manpower. Like the Nazis in Europe, Japanese armies sustained occupation by plunder. Lacking the numbers to administer this at local level they employed the same indigenous social elites as the Dutch.[21] In Java these people helped the Japanese levy up to 40 per cent of the crop of small farmers, and 70 per cent of the wealthier farmers' crop.[22] As cash was given in exchange for this rice, large landowners made large profits and hoarding became rife. The effect on prices (and consequently on the landless) was devastating.[23] Maladministration also left thousands of tons rotting in stores or eaten by rats.[24] Soon the ratio of deaths to births reached 'unexampled heights'.[25] Cloth became so difficult to obtain that in some places women were unable to go out, and farmers worked the fields stark naked.[26]

The Japanese instituted a forced labour system called 'romusha'. By the end of the war Java's entire mobilisable workforce of ten million had served in it at some point. Romusha were, according to one historian, recruited through 'unbelievable and even immoral deceptions':

> The townsmen gathered, thinking there would be special distribution [of food or clothing]. With clever words, the military men loaded them on prepared trucks and took them away to ports where ships awaited them. The men were then shipped to the battlefields of New Guinea, to the Andamans and Nicobars, to Burma, etc. as laborers. They had no idea once they left when they could return home, and they received no opportunity to bid farewell.[27]

Mistreatment of romusha was so extensive that the Japanese had to institute a 'Don't Hit the Natives' campaign amongst their own people.[28] Labourers received just 40 to 60 per cent of a Japanese soldier's food ration.[29] Though most were employed locally, of the hundreds of thousands sent abroad a large number (perhaps 50 per cent) never returned.[30]

Japan's treatment of opposition was sometimes even more cruel than its Axis partners. Thus, 27 per cent of those in its POW camps died compared with 4 per cent in German or Italian camps, while hundreds of Javanese were executed without trial.[31]

In spite of these horrors 'persuasion' could also succeed, though initially the plan was that 'native inhabitants shall be so guided to induce a sense of trust in the imperial forces, and premature encouragement of native independence movements shall be avoided'.[32] Japan altered its stance when its military position deteriorated and sought an alliance with the nationalists. Most were more than willing to collaborate. Pliable nationalist politicians fronted the three successive Japanese campaigns to mobilise Indonesians behind the war effort – Triple A ('Asia's Mother – Japan; Asia's Dawn – Japan; Asia's Leadership – Japan'),[33] Putera (Concentration of the People's Energy), and Java Hokokai. For example, Sukarno addressed 100,000 people at Putera's launch. The event started with a bow towards the Emperor's Palace in Tokyo and ended with three cheers of 'banzai!'[34] In between Sukarno told his followers that the Japanese were 'elder brothers' and that the Indonesian people would 'follow the advice of the elder brothers. We trust Dai Nippon'.[35]

Sukarno registered himself as romusha to encourage others.[36] After the war he confessed that he knew about the tragic fate of those who followed his advice: 'In fact, it was I, Sukarno, who sent them to work. Yes it was I. I shipped them to their deaths … It was horrible, hopeless. And it was I who gave them to the Japanese. Sounds terrible, doesn't it?'[37] Why did Sukarno collaborate if, as one apologist insists, he 'was never a lackey of Japan' and 'at no time subordinated his goal, Indonesian independence, to Japanese interests'.[38] Perhaps he was duped by the Greater East Asia Co-Prosperity Sphere[39] and the sort of widely circulated propaganda that said 'yellow men will come out of the north to liberate the Indonesian people from the slavery of the Dutch. Look for the yellow skins'.[40]

However, the real intention of the authorities in Tokyo remained what it had always been:

> In order to enable the fifty million people of Java to further endure the deprivation of clothing, to deliver foodstuffs while bearing hardships, and to cooperate with the military administration in all aspects, the best policy is to clearly indicate to them that they shall be granted independence when their preparatory education for the postwar future has been completed.[41]

No demand for 'preparatory education' was made of Vietnam, Cambodia, Laos, the Philippines or Burma, which were granted nominal independence.[42] In private Sukarno complained bitterly about the contrast: 'It's beyond our comprehension what evil we've done to be made to face such an insult.'[43] The hurt was personal too. He was beaten by a drunken Japanese officer who claimed not to recognise the Indonesian leader.[44] In truth it was the craven attitude of the Indonesian nationalists, in contrast to the more independent stance taken by nationalists in these other countries, which left the country lagging behind in the movement towards limited independence.

Experience showed that progress did not come from kowtowing to imperialism. When they first arrived the Japanese were uncertain of their reception and dropped Indonesian flags from planes. But as soon as they felt secure they banned such national symbols, all political parties, and any discussion of politics.[45] It was only when they felt their hold on the country was at risk that permission to use the flag and the term 'Indonesia' was given once more.[46]

Sukarno's fawning (and that of the nationalist movement in general) was analogous to the attentists elsewhere. Fearing mass mobilisation might spill over into a challenge to his all-class alliance, he depended on one of the belligerent imperialists in the Second World War bestowing independence. Hatta and Sjahrir were less enthusiastic than Sukarno about Japan, as they disliked its militarism intensely. However, the pair agreed to an ingenious division of labour: Hatta would work with Sukarno and use opportunities that might arise through his channels; meanwhile, Sjahrir would stand aloof so that there was a leader with whom the Allies could do business in the event of Japanese defeat.[47] Neither man offered an alternative to reliance on one or other of the rival imperial powers.

With the communists neutralised by repression there was no other strategy on offer. Consequently Indonesia saw 'no maquis or even underground networks in the sense of groups engaged in sabotage, spying, or subversion'.[48] The only attempt to build a serious resistance movement under Japanese occupation was initiated by Amir Sjarifuddin, leader of the most left-wing of the pre-war legal parties. He accepted 25,000 guilders from Holland to mount a campaign.[49] It was unlikely that any movement that might assist the return of the Dutch would gain a foothold and his organisation was quickly penetrated by the occupation secret police and eliminated.[50] Beyond this, there were only three tiny organised groupings on Java. Merely forums for discussion and composed largely of students studying medicine and law, they drew on an extremely narrow, privileged layer.[51] There were isolated examples of sporadic resistance, from peasants in Aceh, to an Islamic movement in South Kalimantan, but as one author writes: 'none of these forms of popular resistance seriously threatened Japanese rule, and all met with terrible consequences.'[52]

The decision of people like Sukarno or Hatta to tie themselves to the coat-tails of Japanese imperialism did not arise purely from the difficulties of resistance, but was the consequence of a political choice. With the possible exception of Poland, in every country considered so far, people's war was shot through with issues of social change. But the nationalist leaders' stress on national struggle to the exclusion of class issues removed an important motive for ordinary people to resist.[53] In sum, the power and brutality of imperialism (both Dutch and then Japanese), coupled with the character of Indonesia's national leadership, stymied the development of a people's war.

The situation changed dramatically during the closing stages of the Second World War. The people's war may have been a late arrival on the scene, but it was able to simultaneously challenge the Japanese, the Dutch, their British backers, and the Indonesian elite. The turnaround was assisted by the weakening position of Japan. The USA was vastly superior in economic strength and manpower, and Japan suffered defeats at Midway (June 1942), Guadalcanal (February 1943) and the Aleutians (August 1943). The forces occupying Indonesia were now needed elsewhere and soon only eight of the original 23 battalions remained.[54]

The end of Japanese rule was swift. On 24–25 February 1945 the US Air Force began the series of raids that culminated in the Tokyo firestorm that killed 100,000 people – initially more than at Hiroshima. Four days afterwards in Java the Japanese announced the formation of an 'Investigation Committee for the Preparation of Indonesian Independence'. Not only was its title highly tentative, it did not even meet until 28 May, and achieved little. Its successor, the slightly more boldly named 'Preparatory Committee for Independence' was established on 7 August – the day after Hiroshima.[55] Finally Japan promised immediate independence, but before this all-too-obvious manoeuvre could be carried out Japan surrendered. The terms accepted on 15 August 1945 required that in Indonesia Japan must maintain 'the status quo, while firmly securing peace and good order, until the day when the transfer of everything to the Allies is completed'.[56] Previously Japan had chosen to ban the Indonesian flag; now, in a thrilling 360 degree turn, they banned the Indonesian flag once more! The only difference was that this time it was at Allied insistence.[57]

Even though Sukarno's carefully nurtured hopes of backing from Tokyo had turned to dust, he still hesitated to declare independence.[58] Liberation would require a people's war from below, and it was at this moment that it appeared – in the form of the pemuda (youth), a point stressed in Anderson's classic *Java in a Time of Revolution*. 'Youth' may seem a vague and arbitrary category. The age difference between the Sukarno generation and pemuda leaders was only twelve years, for example.[59] One writer therefore objects to Anderson's use of the term, as it is 'a ubiquitous adjective – as in "pemuda consciousness", "pemuda tradition," "pemuda nationalism," and "pemuda revolution" ... abstractions without substantiation'.[60] It is valid because the blot of repression and collaboration had crippled the generation that lived between the destruction of the PKI in the 1920s and 1945. Only the young were free from this past; and their impact was immediate.

In the early hours of 16 August, a group of pemuda kidnapped Sukarno and Hatta to compel them to immediately declare independence.[61] The two leaders temporised and were released. But later that day they approached Japan's Admiral Maeda, who was known to be sympathetic to the national cause. He was one of several officers who thought that if Tokyo granted independence even at this late stage it might secure Japan a long-term ally. Others like Yamamoto, the Japanese commander in Java, intended to strictly enforce the surrender terms. He refused to receive Maeda and the Indonesian nationalists, or even call a meeting of the Preparatory Committee. Instead, he deployed troops to prevent a mass meeting in Jakarta and imposed a radio blackout. Faced with an impasse and the momentum created by the pemuda Sukarno, despite his misgivings, proclaimed independence on 17 August.[62]

It was uncertain this would succeed as former imperialist rivals had reconciled their differences. Sukarno could declare himself President and Indonesia independent, but the Japanese authorities might remain in charge until the Dutch returned. To forestall this the movement of educated urban youth expanded to encompass armed militias and mass insurrection. The people's war was born. Targets ranged from an unholy alliance of British, Dutch and Japanese troops, to local Indonesian officials and individuals who had profited from occupation.

There were also tensions between the pemuda and the very government they had just done so much to establish. At state level youth representatives constituted just one-sixth of the 135 invited to form the new Central Indonesian National Committee (KNIP). The rest, says Anderson, were 'professional men who had been appointed to the various top-level pseudo-legislative and pseudo-party organisations of the Japanese period'.[63] At local level Sukarno declared that the clique of Indonesian administrators who had faithfully served both Dutch and Japanese masters, must not be treated 'as secretaries, clerks or petty foremen [but given] the proper place it deserves'.[64]

International relations were another controversial area. Sukarno and Hatta's closeness to the Japanese put them at a disadvantage when dealing with the Allies. By contrast, Sjahrir had kept his distance and so in his pamphlet, *Our Struggle*, he could plausibly call for a thorough elimination of remaining imperialist influence. The new Republic must start by:

purging itself of the *stains* of Japanese *fascism,* and curbing
the views of those whose minds are still under the influence
of Japanese propaganda and indoctrination. Those who have
sold their *souls* and their *honor* to the Japanese fascists must be
eliminated from the leadership of our revolution [and] regarded
as *fascists* themselves ... .[65]

Such statements won pemuda support and in November 1945
they compelled Sukarno to downgrade his role as President to
a ceremonial one, and appoint Sjahrir to dominance as Prime
Minister.[66]

Our Struggle condemned the Japanese, but embraced the rival
victors of the Second World War:

so long as the world we live in is dominated by capital, we are
forced to make sure that we do not earn the enmity of capitalism
... Indonesia is geographically situated within the sphere of
influence of Anglo-Saxon capitalism and imperialism; accordingly,
Indonesia's fate depends ultimately on the fate of Anglo-Saxon
capitalism and imperialism ... [Indonesia is] in harmony with the
political ambitions of that Giant of the Pacific, the United States.[67]

The timing of this statement was highly significant. At the very
moment it appeared 'Anglo-Saxon imperialism' was engaged in
invading the country to prepare for the return of the Dutch, and
Sjahrir had negotiated an agreement giving 'recognition by the
Republic of all claims by foreign nationals for the restitution and
maintenance of their rights and properties...'[68]

A comprehensive alternative to both the Sukarno and Sjahrir
was penned by the 'the enigmatic and legendary'[69] Tan Malaka, a
former leader of the PKI who had pursued an independent course
in his long exile. His movement 'Persatuan Perdjuangan' (Union
of Resistance – PP) rejected both imperialist camps: 'We are not
willing to negotiate with any one else before we obtain our 100
percent freedom and before our enemy has left our shores and our
seas in good order. We are not willing to negotiate with a thief in
our house.'[70]

If negotiations were excluded, how was it possible to deal
with the imperialist 'thief'? Malaka's solution was to engage the
people in an offensive based on an ambitious social and military
programme: 'Why should the factories and the agricultural estates
not be confiscated before freedom is obtained 100 per cent? Why

should they not be distributed among the masses? Because if they have become the properties of the masses, they will be able to fight as lions if the enemy ever comes back.'[71]

The difference between Sjahrir and Tan Malaka concerned their interpretations of the Second World War. The former saw it as the victory of one imperialism over another, and hoped the Anglo-Saxons could be peacefully persuaded to accept independence. The latter saw the Second World War as a people's war, 'a national revolutionary movement ... backed by the full mobilized force of popular hopes and energies'.[72]

Sjahrir's strategy was discredited within six months of independence. By February 1946 the British had invaded to restore the Dutch, and the Republican government had been forced to flee Jakarta for the relative safety of inland Yogyakarta. Malaka's PP had now grown to massive proportions. Its demonstration in the new capital was 8km long.[73] Isolated and despised, Sjahrir's government resigned, and it seemed the PP programme of people's war would become government policy. But this was not to be. Enormous though it was, the mass movement's birth was very recent, and it lacked the sort of organisational coherence given by experienced communist party cadres to resistance movements elsewhere. Sukarno realised the PP was too heterogeneous to seize power, and banking on its unstable coalition falling apart, he defiantly reappointed Sjahrir as PM. Tan Malaka was arrested on trumped up charges and the PP quickly disintegrated. It seemed the people's war could bring an independent state into existence, but lacked the ability to control it.

This was not the end, however. The pemuda fought on at community level, because they saw independence as more than an affair simply for national politicians. One feature of this second level of action was the so-called 'social revolutions'. For example, on 1 September a pemuda council suggested 'all enterprises (offices, factories, mines, plantations, etc.) must be seized from the Japanese ...'. Over the next fortnight Jakarta's radio and tram workers took control over the enterprises they worked for.[74] So complete was the process on the railways that by October 'it was formally announced that all railway stations in Java were no longer under the control of the Japanese army; not a single Japanese soldier was allowed to enter any railway station, office or workshop'.[75] In Semarang pemuda captured civil buildings while workers did the same in local plantations and factories.[76] Surabaya's oil refinery workers led the way in developing self-organisation in that major port.[77]

Lucas's case study of social revolution in Pemalang gives a sense of events in the countryside. The movement was driven by anger at village heads who had administered Japan's occupation policies.[78] Pemuda groups with titles like Movement of the Arab Youth of Indonesia, the Chinese Youth Irregulars, Hizbullah (Army of God), and the largest – Indonesian Youth Generation – sprang up. The variety of these bodies shows that, as one pemuda explained: 'Ideology was not important … We were united then with the one aim of destroying the corruptor cliques.'[79] The activists carried out tasks ranging from the free distribution of cloth, control of the movement of goods, security, and the staging of community plays.[80]

Pemalang continued to suffer from rice shortages, and revenge was visited upon those local officials and hoarders felt to be responsible. One method was 'dombringing', publicly parading culprits wearing a necklace of rice to the accompaniment of clanging tin pots and wooden clappers. 'The essence, then, of these dombring actions was a symbolic, public unmasking and shaming of officials rather than intimidating or killing them.'[81]

Violence was not excluded, however. An official was killed for his role in cloth distribution under the Japanese, while the homes of others were looted and burnt. At the local sugar refinery the administration was overthrown.[82] As Lucas explains, the strength of this spontaneous mass movement ensured that virtually all officials and collaborators were purged by the end of 1945. However, the weakness that afflicted the people's war nationally – its sudden birth and lack of well-established organisation or cadres – meant that during the social revolutions the 'corruptor cliques' were often replaced by competing 'alternative elites, ethnic and communal groups'.[83]

The comparative success of the 'social revolutions' was not to the taste of the central state, however. Turning on those who had brought him to power, Hatta declared there was 'too much popular sovereignty'.[84] The result in Pemalang was a series of mass arrests by the TKR (the new state army) during December 1945. One of the jailers explained the purpose of repression: 'People were being taught a lesson … They were lined up in the town square and whipped until they were half dead.'[85] Many revolutionaries spent years in captivity.

There was a third level of people's war activity too. This provided the clearest expression of the dual nature of the Second World War, and involved confronting imperialist forces still fresh from settling their internecine conflicts. The former Allied and Axis enemies joined together to attack Indonesia in successive waves, with the Japanese prominent at first, then the British, and finally the Dutch. Each will be considered in turn.

In the last days of their rule Tokyo had recruited local auxiliary forces to assist in repelling an expected Allied invasion. One formation was the Peta which had involved 35,000 in Java and 20,000 in Sumatra.[86] Even during the war it could sometimes turn against its master, as Peta uprisings at Blitar, Kroja and Njomplon showed.[87] After the war it posed a real threat to the Japanese. So before news of the VJ Day surrender had filtered through, 'fully equipped, camouflaged and battle-ready army units' of Japanese disarmed and disbanded such militias,[88] with Sukarno's approval.[89] The next service Japan provided was to facilitate the landing of British forces under Mountbatten's Southeast Asia Command. This went smoothly everywhere except Surabaya.[90]

However, the first clash occurred in October 1945 at Semarang. After independence many former militiamen became pemuda 'irregulars'. Anderson calls them 'a swarming mass of heterogeneous armed groups that grew up from the bottom'. Often led by former officers both the imperialists and the Indonesian government found these very difficult to control.[91] The British regarded them as 'terrorists' or 'extremists'. According to the surrender terms the Japanese in Semarang were instructed to restore order there.[92] However, in many places Japanese troops had little motivation to comply with commands from former enemies, and many were torn between strict adherence to surrender terms of the Allies and facilitating the Indonesian Republic by default. The Japanese lashed out against the Indonesians in Semarang because, on nine separate occasions the British demanded that they do so, and also because the pemuda had forcibly disarmed a nearby Japanese force. The situation escalated into five days of bitter fighting which left Tokyo in control, but at the cost of around 2,000 Indonesians dead, against roughly 500 Japanese.[93]

The Japanese were not the only imperialist army having difficulties in Java. After landing Britain soon realised it was too weak to control the whole island and so confined its forces to key cities. In a conciliatory (but hypocritical) move the commander for all Indonesia, Lieutenant General Sir Philip Christison, gave de facto recognition to the Republic, promising 'the British have no intention of meddling in Indonesian internal affairs ... .'[94]

London had charged Mountbatten's forces with a three-fold duty: firstly, to disarm and repatriate the Japanese; secondly, to rescue Allied internees held in Japanese camps but now menaced by Indonesians; and thirdly, to prepare for the return of the Dutch.[95] The first objective was almost immediately abandoned, because with only 45,000 troops Britain was too weak to confront hostile Indonesians on its own. Japan had required 70,000 soldiers to hold Java and that was when the population was co-operative. The Battle of Semarang led to a new warmth between the former enemies. When a British officer arrived there to investigate Japanese war crimes, Tull, the commander, removed him[96] and reported that the Japanese 'fought with incredible gallantry ...'. Mountbatten's own political advisor praised their 'devotion to duty',[97] and Christison went so far as to recommend one Japanese Major for a Distinguished Service Order.[98]

So instead of repatriating the defeated troops as originally intended, Mountbatten told Christison to 'Re-arm the Japs and take them under command' for use in combat and support roles alongside Anglo-Dutch forces now fighting across the island.[99] To one British officer this was an 'Alice in Wonderland situation'.[100] The policy evoked disgust amongst some of the lower ranks. In January 1946, a Staff Sergeant Barker wrote the following to Ernest Bevin, the current Foreign Secretary:

Two Jap sentries stand at this billet door, as I write, armed with loaded British rifles, and a Bren Machine Gun with 13 full magazines. We sleep securely, thinking 'Hell have we descended to THIS? Our tortured P.O.W comrades must be writhing in their jungle graves; what did they die for?'[101]

The second British objective concerned Japan's prisoners. Many Indonesians were deeply hostile to these Dutch, Eurasians, and their families, a British report warning in typically racist terms, that without protection the natives would 'sally out to indulge their tastes for murder and loot ...'.[102] Nonetheless, the risk of violence was real. For example, in Bandung, between December 1945 and March 1946, 1,500 (including Chinese who were seen as Dutch allies) were kidnapped or murdered.[103]

So, the rescue of internees could be presented as the humanitarian face of the British mission. The truth was more complicated, for as one writer explains, it was intended that few internees would leave Indonesia: 'The vast majority ... would be gathered into areas where they could be given medical treatment ... so that they could, in due course, resume their pre-war lives in a country where Dutch authority was being restored by the British.'[104] Violence against innocent civilians was regrettable, but the fact the British were there to reimpose the old arrangements was undoubtedly a provocation. A promise to end colonialism might well have eliminated the hostility.

In October/November 1945 the issue of evacuating internees precipitated the most important engagement of the independence war. The port of Surabaya was a designated transit point for Japan's former prisoners, and, uniquely for Java, this town had a militant working class tradition associated with employment at its large naval base.[105] When the British landed on 25 October they ignored numerous posters saying 'Remember the Atlantic Charter' because, as one officer wrote: 'My orders were to proceed into Surabaya and secure a position. Anyone not in Allied uniform and carrying arms was to be shot.'[106] The pemuda had other ideas. They had fortuitously obtained large quantities of Japanese arms because a self-important Dutch naval officer, unhappy with relying on Britain, had flown ahead and demanded the Japanese surrender their weapons to him. Since he had no means of holding them they fell into Indonesian hands.[107]

When Britain's Brigadier-General Mallaby realised he lacked the ability to disarm the pemuda, he decided instead to prioritise internee evacuation. The armaments issue was set aside and joint British-Indonesian committees were formed. Mallaby's plan was scuppered when, the very next day, the British authorities in Jakarta airdropped leaflets warning all Indonesians to surrender their weapons within 48 hours or be shot. An eye witness described the Indonesians' reaction: 'Everywhere people were saying the same thing: "Of course, the Allies aren't our enemies, but ... We'll fight!"'[108] The outcome was an uprising in which around 140,000 Indonesian TKR troops and pemuda attacked Britain's 4,000-strong 49th Indian Infantry Brigade.[109] The latter might have been obliterated had not Sukarno again assisted occupying forces, and called a ceasefire.

This time the Indonesian President's authority was challenged. A popular local radio presenter called Bung Tomo used his Allah for Radio Rebellion station to warn the: 'Leaders of the Indonesian people [that] if you gentlemen negotiate with the British and Dutch, this means the possibility that our people will be stripped naked once again ... .'[110] Sukarno's ceasefire broke down almost immediately; Mallaby was killed; and the President had to step in a second time: 'I have ordered all fighting against the Allies to cease ... there is no reason yet for groups among the people to take the law into their own hands... .'[111]

The new ceasefire lasted until the internees were safely evacuated. Then the British tore it up. To revenge Mallaby Christison announced: 'I intend to bring the whole weight of my sea, land and air forces and all the weapons of modern war against them until they are crushed.'[112] Surabaya's punishment lasted three weeks and has been summarised in these terms:

> British forces now consisted of about 6,000 Seaforth Highlanders strengthened by 24,000 'battle-hardened' troops of the Fifth Division, 21 Sherman tanks, eight Thunderbolt and 16 Mosquito planes, and divisional artillery. Indonesian forces were neither countable nor accountable. They took shape from within and against imperial history, Dutch, Japanese and now, incidentally British. They expressed the spirit of Surabaya and the ideal of *merdeka* [liberation]. Their casualties were incompletely numbered. The British counted 1,618 corpses, and another 4,697 Indonesians who died of wounds.[113]

Though Britain won in the short term, the people's battle at Surabaya would ensure their triumph in the longer term.

Elsewhere Christison ordered the destruction of Bekasi, where 20 British troops survived a plane crash but had then been attacked by Indonesians. Air and ground strikes led to 200 houses being burnt down and many dead. As one historian explains: 'Although the British occupation of Indonesia had assumed the character of a war, it is clear that captured Indonesians were not treated as prisoners of war, as the British had treated the Japanese in Burma. Indonesians captured in the act of offering armed resistance were shot as a matter of routine.'[114]

It was events such as these that led Nehru to say '... there is a perilous resemblance between these wars of intervention carried on by Britain and that other war of intervention, which fascist Italy and Nazi Germany waged ...'.[115] By the end of its occupation in 1946 British forces had sustained some 2,400 casualties, but inflicted death and injury on an estimated 31,000 pemuda.[116]

Holland was the last and weakest of the three imperialisms to act. Its government had learnt nothing from its own occupation by the Nazis, the Dutch representative saying of the Javanese: 'We are their father and mother; they can't manage without us.'[117] Whether out of arrogance, natural proclivities, or an attempt to prolong

British assistance by provoking trouble, Dutch troops behaved outrageously whenever possible. One British Major complained that they targeted 'youths and children'. 'Split heads and broken limbs [became] almost hourly occurrences ... Gunshot wounds, generally in the stomach or legs [were] so frequent as to be commonplace.'[118] It was to these forces that the British wished to hand Indonesia.

It might be argued that to use the term 'a *people*'s war against imperialism' in the context of Indonesia is inappropriate. Was this not simply a 'national war' for independence? This would be a mistaken interpretation because the dividing line was between the militant pemuda, and both the imperialists and people like Sukarno, a man who collaborated with the Japanese and later on with the British (as his role in Surabaya showed). The hostility of the new Indonesian government to the 'social revolutions' was symbolised by the Indonesian government representative in Sumatra who requested foreign intervention against his own 'irresponsible youths'. He asked the British commander to 'deal with them severely ... if only Allied troops would teach them a lesson, his position would become much more secure'.[119]

The imperialist war that began with the invasion of Java in 1942 had not faltered in 1945. It only concluded in 1947, but although there is not space here to provide the details, in the end, the combined forces of Japan, Britain and Holland failed to crush the people's war. After a protracted struggle Indonesia consolidated its independence.

14
Vietnam – Anti-Imperialist Breakthrough

Shortly after the formal end of the Second World War, General Vo Nguyen Giap of the Vietnamese Liberation Army met General Leclerc, the (misnamed) 'liberator of Paris',[1] and greeted him with these words: 'the first resistance fighter of Vietnam is happy to meet the first resistance fighter of France.'[2] In 1946 the French returned to shell the port of Haiphong killing 6,000 civilians in a bid to restore their former rule. Vietnam's fightback lasted 30 years and not only expelled the French but humbled America, the world's greatest superpower.[3] The contrast between Giap's rhetoric, and the people's war he was compelled to undertake, symbolised the conundrum that was the Second World War. Was it a struggle for freedom or to preserve established power?

French Indochina had comprised Vietnam's three provinces (Tonkin in the North, Annam in the centre, and Cochinchina in the South) plus Cambodia and Laos. To the world France claimed its officials there were performing an 'immense task ... for the sake of the Indochinese population'.[4] In Paris the language was different: 'No country in the world ... offers as many resources ... There are so many industries to be created! So many brilliant financial operations to be performed! So what are you waiting for? Go ahead!'[5] By the 1930s 'brilliant' financial operations had concentrated two-thirds of the colony's production in foreign hands[6] and provided European civilians with an income 102 times greater than that of the peasants.[7] Such a regime inevitably depended on the sword, so over half of the 42,000 European residents were soldiers.[8]

The impact of this colonial background on the Second World War period is disputed. According to the Indochinese Communist Party (ICP) the growth of an indigenous ruling class was so stunted that meaningful social divisions among the Vietnamese were effaced. Its leader, Ho Chi Minh said he was therefore following 'the instructions in *The Communist Manifesto*: The proletariat of each nation should ... build itself into a national class and make itself become national.'[9] If true it would have ruled out a people's war with its social and economic overtones, and stood Marx's famous dictum – 'Workers of the World Unite!' – on its head. However, the ICP's premise it was possible to 'graft communism on to patriotism'[10] was false.

Though few in number, the *per capita* income of wealthy Vietnamese landowners and businessmen actually exceeded that of European civilians, and was 122 times greater than that of the peasantry.[11] The Second World War further widened this social divide in several ways. As the colony was isolated from France it had to provide its own administrators, and the number of middle and top posts doubled. By 1944 the managing directors of 75 of the 92 corporations operating were Vietnamese.[12] The French had deliberately expanded the power of local landlords so as to provide its regime with a domestic social base, and a mere 6,200 people owned 45 per cent of rice-growing land in the south. In the Red River valley 2 per cent of households possessed 50 per cent of land.[13] The arrival of world war added rising food prices, hoarding, speculation, fabulous profits for the few, and immiseration for the majority.

Establishing the social dimension does not diminish the importance of the national issue. From 1941 Vietnam found itself oppressed by not just one imperialist power, but two! Japan viewed Vietnam as an important staging post for its Chinese campaign. Whereas Tokyo overturned European administrations in the Philippines, Malaya, Burma and Indonesia, in Indochina it signed a treaty with Vichy France. Governor-General Jean Decoux, an arch-Pétainist who imprisoned Jews and Gaullists, was permitted to remain in office in return for allowing Japanese bases.[14] To Vichy's diplomats it was 'a miracle to have maintained, in the midst of the sphere controlled by Japan, a peaceful, prosperous "island" on which western civilization and ideas are successfully asserted'.[15] Astonishingly, when France was liberated de Gaulle retained Decoux's services. He feared that disturbing Decoux's regime would open the way for the Chinese and their US backers to intervene, even more than he disliked Pétainist cronies.

So the Free French government in Paris must take responsibility for Tonkin's famine of 1945. As with Athens or Bengal this was man-made. Equitable food distribution could have avoided starvation[16] even though poor weather and pests had reduced the northern rice crop by one-fifth.[17] But the French army shipped ten or more boatloads of rice out of the affected area every day.[18] Hoarders and speculators, many of them local, completed the job. In Tonkin's capital, Hanoi, food prices rose 373 per cent in just three months.[19] Officials described seeing 'corpses, which are shrivelled up on the roadsides with only a handful of straw for clothes as well as for their burial garment. One feels ashamed of being a human.'[20] Estimates of the death toll reach up to two million.[21]

Then the Japanese swept away what remained of French power. In November 1944, with the US poised to re-take the Philippines, Japan's Southern Army transferred its General HQ from Manila to Saigon, and on 9 March it took sole control of Vietnam.[22] Tokyo's takeover had a significant political impact (although famine victims noticed little difference as grain requisitions continued).[23]

The Japanese restored the Annamese Emperor Bao Dai to his palace in Hue and endowed him with fictitious independence and nominal powers over all Vietnam. By collaborating with the Axis Bao Dai, and the various nationalist parties who worked with him, sacrificed any claim to leadership in a future people's war. That made it easier for ICP to become the undisputed leader of the struggle for independence.

However, the ICP did not adopt this position in a straightforward manner. Its strategy gradually evolved from subservience to the Allies to open people's war against them. To understand why, it is necessary to follow the Party's tortuous course under the twin impact of French repression and Stalinist politics.

The ICP's founding statement in 1930 aimed: 'To make Indochina completely independent', by overthrowing 'French imperialism *and* Vietnamese feudalism and reactionary bourgeoisie'. The ICP would 'confiscate all the plantations and property belonging to the imperialists and the Vietnamese reactionary bourgeoisie and distribute them to the poor peasants'.[24] These aspirations gave the Party a difficult start in life, and that same year defeat of the 'Nghe Tinh Soviet' movement led to the detention of thousands of communists.

A decade later the ICP loyally committed itself to the Communist International's popular front policies that were an exact opposite of the 1930 position:

1. For the time being the Party should not put forward too exacting demands (national independence, parliament, etc.). To do so is to play into the Japanese fascists' hands. It should only claim democratic rights, freedom of organization, freedom of assembly, freedom of the press and freedom of speech, general amnesty for all political detainees, and freedom for the Party to engage in legal activity.

2. To reach this goal, the Party must strive to organize a broad Democratic National Front. This Front should embrace not only Indochinese but also progressive French people residing in Indochina, not only the toiling people but also the national bourgeoisie.
3. The Party must assume a tactful, flexible attitude towards the national bourgeoisie, strive to draw them into the Front and keep them there ... .

If the national bourgeoisie were now welcome allies, Trotskyists, who still advocated many policies the ICP itself embraced in 1930, were the enemy: 'there can be no compromise, no concession. We must do everything possible to unmask them as agents of fascism and annihilate them politically.'[25]

Despite revising its policies and making overtures to the French, the ICP did not escape anti-communist repression following the Hitler–Stalin Pact.[26] Arrests so disrupted internal links that the party's central apparatus no longer exerted the monolithic authority common to communist organisations.[27] The leadership were unable to prevent members from being drawn into doomed uprisings against the French at Bac Son in the North and Cochinchina in the South. Marr describes how the latter was crushed:

[A]ircraft, armoured cars, and artillery were used to destroy whole villages ... For want of sufficient handcuffs or chains, detainees had their hands and feet pierced with telegraph wire. When all existing prison facilities were full, the French packed detainees onto ships moored in the Saigon River. No one knows how many people died in this 'white terror,' but the number almost surely exceeded two thousand. Up to eight thousand were detained, some later dying in jail or being executed. On the other side, three Frenchmen and thirty militamen or local Vietnamese notables were killed.[28]

Such experiences reinforced the ICP leadership's wariness of engaging in a people's war.

As evidence of the difficulties the ICP faced, Ho Chi Minh was compelled to live abroad from 1911 to 1941 under numerous aliases. A leading opponent of colonialism rebuked him with these words: 'we shouldn't reside overseas and introduce back our leadership. Instead we should return to the homeland'. He answered that this was pointless since: 'local combatants are all closely watched and hotly pursued on their own soil.'[29] He changed his outlook during the Second World War. Ho then issued this 'Letter from Abroad':

> Now the opportunity has come for our liberation. France itself is unable to help the French colonialists rule over our country. As for the Japanese, on the one hand, bogged down in China, on the other hampered by the British and American forces, they certainly cannot use all their strength against us. If our entire people are solidly united we can certainly get the better of the best-trained armies of the French and the Japanese. Fellow-countrymen! Rise up![30]

Even now progress was slow. On the eve of gaining power in the August 1945 revolution, the party still counted no more than 5,000 members (a third of whom were in jail). Its army was of a similar size.[31] The Japanese had 57,000 troops in Vietnam, and thousands more seasoned Allied troops were waiting in the wings to crush any post-war independence movement.[32] These conditions led the Vietnamese ICP to adopt a cautious strategy.

Playing down popular initiatives Ho cautioned against precipitate mass struggle as this was 'likely to lead to the dispersal of physical and human resources'.[33] Instead, he advocated a three-stage plan following the Chinese CP model. First, the party cadre would establish a revolutionary base in a secluded spot.[34] Later the peasantry would be recruited, and in the final stage the party would launch an assault on the towns and seize power. Ho Chi Minh had been a Comintern functionary for many years, and if he still paid lip service to the proletariat, in practice he relegated mass action to rubber-stamping the actions of the Party and wrote off the urban working class.

The first tentative step in his programme was the formation of an 'Armed Propaganda Brigade for the Liberation of Vietnam'. Its title boldly pointed to the eventual goal but expressly fell short of direct confrontation. As Ho put it, 'the name ... shows that greater importance is attached to its political than to its military action'.[35] Then, in May 1941, came the decision to create the Viet Nam Doc Lap Dong Minh (Hoi) [Vietnam Independence League], or Vietminh. Marr explains how this positioned:

> [W]orkers and peasants side by side with those landlords, capitalists, mandarins, soldiers, intellectuals, clerks, and

shopkeepers increasingly antagonized by outrageous Franco-Japanese behaviour and prepared to struggle for Vietnam's national liberation ... The Viet Minh would identify itself entirely with one side in the global confrontation, those who soon styled themselves the Allies.[36]

The price for seeking friendship with this faction (which, it must be remembered, included de Gaulle's French) was to defer working-class and poor peasant demands in favour of a 'national liberation revolution'.[37] Therefore the Vietminh renounced redistribution of land, a key issue, as it provided the livelihood of 90 per cent of the population. According to Neale, part of the explanation for the stance of the ICP can be put down to its social origins:

> First it recruited educated men ... Then those people recruited and led the villagers they knew... They were the decent minority of the landlord class. They hated the corruption and brutality of their class. They wanted to sweep away the old order and replace it with a modern industrial state ... This meant the Communist Party was always deeply ambivalent about land reform.[38]

So strenuous were Ho's efforts to forge a cross-class alliance that foreign commentators were uncertain as to whether he was a communist or not. *The Times*, for example, published this report: 'There seem to be only two parties of any significance at the moment, the Viet-min and the Communists.'[39] Ho's 'frontist' strategy went so far as the formal dissolution of the ICP (in November 1945), which, as one writer says, 'was a gesture without precedent or parallel in the history of the international Communist movement'.[40]

Modifying policies did not guarantee that Allied assistance, however. With Russia out of reach, Ho turned to warlords linked to Chiang Kai Shek, the Chinese nationalist leader. They operated on the Sino-Vietnamese border and could provide weapons and a safe haven if retreat became necessary. Hopeful of their support, in February 1941 he established himself in a cave in Cao Bang, a mountainous border area.[41] The precarious nature of Ho's position was underlined when he was held captive for a year by a previously co-operative warlord. Since Chinese help had proved unreliable[42] he sought alternative sources of aid. At one point he even declared himself 'ready to shake hands with the French who are truly and thoroughly resolved to resist the Japanese ...'.[43] General Giap duly made contact with France's Commander Reul, but an accord proved elusive.[44]

American aid was a better option. There were signs the USA might help the Vietminh and oppose the restoration of French colonialism. When Roosevelt discussed Vietnam with Stalin at the Teheran Conference in 1943 they agreed '100% [that] France should not get back into Indochina'. The President added that the USA was considering with its Chinese client 'a system of trusteeship which would have the task of preparing the people for independence within a definite period of time, perhaps 20 to 30 years.'[45] Such paternalism fitted post-war plans. Europe's Asian possessions were to be cracked open and subjected to America's overwhelming economic dominance, with four policemen ultimately ruling the world: Russia, Britain, USA and China. France was not yet part of this future.[46]

But American friendship towards the Vietminh would be shortlived. As the Second World War drew to a close Cold War winds began blowing. Chiang's Nationalist China collapsed while de Gaulle's France was needed to counter Russian influence in Europe. Therefore, four days before he died in April 1945, Roosevelt killed off his trusteeship plan.[47] By May the US Secretary of State was claiming, disingenuously, that his government had been 'entirely innocent of any official statement ... questioning, even by implication, French sovereignty over Indo-China.'[48]

These shifting sands of US government policy sowed confusion in the East Asian theatre. For example, the US Air Force flew many sorties to help the French during their brief resistance to Japan's 9 March coup.[49] Yet soon afterwards OSS agents worked with Ho Chi Minh and even enrolled him as an agent[50] and a team under Major Allison Thomas parachuted in to train Vietminh fighters.[51] Although the US supplied only 12 per cent of its weapons[52] the psychological boost for the Vietminh was considerable as it became associated with the victorious Americans.[53]

By VJ Day the US had swung decisively towards supporting French claims and abandoning Ho. Major Thomas was the Allied officer best placed to receive the Japanese surrender in Hanoi, but was told by his superiors that 'under no circumstances' was he to do so. He found this 'stunning news' and 'extremely disheartening' but discerned the reasoning behind his orders. America dare not be seen co-operating with Ho because 'the French were our Allies and the Vietminh party was a secret party working against the French ...'.[54]

So despite all efforts Ho failed to obtain consistent support from any of the relevant Allies – France, China or the US. Yet his strategy remained attentist and tied closely to an expected Allied landing. As late as 12 March 1945 the ICP Central Committee said:

> we should not only wait for the Allied forces to get a firm foothold, we must also wait until they are advancing. At the same time, we must wait until the Japanese send forces to the front to intercept the Allied forces, thus relatively exposing their rear, before we launch the general insurrection.[55]

Nonetheless Ho's approach was not bound hand and foot to imperialism. He was not so naïve as to take announcements such as the Atlantic Charter at face value and, while waiting for the Allies, also envisaged a mass movement to counter any re-imposition of French rule.

In the meantime the Vietminh generally avoided conflict with Japanese forces. Between March and May its operations cost Tokyo around 50 men.[56] Tonnesson suggests that the Japanese found this 'a nuisance', but not one comparable to the resistance in Yugoslavia, or to the Chinese Red Army: 'the few clashes do not amount to more than incidents. There was never enough fighting to speak of armed struggle.'[57]

Everything changed when looming defeat loosened the grip of Japan. A power vacuum suddenly developed enabling the aspirations of ordinary Vietnamese to find expression. The Vietminh benefited from this despite its miniscule size and orientation on tightly organised military formations. It became the rallying point for a people's war in the North, and also a major force in the South. Marr describes the complex relationship between the mass popular movement from below and the narrow layer of communists:

> While most of the upheavals in August were sparked by Viet Minh slogans (created or cleared by experienced ICP members), and while almost everyone came to identify with the Viet Minh flag, soon to become the national standard, many local groups calling themselves Viet Minh had almost no idea of what the organization stood for, much less possess any connections with the Tong Bo (General Headquarters). The hundreds of 'people's committees' and 'revolutionary committees' that replaced the assorted royal mandarins and appointed councils … were far from being mere appendages of the central authority or fronts for ICP cadres.

Many of these committees sought revenge for past injustices or projected radical social revolutionary aspirations ... .[58]

People's war occurred because official ICP policy was disregarded on a mass scale. Rejecting the politics of class compromise many demanded land redistribution and started 'a property upheaval from below that no government could control'.[59] The French authorities in Tonkin noted the accelerating rhythm with just four 'Vietminh incidents' recorded during 1942–43, but 80 in 1944.[60] In famine districts the local Vietminh gave organised expression to the widespread need for grain. Demonstrations armed with spears and machetes became commonplace, with over 75 warehouses affected in the Red River Delta alone.[61]

By the summer of 1945 this seething discontent had intensified and the ICP had to respond. In June the Vietminh declared a 'liberated zone' in the North and 100,000 people, or one in ten of the population there, enrolled in its militia.[62] At this time the Vietminh had only 80,000 adherents in the rest of the country. On 12 August it called for a general uprising, and the next day 'Military Order No. 1' ordered an attack on the Japanese with a view to seizing their arms.[63]

Nonetheless, the ICP's ability to control and direct the on-going people's war remained limited. In particular, the difficulty of communicating across this 1,650km strip of a country meant that between late 1940 and June 1945 there was no direct contact between the leadership in the North and Cochinchina![64] Different southern currents challenged the Vietminh organisation for leadership. One was the Vanguard Youth. Originally a French-inspired scouting and sports organisation, it was politicised by war and had a mass following, but it lacked the Vietminh's coherence due to the great variety of political currents and religious sects that jostled for dominance within its ranks.

Another rival was Trotskyism which rejected the ICP strategy of a cross-class alliance working in stages (from revolutionary base, to the countryside, and finally the towns). This current had many adherents in Cochinchina, and in the 1939 elections to the Colonial Council eclipsed the communists by attracting the overwhelming majority of votes.[65] The Trotskyist leader, Ta Thu Thau, rejected the notion that one could 'graft communism on to patriotism'. He insisted a choice must be made between 'socialism or nationalism' because, although the world was 'divided politically into nations, [it] tends to form an economic whole ...'. So the division between exploiters and exploited was greater than between capitalist states. In Vietnam this meant workers and peasants faced a two-headed enemy – colonialism 'dragging behind it the native bourgeoisie'.[66] Ta Thu Thau believed that the Second World War presented an opportunity 'to take advantage of the war between the capitalist nations to emancipate the proletariat'.[67] For this to happen clear class demands had to be put forward.

Japan's sudden surrender wrecked Ho Chi Minh's strategy of co-operating with advancing Allied forces as a step towards eventually gaining power. The Vietminh did triumph, but events occurred in reverse order to the leadership's expectations. As Tonnesson writes, the ICP found itself:

> on the sidelines in August, when the opportunity for a classical city-revolution suddenly presented itself. In Hanoi, Hue and many provincial centres, the August Revolution was carried out – more or less spontaneously – by enthusiastic youth and second-level cadres while the party leaders were stuck in their 'war capital', an out of the way little place they called Tan Trao.[68]

It was the nationalist Democratic Party in Hanoi which called the first mass demonstration, on 16 August, insisting that only a 'revolution by all citizens' would be enough to frustrate the ambitions of the various imperialist forces. However, that Party was outmanoeuvred by a Vietminh supporter. She took the rostrum and led the crowd in cheers for her organisation. As the only nationally organised, disciplined, cadre party in the revolutionary mix, the ICP and its Vietminh front held a trump card. It quickly made up for lost time. Defying the central leadership's attentism, the Communist Regional Committee called for a seizure of power. On 19 August a crowd of 200,000 accomplished this while demoralised Japanese troops stood aside.[69]

Again, contrary to Ho's ideas, action in towns inspired the countryside, not *vice versa*. Rural activists poured into Hanoi for advice, followed by tens of thousands of villagers.[70] At the same time the revolution burst through the limitations of ICP policy. Marr writes that despite the Vietminh leaders' determination to avoid radical demands:

> Events in many rural districts of Vietnam in late August went well beyond political transfer of power, involving social revolutionary behaviour the consequences of which no one could

predict at the time. The administration established by the Viet Minh in Hanoi became as much a prisoner of the thousands of revolutionary committees emerging around the country as the directing authority.[71]

The contradictions opening up between the people's understanding of the purpose of the Second World War and the ICP brought in the question of land. On 30 July 1945 the Party reiterated its programme, such as preservation of existing land tenure:

> After the victory of the Revolution, when our country becomes independent, the land of rich people is not to be distributed to the poor people. We will confiscate only the land and property of aggressors and traitors. Anyone who says that the land of rich people must be distributed to the poor deliberately divides the people's united front and certainly deserves punishment.[72]

But the revolution ignored such strictures. In North Annam and Tonkin committees shared out land and confiscated the wealth of the rich. Elsewhere, 30,000 miners formed a 'workers' Commune' establishing equal pay for all, and controlling not only the collieries but public services, railways and telegraphs. This organisation survived until the Vietminh arrested its leadership in November 1945.[73]

Still more troubling for the ICP was the turn of events in the south, where competition was strongest. When Japan surrendered here local communists mobilised in a village 40km from Saigon. They intended to approach it only later.[74] But 100,000 marched through the Cochinese capital behind the banner of a 'United National Front'[75] and the Vanguard Youth led the way in seizing power.[76] For a time it looked as if the ICP had lost the initiative entirely.[77]

In this maelstrom Trotskyist slogans were popular: 'Land to the peasants! Nationalisation of the factories under workers' control! People's committees!'[78] These calls both reflected and inspired the actions of the landless in the provinces of Mytho, Travinh, Sadec, Longxuyen and Chaudoc.[79] Workers in the Phu Nhuan district declared their committee to be the 'sole legal power in the area', an example followed elsewhere.[80] Within three weeks over 150 independent revolutionary committees were established.[81]

But the ICP, with its Stalinist roots, was not about to abandon the South to others. After half a million marched through Saigon on 25 August, a Southern Provisional Executive Committee was formed to unite the various currents in one body. The Vietminh quickly manoeuvred to win most positions[82] and then turned on its rivals. Following Ho Chi Minh's policy that 'All those who do not follow the line set out by me will be broken',[83] several Trotskyists were executed, a notable early casualty being Ta Thu Thau.

As well as reining in the revolution, Ho wooed the imperialists. On 2 September he broadcast from Hanoi the 'Declaration of Independence of the Democratic Republic of Vietnam' (DRV). This began with a direct quotation from the USA's Declaration of 1776, and followed up with words lifted from France's 1791 'Declaration of the Rights of Man'.[84] Ho predicted that since the 'Allied nations … have acknowledged the principles of self-determination and equality of nations [so they] will not refuse to acknowledge the independence of … a people who have fought side by side with the Allies against the fascists during these last years'.[85]

Following this line in Cochinchina, Tran van Giau, the ICP leader of the Provisional Executive Committee discouraged the only thing that could counter imperialism – mass activity.[86] He announced the disarming of all non-governmental organisations on 7 September, saying: 'Those who call the people to arms and above all to fight against the imperialist Allies will be considered provocateurs and saboteurs.'[87] This was the day after the first Allied troops had disembarked, but before they could establish their authority.

In Hanoi the DRV survived, not so much through an alliance with imperialism but because arguments amongst the Allied powers provided a breathing space. Roosevelt was determined to bolster China, and the US Commander, General Wedemeyer was ordered 'to prevent any British and French political activities' in areas under his control.[88] By contrast, the commander of British forces, General Gracey was told to 'liberate Allied territory in so far as your resources permit'.[89] Of course, the 'Ally' was France, and the territory in question was to be 'liberated' from the Vietnamese themselves. To resolve this row the US and Britain struck a deal at the Potsdam Conference. Vietnam was divided between 'the China Theater' of operations north of the 16th parallel, and Mountbatten's South East Asian Command in the south. De Gaulle was disappointed but too weak to intervene. He thought, rightly, that these divisions 'fatally compromised' imperialist efforts.[90]

Ho was fortunate that the Chinese were more interested in corruption and plunder than long-term occupation of North Vietnam on their own account, and they tacitly recognised the Hanoi government.[91] It was a different story in Cochinchina. Although the Vietnamese reminded General Gracey that they 'fought side by side with the Allies against the fascists', his response could not have been more blunt: 'I was welcomed on arrival by the Viet Minh, who said "Welcome" and all that sort of thing. It was a very unpleasant situation, and I promptly kicked them out. They were obviously communists.'[92]

Gracey had no qualms about following Mountbatten's injunction to 'rely on the Japanese and French forces to enforce your orders'.[93] He had a Japanese unit assist his Gurkhas in expelling the Provisional Executive Committee from its offices.[94] On 21 September, he banned all demonstrations, processions, public meetings and the carrying of arms by Vietnamese. The day after martial law was imposed groups described by *The Times* as 'members of the French *maquis*'[95] were unleashed on the southern capital. In fact most were French soldiers and Legionaries linked to the Vichy regime from the time of Decoux. Some were even Waffen-SS newly freed from Japanese prisoner of war camps.[96] They ran 'rampage through the city, cursing, beating up, detaining, and otherwise offending any native encountered'.[97]

In response the Vietminh called a general strike. Open war followed. One eyewitness recounted: 'The crackle of gunfire and the thud of mortars soon resonated through the city, as armed Vietminh squads attacked the airport, burned the central market and stormed the local prison to liberate hundreds of Vietnamese inmates'.[98] Numerous French civilians were killed soon after.

Since local French forces were so chaotic Gracey withdrew them (pending the arrival of units from France on 5 October) and fell back more heavily on the Japanese. They were deployed in combat roles, the official history of 20th Indian Division recording that: 'All the dirty work, to fight and disarm the Annamites (Vietnamese), was assigned to the Japanese troops.'[99] Thus a bizarre coalition of Allied victors and defeated Axis, Japanese jailers and jailed collaborators, worked together to oust Vietnamese rule in their own country. By Febuary 1946 British forces had lost 40 soldiers, France 106, and Japan 110. Against this were set at least 3,026 Vietnamese. 1,825 were victims of the French, 651 of British forces, and 550 died at the hands of the Japanese.[100] The last British forces withdrew in March 1946, leaving the French in control south of the 16th parallel and determined to extend their power north of it.

Ho's attempt to straddle the two wars proved unsuccessful. Wooing imperialism to assist independence did not bear fruit. Though the belated promotion of mass action did bring victory in Hanoi, it left the enemy in power in the south. As we saw at the beginning of this chapter, the presence of two wars was summed up in the contradiction between the hopes of General Giap and his eventual actions. This can now be elaborated upon. In early September 1945 he had argued:

> The great powers in the democratic front have declared that they were fighting for equality among nations, so there is no reason why they would help French imperialism return to repress and exploit the Vietnamese people.
>
> We and the whole world cannot imagine that after having, of our own volition, stood on the allied side to fight the Japanese fascists in Indochina, after having contributed bones and blood to the struggle of the allies on the Pacific front, we would be considered by the allies as having to live under the yoke of slavery of the French colonialists, who were the very ones who agreed to let Fascist Japan occupy Indochina in order to make it a base for attacking the Philipines, Malaya, Burma, South China ... .[101]

Yet it was this same man who masterminded the stunning defeat of the French army at Dien Bien Phu in 1954 and the eventual defeat of the Americans who stepped in afterwards. The thirty-year Vietnam War became the most important anti-imperialist episode of the twentieth century and a stirring example of the people's war. The final outcome was an independent country, though one ruled by a dictatorial state capitalist regime. Many of the social and economic demands of ordinary people went unanswered in the process, and in the challenge set by Ta Thu Thau of 'nationalism or socialism', the government came down firmly on the side of the former.

In Vietnam, as elsewhere, the Second World War saw political, social, and economic elements blended in unpredictable combinations and producing unpredictable results. Ho Chi Minh's initial policy of relying on various imperialist powers turned out to be flawed, and he came to a grudging acceptance that a people's war was the only solution to the problem of independence: 'The war is won. But we small and subject countries have no share, or very very small share, in the victory of freedom and democracy. Probably, if we want to get a sufficient share, we have still to fight.'[102]

Conclusion

The conventional view of the war against the Axis admits the co-existence of official armies and the resistance, generals and privates, rich and poor, but stresses their harmony and joint endeavour to end the evils of the Axis regimes. However, differences between the participants were not variations upon a common theme, but reflected fundamentally contradictory processes at the level of aims, ideology, tactics, military and social structures. Between 1939 and 1945 parallel wars were not an exception to the rule but occurred generally, if not universally. Apparent unity merely papered over the underlying cracks, the notion of the Second World War as a 'single whole' was a convenient myth.

An example of the disparity between the two elements was the presumed shared opposition to fascism. During the Spanish Civil War the Western Allies chose Franco over the Republic, and they continued to support him after the Second World War. Conflict with Germany only began after appeasement policies failed to curb Hitler's territorial expansion into spheres of Franco-British influence. During and after the war the Allies were happy to work with Axis forces indirectly (take the example of Darlan, the abandonment of the Warsaw uprising or the collaborationist militias in Greece), or directly (using Japanese troops in Indonesia and Vietnam). So, despite the common commingling of the two together, the people's anti-fascist war did not correspond to the Allied governments' war on the Axis.

The parallel wars differed in other ways too. Allied ruling classes battled to defend their privileged *status quo* from internal and external threats, while popular armed struggle strove for real, all-encompassing, human liberation and a more just, democratic future. Imperialists sacrificed life indiscriminately to achieve their ends; partisans and guerrillas defended local populations from aggression and agonised over the risks their actions posed for civilians. Conventional soldiers were subordinate to a rigid hierarchy and sworn to unquestioning obedience; fighters of the people's war, whether in the soldiers' parliament in Cairo, the ghettos of Detroit, or the mountains of Greece, Yugoslavia and Italy, were conscious volunteers driven by ideological commitment.

The reader might justifiably ask whether categorising the Second World War as parallel wars on the Allied side is not the imposition of a blanket theoretical construct on what are simply disparate events. Why not, as most standard histories do, simply narrate 'the facts' (although in so doing they move from the extreme of assigning a single label to the entire 1939–45 conflict, to the other extreme of pulverising the period into a series of unrelated incidents connected only by military action)?

In one sense every historical event is unique and defies comparison with any other, because circumstances never repeat exactly. All overarching concepts shoehorn the richness of detail into an analytical framework. Nonetheless, history, and modern history especially, consists of interactions that are not limited to one moment or place and are not comprehensible without reference to a wide framework. The Second World War was the most graphic possible example. It was 'the largest single event in human history, fought across six of the world's seven continents and all its oceans'.[1] Therefore, alongside the detail, a discussion of connections between its manifold episodes reveals an historical truth. There was such a thing as the Second World War, so its underlying character can and should be investigated. And the discovery of parallel wars within it shows, to use the language of dialectics, that the Second World War represented a 'unity of opposites'.

There is nothing startling about the idea that different sections of society had varying interests or behaved in different ways; nor that the formal declaration of war did not automatically suspend these differences. What was unique about the Second World War was that these tensions amounted to parallel wars rather than tensions within the same war. To understand why, it is necessary to briefly trace the long-term history of the state and warfare, arms and the people.

In the Middle Ages state military power was decentralised, with barons running local armies in a loose relationship to the monarch. Wars involved relatively small numbers because primitive transport methods and weak central government meant large national armies could be neither assembled nor supplied on a long-term basis. The situation changed in 1789. The modern nation was born with the French Revolution whose motto was 'liberty, equality, fraternity'.

'Fraternity' included the idea that war (or at least defensive war, and all wars would henceforth be described as defensive) was for the people; but it was deeply ambiguous. Fraternity was symbolised by the newly founded nation state that the masses defended from the surrounding aristocracies. But this self-same institution was also the embodiment of ruling-class interests, what Marx's *Communist Manifesto* calls 'a committee for managing the common affairs of the whole bourgeoisie'. Insofar as national states maintained freedom from foreign oppression they represented the interests of masses of people; insofar as they were a ruling-class instrument they protected domestic capitalism from external competitors.

The year 1789 also revolutionised army organisation. The assembled monarchies of Europe were fought off by a close alliance of the French government and the population. This involved the '*levée en masse*'. Mobilisation on a scale hitherto unknown was the basis for Napoleon's quarter-of-a-million strong *Grande Armée*, a body which showed the effectiveness of huge numbers, but also bumped up against the technical limits of the time. Aristocratic-led mercenary forces tumbled before the Napoleonic juggernaut, and in 1812 its hundreds of thousands of soldiers, on foot and horseback, defeated Russia at Borodino and captured Moscow. However, over-extended communication lines, bad weather, and starvation eventually destroyed the *Grande Armée*. Only 90,000 survived and Napoleon commented ruefully, that 'an army marches on its stomach'. Advances in productive force had not kept pace with destructive force.

The nineteenth-century's industrial revolution burst through these technical obstacles. Railways now moved troops and supplies rapidly and the scale of warfare expanded exponentially. This made possible the largest battles of the nineteenth century, at Gettysburg (1863) and Sadowa/Koeniggratz (1866). These had 170,000 and 425,000 in the field respectively. By the First World War Russia deployed an army of 16 million, and Germany 13 million. Weaponry also became more deadly. Napoleonic-era muskets had a range of 150 yards and fire rate of two rounds per minute. The First World War rifles reached up to a mile at a rate of ten per minute; machine guns 400.[2] Casualties at the battle of the Somme in 1916 came to 1.9 million alone, and on the first day the British army fired 943,837 shells weighing 40,000 tons.[3] Total war, launched by governments, but sustained by entire populations on the 'home front', had arrived.

During the French Revolution no-one could know if the language of national war of the people would be a durable concept, or depended on a particular political conjuncture – the life-and-death struggle between aristocratic society and modernising forces. In a prescient passage written at the time, Clausewitz noted that contemporary warfare, being: 'an affair of the whole Nation, has assumed quite a new nature' but wondered if:

> all Wars hereafter in Europe will be carried on with the whole power of the States, and, consequently will only take place on account of great interests closely affecting the people, or whether a separation of the interests of the government from those of the people will again gradually arise … .[4]

By the twentieth century the threat of the *ancien régime* was largely destroyed, and capitalism (now in its imperialist phase) was fully established. In Europe nationalism was consistently used to divide and rule the working class; exploitation by a local capitalist was much the same as exploitation by a foreign one; so it might be assumed that the readiness of ordinary people to sacrifice themselves in defending 'their state' would diminish. However, a countervailing tendency was equally influential. The predatory nature of capitalist competition and capitalist states drove many people to support their national governments against outside aggression. Therefore, in 1914 the question Clausewitz had posed about the stability of the government/people consensus in wartime was still unresolved.

The First World War began with a frenzy of enthusiasm, as symbolised by the famous slogan on the Kitchener recruitment poster: 'Your Country Needs You!' Yet by 1918 millions would have agreed with the Bolshevik statement that: 'Official patriotism is a mask for the exploiting interests.'[5] The separation of people and governments that Clausewitz had postulated, manifested itself in revolutions that ended the war by sweeping away governments in Russia, Germany and Austria. Meanwhile, in the victor countries, mutinies, mass strikes and factory occupations were commonplace. The First World War did not create a people's war *alongside* an imperialist war, but its opposite – people's uprisings *to stop* an imperial war.

The Second World War differed significantly from the First World War in many other ways. Firstly, because the appalling memory of 1914–18, broken promises of post-war reforms, and inter-war socio-economic crisis, left a deep imprint on ordinary people, in 1939 Allied governments knew that repeating simplistic pleas to patriotism would fail. So in documents like the Atlantic Charter they emphasised the fight for freedom even more insistently and threw out still more lavish promises of post-war improvements, both to engage the energies of the population and avoid a repetition of the upheavals of 1917–19. Though Allied government intentions were no less imperialist than before, the people's expectations of liberation and reform were at a higher level than during the First World War and more difficult to restrain.

Secondly, fascism and communism established a new ideological context. Fascism was explicitly a counter-revolutionary attempt to break working-class organisation at home, and also a policy of aggressive expansion at the cost of established imperialist powers. This first element was new and spurred ordinary people to fight fascism and uphold their freedoms and rights. The second element was not novel and in this sense the Second World War was, like the First World War, another round of jockeying for competitive advantage.

Thirdly, there were differences at the military level. The First World War often involved large-scale trench warfare that established clearly delineated, and fairly static, military fronts. The Second World War's *Blitzkrieg* techniques made warfare far more mobile, bringing aerial bombardment and enemy rule to millions. Germany and Japan deliberately shifted military costs on to those they conquered. The result was famines and the hunt for manpower, the latter playing an important role in driving young men to join partisan bands. The immediacy of Axis aggression, whether in the London Blitz or under direct occupation, meant that fighting would not be left to government action alone, but became an urgent necessity for ordinary people.

Fourthly, Axis seizure of huge swathes of territory was usually accompanied by the emergence of quislings. The ruling-class instinct for survival was supplemented by their desire to have the Gestapo help them destroy working-class movements. Such collaboration disrupted the national illusion and the ideological hegemony that capitalism usually enjoys. Even those ruling classes that preferred Allied imperialism feared mobilising their own poor. The outcome was an attentism which left space for new forces to flourish. In Asia an additional factor was that the swift Axis onslaught in Europe weakened colonial states and opened new vistas for independence.

To sum up, alongside a brutal imperialist war, the situation was uniquely favourable to movements from below seeking national and social freedom. That some of the fighting of 1939–45 exceeded a traditional defence of the capitalist state was therefore no aberration, but a logical outcome of prior development.

The people's war had both weaknesses and strengths. As an amalgam of class and nation it was not viable in the long term. Often its forces were rapidly dissolved (such as in Germany, or France). Even where it gained state power (e.g. Yugoslavia and Vietnam), the new governments would reassert the 'national state' as the managing committee of capitalism, and the 'people' would become the object of exploitation. And its military impact on the defeat of the Axis is debatable. Keegan is surely too critical when he writes that the contribution of resistance movements to Allied victory was minimal and 'must be seen, by any objective reckoning, as irrelevant and pointless acts of bravado'.[6] In January 1944 Yugoslav partisans were tying down 15 German divisions, and the French resistance blocked the movement of twelve during D-Day.[7] Nonetheless, these achievements pale against the hundreds of divisions deployed by Allied governments who enjoyed the inestimable advantages of taxation, the backing of wealth, arms industries, and the 'legitimate force' of well-equipped conventional armies.

But the people's war was not confined to resistance movements alone. Millions in the conventional armies were determined to confront Axis oppression (and by implication oppression generally). This was clearly understood by the Allied governments who collectively donned the cloak of anti-fascism. Overy is correct to say that for ordinary people everywhere 'the belief that they fought on the sight of righteousness equipped them with powerful moral armament'.[8] This weapon was used against Germany, Italy and Japan, but could be turned on the Allies too.

To the question 'Was the Second World War an imperialist war or a people's war?' the answer is 'It was both'. However, it does not follow that the balance between the two was the same everywhere. Variations were partly due to subjective factors such as the communists. While the Hitler–Stalin pact was in force the CPs denounced the Second World War as imperialist, but they rapidly moved to spearhead people's war after Operation Barbarossa. The prestige of association with the victorious Red Army helped build their following thereafter. The communists' willingness to take the lead, at great personal risk, arose from a genuine commitment to social progress and justice. Yet this was tempered by their leaders' slavish adherence to Moscow that often proved injurious to the very movements they did so much to build. That does not mean the people's war was a manipulated communist construct. It is important to remember that it encompassed movements as diverse as the Quit India struggle (which the Indian CP opposed), the Warsaw insurgents, and the Double V campaign in the US.

Objective factors also played a role. Countries caught between imperialist blocs – Yugoslavia, Greece, Poland and Latvia – provided the greatest variety in relations between people's war and imperialist war. In Yugoslavia Mihailovich feared the partisans more than the enemy and collaborated with the latter. This left the British and Russians little choice but to back Tito's partisans as the only force challenging the Axis. So ultimately people's war and imperialist forces worked together. In Greece the communist-influenced EAM/ELAS received some support from the Allies. However, since the 'percentages agreement' assigned Greece to the British camp, Churchill bombed Athens and re-imposed the hated monarchy. The opposition between the two wars here was total and violent.

In Poland, the callous manoeuvring of Stalin, and the indiscriminate character of Nazi violence, united those Poles linked to imperialism with the mass of the population, in a common enterprise. The outcome was the Warsaw uprising that reflected both types of war, but which Stalin abandoned to German revenge. Latvia was so crushed between two rival imperialist blocs that its population chose to identify with one or other of these appalling alternatives. So a people's war never materialised.

In the homelands of the Allied powers it was sometimes hard to spot the difference between those fighting fascism and those upholding empires. For the USA the fissure was along race lines with riots and armed clashes at home. In Britain the results of the 1945 general election confirmed that the population and ruling class had been fighting separate, parallel wars. The widest gap was seen in France, where not only was the ruling class split between de Gaulle and Pétain, but the resistance grew up independently of both.

The situation in Axis countries was generally less favourable to parallel wars. In Germany, a ruling class opposition only emerged at points when the country's imperial interests were endangered. It did not welcome people's war. Furthermore, repression so restricted mass action from below that it could only emerge after the Nazi regime was shattered from outside. The two wars then appeared as a clash between the Allies and Antifa resistance. A similar process might have happened in Austria had not the Allies, in an attempt to divide it from Germany, identified its ruling class (with its rotten track record of fascism and collaboration) with the anti-Nazi cause. It was therefore difficult for the people's war to make headway there.

Italy was the exception because the hold of Mussolini slipped before the Allies could reach the north. The people's war could therefore mount an effective challenge to both Nazi occupiers and

214 OF THE SECOND WORLD WAR

their Republic of Salò collaborators. Although General Alexander came close to inviting the Nazis to destroy the CLNAI, and it was hurriedly dissolved once the war ended, the Italian resistance left a lasting political legacy.

In Asia the relationship between imperialist war and people's war was conditioned by the weakened hold of the European colonialists, and the false claim of the Japanese to be anti-imperialist themselves. In India resistance took the form of either a straightforward anti-colonialist struggle (Quit India) or an attempt to use Japanese leverage to expel Britain (the Indian National Army). After hesitation on the part of Sukarno, Indonesia's people's war involved armed conflict with all the imperialist forces present – Japanese, British and Dutch. The Vietnamese Communist Party sought support from the Allies, but after failing to obtain this, engaged with mass pressure from below to develop a powerful anti-imperialist struggle.

In conclusion, the Second World War was unlike any other war. It brought unimaginable horrors – the Holocaust, nuclear annihilation, great famines, and civilian death on an enormous scale; but it is also remembered as 'the good war' that destroyed Nazism and fascism. As Clausewitz showed, warfare is not just a technical matter but reflects deeper political currents, and so these dual characteristics of the Second World War persisted after 1945. If we can reverse his aphorism for a moment: in peacetime 'politics was a continuation of war, a carrying out of the same by other means'. So even after the guns fell silent inter-imperialist competition continued. The result was the Cold War. For its part, the people's war transmuted into a successful, sometimes violent, struggle for decolonisation, plus a movement for the establishment of welfare states and decent living conditions.

In the twenty-first century these components are still present. Imperialism lives on through interventions in Iraq, Afghanistan and elsewhere, accompanied by a domestic onslaught on living standards occasioned by economic crisis. Fortunately, the people's war also lives on through the struggle against imperialist wars, anti-racism and anti-fascism, as well as in defence of the welfare provisions bequeathed after 1945. As one veteran of the Second World War wrote recently: 'The Resistance came at a very specific point in history ... people had to fight back against a situation they found intolerable. But today we are facing intolerable situations, and against these we need the same sort of response.'[9]

Chronology

Year	Imperialism & Imperialist War	Interaction	Popular Movements & People's War
1931	Japanese occupy Manchuria.		
1933	Hitler becomes German Chancellor.		
1934	Schuschnigg replaces assassinated Austrian Chancellor.		Viennese uprising against fascism. Paris mass anti-fascist demo.
1935	Italian invasion of Abyssinia.		
1936	Greek King installs fascist Metaxas. Franco's coup in Spain.		Spanish Revolution.
1937		Stalinists lead counter-revolution in Barcelona.	
1938	Japanese extend occupation of China. Rape of Nanjing.		
	Germany annexes Austria (March). Appeasement at Munich (September).		
1939			
January			
February			
March	Czechoslovakia dismembered. Poland participates.		
April		Spanish Civil War ends with Franco's victory.	
May			
June			
July			

Year	Imperialism & Imperialist War	Interaction	Popular Movements & People's War
August	Hitler–Stalin pact.		
September	Second World War begins. Germans and Russians partition Poland. Phoney war period.		
October			
November	Russo–Finnish War.		
December			
1940			
January			ZWZ (basis of Polish Home Army) formed.
February			
March			
April	Nazis occupy Denmark.		Rescue of Danish Jews begins.
May	British evacuation at Dunkirk. Churchill British PM.		
June	Italy joins war on Axis side. German defeat of France. Phoney war ends.	De Gaulle calls for resistance on BBC radio.	Beginning of French resistance.
July	Baltic states made part of USSR.		
August	Russian absorption of Latvia complete.		
September	Blitz of Britain begins.		
October			
November			
December			
1941			
January			'March on Washington' movement.
February			Ho Chi Minh returns to Vietnam from exile.

Year	Imperialism & Imperialist War	Interaction	Popular Movements & People's War
March	Yugoslavia joins Axis, counter-coup next day.		
April	Axis invasion of Yugoslavia and Greece. Yugoslavia dismembered.		Mihailovich commences chetnik resistance.
May	Germany completes occupation of Greece.		Vietminh formed.
June	Russia deports many Latvians. Germany invades Russia (Barbarossa).		Communists everywhere promote resistance.
July	Japanese invasion of French Indochina begins.		Popular uprising – Montenegro.
August	Atlantic Charter (USA and Britain). First Holocaust phase complete in Latvia.		
September			EAM/ELAS founded.
October	Russian government begins to evacuate from Moscow.		
November		Partisan–chetnik civil war.	
December	Japanese attack Pearl Harbor and Indonesia. USA joins war.		
1942			
January			
February	Order interning US Japanese. Java & Singapore fall to Japan.		Indian National Army formed.
March	Cripps mission to India. Japanese interned in US. Japan takes Java.	Ethnic conflict in Detroit.	'Double victory' campaign in US.
April			
May			
June			

Year	Imperialism & Imperialist War	Interaction	Popular Movements & People's War
July	First battle of El Alamein. Tide turns against Axis in North Africa.		
August			Quit India resolution passed.
September			Leadership of Quit India falls to Congress Socialists.
October			
November	Anglo-US landing at Algiers (Operation Torch).		Gorgopotamus viaduct destroyed, Greece.
December			British soldiers' 'Parliament' in Cairo.
1943			
January			
February	German defeat at Stalingrad.		
March			Mass strikes begin in Italy.
April		Soldier's Parliament in Cairo dissolved.	Warsaw Ghetto uprising.
May			
June			
July	German defeat at Kursk. Hamburg firestorm. Mussolini replaced.	Jubilant Italians repressed by new government.	Italians celebrate hoped-for end of fascism and war.
August			
September	Eisenhower broadcasts Italian surrender. Germans occupy north.		Partisan struggle begins in north Italy.
October	Italy declares war on Germany.		Corsica becomes first part of France liberated.

Year	Imperialism & Imperialist War	Interaction	Popular Movements & People's War
November		Tehran conference. Allies support Tito's partisans.	
December			
1944			
January	Red Army enters Poland. Japan's offensive at Imphal.		INA in action at Imphal.
February	Yalta conference confirms spheres of influence.		
March		Togliatti's 'Salerno turn'.	
April		Right-wing purge of Greek army.	
May			
June	D-Day landing in Normandy.		French resistance launch uprisings to support D-Day.
July		Operation 'Valkyrie' fails to kill Hitler.	Poland – Operation Burza (Tempest).
August			Paris liberated. Warsaw Rising begins.
September			ELAS gains control of most of Greece.
October	Churchill–Stalin 'Percentages Agreement'. British land in Greece.	Crushing of Warsaw uprising aided by Russian hostility.	Greece and Yugoslavia liberated.
November		Alexander orders Italian partisan ceasefire.	
December	Germans launch 'Battle of the Bulge'. Tonkin famine begins.	Battle for Athens. ELAS destroyed.	
1945			
January	Red Army takes Warsaw.		

Year	Imperialism & Imperialist War	Interaction	Popular Movements & People's War
February	Firestorm in Dresden.		
March	Japan takes direct control of Indochina. Red Army enters Austria.		
April	Hitler commits suicide. Roosevelt dies. Replaced by Truman.	Mussolini killed by partisans.	Italian 'national insurrection'.
May	Victory in Europe Day (8th) – VE Day.	Demonstrating Algerians massacred at Setif on VE Day.	Antifa movement in Germany.
June			Vietminh creates liberated zone in N. Vietnam.
July	Potsdam Declaration.		Labour defeats Churchill in UK general election.
August	Atom bombs on Japan. VJ Day (15th).		Indonesian independence. Revolution in Vietnam.
September	Allies disembark in Saigon.	Fighting in Saigon – Vietnamese v. France, Britain, Japan.	Ho declares Vietnamese independence.
October		Battle of Semarang – Indonesia.	
November		Battle of Surabaya.	INA trial in Delhi.
December			

Notes

INTRODUCTION

1. The numbers for peace with Hitler were 20 per cent in 1941 and 15 per cent in 1945. H. Cantril, *The Human Dimension: Experiences in Policy Research*, New Jersey, 1967, p. 48.
2. Mass Observation, File report 301A, June 1940. First weekly morale report, p. 4.
3. File report 301A, June 1940. First weekly morale report, p. 34.
4. File Report 2131, July 1944, p. 2.
5. File Report 2149(1), May 1945 Changes of outlook during the war, p. 8.
6. D. Loza, *Fighting for the Soviet Motherland. Reflections from the Eastern Front*, Nebraska, 1998, p. 211.
7. Loza, p. 213.
8. Survey of the Internet Movie Database at www.imdb.com. Search conducted on 20 January 2008. 5,526 war films were listed and 10 per cent were sampled.
9. Quoted in H.T. Cook and T.F. Cook, *Japan at War: An Oral History*, New York, 1992, p. 335.
10. J.G. Royde-Smith (ed.) in *Encyclopaedia Britannica Online*, Academic Edition, 'World War One' p. 50, and table 4. Accessed 15 January 2008.
11. Agence France Presse, news release, 4 April 1995.
12. According to a team of American and Iraqi epidemiologists. D. Brown, 'Iraq war: Study Claims Iraq's "Excess" Death Toll Has Reached 655,000', in *Washington Post*, 11 October 2006.
13. I.C.B. Dear and M.R.D. Foot (eds), *The Oxford Companion to the Second World War*, Oxford, 1995, p. 289. *Encyclopaedia Britannica* puts the figure at between 35 and 60 million.
14. S. Terkel, *'The Good War': An Oral History of World War Two*, New York, 1984, p. 13.
15. Loza, p. 211.
16. Released 27 May 1943. Also known as *Prelude to War* this was the official World War II US Government film and was used in US Army training before it was shown publicly.
17. A. Tusa and J. Tusa, *The Nuremburg Trial*, London, 1983, p. 200.
18. M. Gilbert, *The Holocaust: The Jewish Tragedy*, London, 1987, p. 457.
19. Vittorio Mussolini (son of the Duce) quoted in R. Cameron, *Appeasement and the Road to War*, Fenwick, 2002, p. 23. See also T. Behan, *The Italian Resistance*, London, 2009, p. 25.
20. According to the Tokyo War Crime Tribunal, 1946. Details in S.H. Harris, *Factories of Death*, London, 1994, p. 102. Chang puts the figures at between 260,000 and 350,000 deaths (I. Chang, *The Rape of Nanking*, Harmondsworth, 1997, p. 6). Japan also engaged in biological warfare research during which British prisoners were deliberately infected with

anthrax, typhus and tetanus and often dissected while still alive (quoted in Harris p. 113).

21. *The Times*, 25 August 1941.
22. Maisky, the Soviet ambassador to Britain, quoted in *The Times*, 25 September 1941.
23. *The Times*, 10 September 1941.
24. W. Churchill, *The Second World War*, Vol. 6, London , 1954, p. 202.
25. Churchill, *The Second World War*, Vol. 6, p. 198.
26. A. MacLeish, quoted in H. Zinn, *A People's History of the United States*, New York, 1980, p. 414.
27. C. Hull, quoted in Zinn, p. 414.
28. C. von Clausewitz, *On War*, Harmondsworth, 1968, p. 119.
29. *Ibid.*, p. 406.
30. BBC broadcast, London, 22 June 1941.
31. J. Stalin, 6 November 1942, quoted in A. Marwick and W. Simpson (eds), *War, Peace and Social Change: Europe 1900–1945*, Buckingham, 1990, p. 84.
32. L. Trotsky, *Writings 1939–40*, New York, 1973, p. 221.
33. *Ibid.*, p. 84.
34. *Ibid.*, p. 104.
35. H. Zinn, *On War*, New York, 2001, p. 103.
36. My emphasis. H. Michel, *The Shadow War*, London, 1972, p. 7.
37. Two other interpretations of the Second World War should be mentioned. The first is put forward by Arno Mayer in his *Why Did the Heavens Not Darken?* (New York, 1988). This sees the Second World War as the end point of a 'Thirty Years War' in Europe and stresses elements of continuity stretching back to the First World War and its outcome. The merit of this thesis lies in its explanation of the background to the Second World War. However, it does not encompass the unique character of the 1939 to 1945 period which made it so different to wars before or since, and is the subject of this book. The second interpretation was advanced in *The Meaning of the Second World War* (London, 1986), by Ernest Mandel. His argument is close to ours in that he sees the Second World War as 'a multifarious affair', going so far as to see it as a 'combination of five different conflicts: inter-imperialist war; self-defence by the Soviet Union; a just war of the Chinese people, of Asian colonial peoples and national liberation. [E. Mandel, *The Meaning of the Second World War*, London 1986, p. 45]. Seeing Russia's role as fundamentally socialist is mistaken and makes it difficult to understand what happened in many instances. Furthermore, rather than seeing the Second World War as a 'combination' of conflicts, the focus of this book is on the inner contradictions which pitted inter-imperialist war against people's war within a dialectical 'unity of opposites'.
38. J. Newsinger, *The Blood Never Dried: A People's History of the British Empire*, London, 2006, frontispiece.
39. C.L. Sulzberger and Stephen E. Ambrose, *American Heritage New History of World War II*, New York, 1997, p. 27.
40. According to Sulzberger and Ambrose, p. 42.
41. Quoted in Zinn, p. 411.
42. Quoted in Sulzberger and Ambrose, p. 57.
43. Quoted in Sulzberger and Ambrose, p. 623.

44. The list of those countries which would yield further evidence of parallel wars is almost co-terminous with the Second World War itself. It includes Albania, Algeria, Belgium, Burma, China, Czechoslovakia, Denmark, Holland, Lebanon, Norway, the Philippines, Slovakia and Syria. No doubt others could be added to the list.

CHAPTER 1

1. Quoted in D. Wingate Pike, 'Franco and the Axis Stigma' in *Journal of Contemporary History*, Vol. 17 No. 3, July 1982, p. 381.
2. M. Wolff, quoted in S. Terkel, *'The Good War': An Oral History of World War Two*, New York, 1984, p. 480.
3. A. H. Landis, *The Abraham Lincoln Brigade*, New York, 1967, p. 598, and John Ciardi in Terkel, p. 194 and Wolff, p. 486.
4. Wingate Pike, p. 371.
5. These planes were provided in even greater numbers than Franco had requested. Within a couple of weeks 15,000 troops had been transported, with devastating effect in Southern Spain.
6. M. Tuñon de Lara, J. Aostegui, A. Viñas, G. Cardona and J. Bricall, *La Guerra Civil Española, 50 años despues*, Barcelona, 1985, pp. 136–7. See also J. Coverdale, *Italian Intervention in the Spanish Civil War*, Princeton, 1975.
7. Speech of 18 July 1936 at Santa Cruz de Tenerife at www.generalisimofranco.com.
8. Quoted in R. Fraser, *Blood of Spain*, Harmondsworth, 1981, p. 309.
9. A. Durgan, *The Spanish Civil War*, Houndmills, 2007, p. 105.
10. Quoted in Fraser, p. 320.
11. H. Graham, *The Spanish Republic at War*, Cambridge, 2002, p. 205.
12. Durgan, p. 107.
13. Tuñon de Lara *et al.*, p. 423.
14. Wingate Pike, pp. 372–86.
15. Tuñon de Lara *et al.*, p. 47.
16. M. Garcia, *Franco's Prisoner*, London, 1972, p. 18.
17. Durgan, p. 82.
18. 'Collectivisation Decree of Catalonia', 24 December 1936, quoted in Fraser, p. 209.
19. G. Orwell, *Homage to Catalonia*, London, 1967, pp. 2–3.
20. Quoted in Fraser, p. 286.
21. Durgan, p. 40.
22. The issue was raised in Moscow as early as 22 July by the French Communist leader Thorez. See Tuñon de Lara *et al.*, p. 152.
23. Tuñon de Lara *et al.*, p. 153.
24. Labour Party Conference resolution, quoted in *The Times*, 21 July 1936. Unfortunately, this position was not retained and the Party fell in behind non-intervention.
25. T. Buchanan, *Britain and the Spanish Civil War*, Cambridge, 1997, p. 23.
26. Graham, p. 125n.
27. *The Times*, 3 October 1936.
28. Arthur Bryant, biographer and confidant of Tory Prime Minister, Stanley Baldwin, quoted in D. Little, 'Red Scare, 1936: Anti-Bolshevism and the

Origins of British Non-Intervention in the Spanish Civil War' in *Journal of Contemporary History*, Vol. 23, No. 2, April 1988, p. 296.

29. See P. Broué and E. Temimé, *The Revolution and the Civil War in Spain*, London, 1970, p. 329.

30. G. Warner, 'France and Non-Intervention in Spain, July–August 1936', *International Affairs*, Vol. 38, No. 2, April 1962, p. 210.

31. Acting Secretary of State, William Phillips quoted in G. Finch, 'The United States and the Spanish Civil War' in the *American Journal of International Law*, Vol. 31, No. 1, Jan 1937, p. 74.

32. Quoted in H. Jablon, 'Franklin D. Roosevelt and the Spanish Civil War', *Social Studies*, 56:2, February 1965, p. 63.

33. G. A. Stone, *Spain, Portugal and the Great Powers, 1931–1941*, Houndmills, 2005, p. 68.

34. See D. Tierney, 'Franklin D. Roosevelt and Covert Aid to the Loyalists in the Spanish Civil War, 1936–39' in *Journal of Contemporary History*, Vol. 39 (3), 2004, pp. 299–313.

35. Landis, p. 15.

36. Durgan, p. 60. See also Stone, p. 71.

37. H. Thomas, *The Spanish Civil War*, Harmondsworth, 1974, p. 284.

38. Durgan, p. 41.

39. See G. Howson, *Arms for Spain. The Untold Story of the Spanish Civil War*, London, 1998.

40. Quoted in Landis, p. xiii.

41. Donald Renton, in I. MacDougall (ed.), *Voices from the Spanish Civil War. Personal recollections of Scottish Volunteers in Republican Spain, 1936–1939*, Edinburgh, 1986, p. 23.

42. P. Preston, review of B. Bolleten, *The Spanish Civil War: Revolution and Counter-Revolution* in *The English Historical Review*, October 1993, p. 990.

43. Stone, p. 148.

44. *The Times*, 9 October 1940.

45. *The Times*, 19 July 1941.

46. *Ibid.*

47. Sir Samuel Hoare, quoted in Stone, p. 150.

48. See R. Wigg, *Churchill and Spain: The Survival of the Franco Regime, 1940–1945*, Oxford, 2005.

49. Wigg, pp. 102–3.

50. Wigg, p. 148.

51. Stone, p. 205.

52. Wigg, p. 153.

53. Wigg, pp. 170–1.

CHAPTER 2

1. A. Donlagic, Z. Atanackovic and D. Plenca, *Yugoslavia in the Second World War*, Belgrade, 1967, pp. 11–14.

2. T. Judah, *The Serbs*, New Haven, 1997, pp. 110–112.

3. H. Williams, *Parachutes, Patriots and Partisans*, London, 2003, p. 27.

4. P. Auty, *Tito: A Biography*, Harmondsworth, 1974, p. 193; Donlagic *et al.*, p. 29.

5. H. Williams, *Parachutes, Patriots and Partisans*, London 2003, p. 32.

6. Milan Grol, a government minister, at a meeting of Royal government on 28 April 1941. Donlagic *et al.*, p. 32n.
7. M. Djilas, *Memoir of a Revolutionary*, New York, 1973, p. 383.
8. Djilas, pp. 384–5.
9. Quisling was the notorious leader of the Norwegian Nazis whose name became a by-word for collaboration.
10. Judah, p. 117.
11. Judah, p. 120.
12. K. Ford, *OSS and the Yugoslav Resistance 1943–1945*, Texas, 1992, p. 170.
13. Donlagic *et al.*, p. 58n.
14. Williams, p. 7.
15. Williams, p. 46.
16. C. Wilmott. *The Struggle for Europe*, Hertfordshire, 1997, p. 118.
17. Ford, pp. 32–3.
18. W. Jones, *Twelve Months with Tito's Partisans*, Bedford, 1946, p. 22.
19. Djilas, *Memoir*, p. 6.
20. Djilas, *Memoir*, p. 21.
21. Djilas, *Memoir*, p. 228.
22. Auty, p. 184n and p. 185. Donlagic *et al.*, p. 46.
23. Djilas, *Wartime with Tito and the Partisans*, London, 1977, p. 419.
24. See B. Davidson, *Scenes from the Anti-Nazi War*, New York, 1980, pp. 236, 181–2.
25. Stjepan Radic, quoted in Judah, p. 106.
26. Jones, p. 11.
27. Judah, p. 120.
28. Djilas, *Memoir*, pp. 228–9.
29. Djilas, *Wartime*, p. 79.
30. YCP statement of June 1942 quoted in Donlagic *et al.*, p. 90.
31. Auty, p. 228.
32. Williams, p. 60.
33. Williams, p. 44.
34. For Keitel's directive on this see Auty, p. 225. See also Williams, pp. 60–1, Judah, p. 118 and Ford, p. 6.
35. Williams, p. 60.
36. Williams, p. 110.
37. Djilas, *Wartime*, p. 147.
38. Djilas, *Wartime*, p. 23.
39. Auty, p. 229.
40. Donlagic *et al.*, p. 68. Williams gives the earlier date of 11 November, p. 63.
41. Ford, p. 53.
42. Ford, pp. 53–4.
43. Farish, quoted in Ford, p. 34.
44. Ford, p. 55.
45. These figures are for 1944. Mihailovich claimed 57,440 men mobilised and the possibility of mobilising over 450,000, though the US liaison officer thought there were probably only 35,000 under arms. Ford, p. 46.
46. Williams, p. 63.
47. Ford, p. 46.
48. Donlagic, *et al.*, p. 58.
49. Donlagic *et al.*, p. 121.

50. Jones, p. 31.
51. Williams, p. 39.
52. Auty, pp. 256, 258. Ford, p. 66. These figures are inevitably imprecise and disputed.
53. Donlagic *et al.*, p. 212.
54. Djilas, *Wartime*, p. 149.
55. Djilas, *Wartime*, p. 231.
56. Djilas, *Wartime*, p. 244.
57. B. Davidson, *Scenes from the Anti-Nazi War*, New York, 1980, p. 199.
58. Djilas, *Wartime*, p. 311.
59. Auty, p. 245.
60. Ford, p. 32.
61. Ford, p. 34.
62. Davidson, p. 103.
63. Eden on 3 January 1943, quoted in E. Barker, 'Some Factors in British Decision-making over Yugoslavia 1941–4' in P. Auty and R. Clogg (eds), *British Policy towards Wartime Resistance in Yugoslavia and Greece*, London 1975, p. 52n.
64. Auty and Clogg, p. 47.
65. My emphasis. Quoted in Barker, in Auty and Clogg, p. 52n, and Davidson, p. 106.
66. Barker, in Auty and Clogg, p. 40.
67. Williams, p. 180.
68. Ford, p. 33.
69. 28 November 1943. Quoted in Donlagic *et al.*, p. 145.
70. Auty, p. 252.
71. Ford, p. 29.
72. G. Kolko, *The Politics of War*, New York 1990, p. 133.
73. Kolko, p. 134.
74. R. Medvedev, *Let History Judge*, London, 1971, p. 221.
75. Auty, p. 179.
76. Djilas, *Wartime*, p. 123.
77. Tito in December 1942, quoted in Donlagic *et al.*, p. 138.
78. Donlagic *et al.*, p. 71.
79. Auty, p. 248.
80. Djilas, *Wartime*, p. 144.
81. Auty, p. 238.
82. Auty, p. 254.
83. Djilas, *Wartime*, p. 199.

CHAPTER 3

1. See C. Tsoucalas, *The Greek Tragedy*, Harmondsworth, 1969, p. 18, and E. Thermos, 'From Andartes to Symmorites: Road to Greek Fratricide' in *The Massachusetts Review*, Vol. 9, No. 1, 1968, p. 114.
2. M. Mazower, *Inside Hitler's Greece*, Yale, 1993, p. 98, Tsoucalas, p. 52 and E.C.W. Myers, *Greek Entanglement*, London, 1955, p. 105.
3. 'The Communist Party history of Giannis Ioannidis', in P. Auty and R. Clogg (eds), *British Policy towards Wartime Resistance in Yugoslavia and Greece*, London 1975, pp. 43–67.

4. See Tsoucalas, p. 55.
5. C. Woodhouse, *The Apple of Discord*, London, 1948, pp. 16–17.
6. *New York Times*, 30 January 1941, quoted in Tsoucalas, p. 63.
7. Quoted in L. Baerentzen (ed.), *British Reports on Greece 1943–1944*, Copenhagen, 1982, p. 151.
8. Quoted in W. Deakin, E. Barker, J. Chadwick (eds), *British Political and Military Strategy in Central, Eastern and Southern Europe in 1944*, Houndmills, 1988, p. 89.
9. Yugoslavia was conquered in one week, but it took almost a month to subdue Greece. This prolonged struggle delayed Operation Barbarossa, which meant the Wehrmacht was caught out by the harsh Russian winter, with decisive results for the entire war (D. Eudes, *The Kapetanios*, London, 1972, p. 10).
10. Tsoucalas, p. 91.
11. Mazower, *Inside*, p. 41, Tsoucalas, p. 59, Eudes, p. 33.
12. D. Glinos, 'What is the National Liberation Front (EAM), and what does it want?' in Clogg, p. 82.
13. Woodhouse, *Apple*, p. 28.
14. Glinos, in Clogg, p. 90. See also Mazower, *Inside*, p. 98, and Myers, p. 103.
15. Sarafis was initially arrested by ELAS forces and had to be convinced to take command, though he did join the KKE later on. See S. Sarafis, *ELAS: Greek Resistance Army*, London, 1980, pp. vi, 100.
16. Mazower, *Inside*, p. 330.
17. Zachariadis, quoted in Eudes, p. 238.
18. The Caserta Agreement, 26 September 1944, in Woodhouse, *Apple*, p. 306 and Clogg, p. 174.
19. Mazower, *Inside*, p. 125.
20. Woodhouse, *Apple*, p. 66, Mazower, *Inside*, p. 316.
21. Myers, p. 73.
22. According to Spiro Meletzis, the official resistance photographer, quoted in J. Hart, *New Voices in the Nation. Women and the Greek Resistance, 1941–1964*, Ithaca, 1996, p. 201.
23. Myers, p. 73.
24. Mazower, *Inside*, p. 325. However, it is worthwhile noting that the killing of EKKA's commander, Psarros, was carried out by Aris in defiance of the other ELAS leaders, because of a factional dispute (which will be discussed later). See Tsoucalas, p. 68n and Sarafis, p. 111.
25. Woodhouse, *Apple*, p. 136 and Myers, p. 102.
26. C. Woodhouse, 'The Situation in Greece – January to May, 1944' in L. Baerentzen (ed.), *British Reports on Greece 1943–1944*, Copenhagen, 1982, p. 73, and Woodhouse, *Apple*, p. 61. See also Mazower, *Inside*, p. xix.
27. D. Glinos, 'What is the National Liberation Front (EAM), and What Does it Want?', in Clogg, p. 91.
28. Tsoucalas, p. 66 and L.S. Stavrianos, 'The Greek National Liberation Front (EAM): A Study in Resistance Organization and Administration', *Journal of Modern History*, Vol. 24, No. 1, March 1952, p. 44.
29. M. Hadas, 'OSS Report of 13 September 1944', in Clogg, p. 182.
30. Eudes, p. 66.
31. Hart, p. 197. Hart estimates that in the Peleponnese approximately 25 per cent of EAM's leadership was communist. See p. 149.
32. Sarafis, p. iii.

33. Hart, p. 187.
34. Woodhouse, *Apple*, p. 32.
35. Eudes, pp. 37–8.
36. Sarafis, p. 318, and Eudes, 33–40.
37. This was reported by an Athenian woman who was twelve years old in 1941. Quoted in Hart, p. 88.
38. See Hart, p. 201.
39. See Hart, p. 153–61.
40. See Hart, p. 24.
41. Mazower, *Inside*, p. 279 and Hart, p. 31.
42. Quoted in Hart, p. 31.
43. Stavrianos, 'The Greek National Liberation Front', p. 53.
44. Quoted in Hart, p. 174.
45. Quoted in Hart, p. 168. Mazower makes an identical point in M. Mazower, 'Structures of authority in the Greek resistance, 1941–1944,' in T. Kirk and A. McElligott, *Opposing Fascism*, Cambridge, 1999, p. 130.
46. Hart, p. 176. In the Democratic Army, the successor to ELAS in the post-'45 civil war, women formed a significant proportion of the fighters and participated on equal terms with the men (A. Nachmani, 'Civil War and Foreign Intervention in Greece, 1946–49' in *Journal of Contemporary History*, Vol. 25, 1990, p. 495).
47. Woodhouse, 'The Situation in Greece', in Baerentzen, p. 81.
48. The pattern was set by the village of Kleitsos in Eurytania on 11 October 1942 and it spread rapidly first to EAM districts and eventually to all resistance controlled areas. See Stavrianos, 'The Greek National Liberation Front', pp. 47–51, Mazower, *Inside*, pp. 271–2, Hart, p. 207, Sarafis, p. 324.
49. Eudes, p. 121.
50. Mazower, *Inside*, pp. 293–4.
51. Stavrianos, 'The Greek National Liberation Front', p. 53.
52. Mazower, *Inside*, p. 132.
53. Woodhouse, 'The Situation in Greece', p. 84.
54. Woodhouse, *Apple*, pp. 146–7.
55. Quoted in Tsoucalas, p. 63.
56. C.M. Woodhouse, 'Summer 1943: The Critical Months', in P. Auty and R. Clogg (eds), *British Policy towards Wartime Resistance in Yugoslavia and Greece*, London 1975 , p. 127.
57. Compare the figures given by Sarafis of 19,355 (Sarafis, p. 427), and Myers combined resistance tally of 25,000 (Myers, p. 280).
58. This is according to Sarafis (see Sarafis, p. 427). Myers suggests a resistance total of 150 locomotives were damaged or destroyed, over 100 bridges blown up and over 250 ships of above 68,000 tons sunk or damaged (Myers, p. 280).
59. Sarafis, pp. 265, 402, Myers, p. 281.
60. Myers, p. 280.
61. Myers, p. 220.
62. Stavrianos, 'The Greek National Liberation Front', p. 43.
63. Myers, p. 281. See also Mazower, *Inside*, p. 140.
64. C.M. Woodhouse, 'Summer 1943', in Auty and Clogg, p. 119.
65. Myers, pp. 267–8.
66. Sarafis, pp. 303, 426.
67. Woodhouse, *Apple*, p. 61. See also Mazower, *Inside*, pp. 77–81.

68. Sarafis, p. 224.
69. Woodhouse, *Apple*, p. 75, See also Mazower, *Inside*, pp. 140–1.
70. This is according to US reports, quoted in L.S. Stavrianos, 'Two Points of View: I. The Immediate Origins of the Battle of Athens', in *American Slavic and East European Review*, Vol. 8 No. 4, 1949, p. 244n.
71. Woodhouse, 'The Situation in Greece', in Baerentzen, p. 112–114, and Myers, p. 272.
72. W. Churchill, *The Second World War*, Volume 6, London, 1954, pp. 194–5.
73. See Eudes, p. 21 and Myers's account as leader of the operation, Myers, p. 85, and Sarafis, p. 49.
74. Quoted in W. Deakin, 'Resistance in Occupied Central and South-eastern Europe', in Deakin *et al.*, pp. 131–2. After the event both Woodhouse and Myers argued in similar terms about the reasons for a switch in policy. Myers wrote:

    Whilst Allied strategy on the main battle-fronts was defensive, every act of sabotage, almost every bang, in enemy-occupied territory reaped a moral reward out of all proportion to the military gain – great even though the latter often was by itself – and fully justified our policy. When the Allies changed over to the offensive, however, morale-raising bangs and propaganda were comparatively unimportant ... But by then it was too late to try to send back to their homes the many thousands in the guerrilla forces ... (Myers, p. 279).

75. Quoted in Sarafis, p. 153.
76. Quoted in Tsoucalas, p. 73.
77. Discord, p. 152.
78. The Ango-American action was in defiance of a unanimous agreement between the Greek political parties, including the Royalists! See L.S. Stavrianos, 'The Mutiny in the Greek Armed Forces, April 1944', in *American Slavic and East European Review*, Vol. 9, No. 4 1950, pp. 305–6.
79. Tsoucalas, p. 73.
80. Stavrianos, p. 310.
81. Churchill, 14 April 1944, quoted in Tsoucalas, p. 73.
82. Tsoucalas gives the figure of 20,000 (Tsoucalas, p. 73) while Thermos suggests it was 12,000. (Thermos, p. 117).
83. Eudes, pp. 77–85, 121–30.
84. Neubacher, on 14 September 1944, quoted in Deakin *et al.*, p. 141.
85. Deakin *et al.*, p. 141.
86. Mazower, *Inside*, p. 329.
87. Quoted in Deakin *et al.*, p. 143.
88. Quoted in L. Karliaftis, 'Trotskyism and Stalinism in Greece' in *Revolutionary History*, Vol. 3, No. 3, spring 1991, p. 6. See also the translation in S. Vukmanovic, *How and why the People's Liberation Struggle of Greece met with Defeat*, London, 1950, p. 13.
89. Quoted in Tsoucalas, p. 83.
90. Vukmanovic, p. 13.
91. Clogg, pp. 171–3.
92. Woodhouse, *Apple*, p. 150.
93. R. Clogg, '"Pearls from Swine": the FO papers, SOE and the Greek Resistance', in Auty and Clogg, p. 197.

94. Quoted in C.M. Woodhouse, 'Summer 1943: The Critical Months' in Auty and Clogg, p. 38.
95. K. Pyromaglou, quoted in L.S. Stavrianos, 'Two Points of View', p. 307.
96. The KKE leadership had used the PEEA as a lever to gain ministers in the Cairo government. Thus the PEEA's first meeting had also been its last. Stavrianos, 'The Greek National Liberation Front', p. 54.
97. Clogg. p. 174 and Sarafis, p. 387.
98. Clogg, p. 174.
99. Eudes, p. 145–8.
100. Woodhouse, *Apple*, p. 199.
101. Tsoucalas, p. 77.
102. Mazower, *Inside*, pp. 295–6.
103. Woodhouse, *Apple*, p. 196.
104. Eudes, p. 105. See also Vukmanovic.
105. Sarafis, p. iii.
106. Woodhouse, *Apple*, p. 214.
107. Tsoucalas, p. 134.
108. Quoted in Stavrianos, 'Two Points of View', p. 242.
109. Quoted Deakin *et al.*, p. 136.
110. Deakin *et al.*, p. 135.
111. General Alexander, quoted in T.D. Sfikas, 'The People at the Top Can Do These Things, Which Others Can't Do: Winston Churchill and the Greeks, 1940–45', *Journal of Contemporary History*, Vol. 26, 1991, p. 322.
112. Clogg, p. 187.
113. J. Iatrides (ed.), *Ambassador MacVeagh Reports, Greece, 1933–1947*, Princeton, 1960, p. 656.
114. Sfikas, p. 321.
115. Clogg, p. 174.
116. http://politikokafeneio.com/Forum/viewtopic.php?=114187&sid=040bbd7 98e8d1b12e85459197e9d8b1b, accessed 8 August 2009.
117. Quoted in Sfikas, p. 324.
118. *The Times*, 6 December 1944.
119. Stavrianos, 'Two Points of View', pp. 245–6, and Sarafis, pp. 494–5.
120. Professor Svolos, quoted in Iatrides, p. 657.
121. Mazower, p. 352.
122. My emphasis. Stavrianos, 'Two Points of View', p. 244.
123. *The Times*, 6 December 1944.
124. Thermos, p. 119.
125. *The Times*, 21 December 1944.
126. Nachmani, p. 495.
127. *The Times*, 6 December 1944.
128. *The Times*, 9 December 1944.
129. Editorial, *The Times*, 14 December 1944.
130. See the report of Charles Edson, OSS, in Clogg, p. 191, and Woodhouse, *Apple*, p. 218.
131. Iatrides, pp. 660–1.
132. *The Times*, 21 December 1944.
133. Woodhouse, *Apple*, p. 218.
134. Quoted in Stavrianos, 'Two Points of View', p. 240.

135. *Ibid*. Stavrianos points out that Churchill won the vote by 279 to 30, but notes that 'although over 450 members were present, only 309 voted'.
136. Mazower, p. 370.
137. *The Times*, 1 January 1945.
138. See the text of the Varkiza agreement in Woodhouse, *Apple*, pp. 308–10, Clogg, pp. 188–90, Sarafis, pp. 530–4.
139. Thermos, p. 120.
140. Tsoucalas, p. 94, and Thermos, p. 120.
141. Quoted in Thermos, p. 121.
142. Hart, p. 252.
143. Senator McGee to US Senate, 17 February 1965, quoted in T. Gitlin, 'Counter-Insurgency: Myth and Reality in Greece', in D. Horowitz (ed.), *Containment and Revolution*, London, 1967, p. 140.
144. Hart, p. 257.
145. Eudes, p. 354.
146. *New Republic*, 15 September 1947, quoted in Thermos, p. 121.

CHAPTER 4

1. J. Rothschild, *East Central Europe between the Two World Wars*, Seattle, 1974, p. 27.
2. See J. Ciechanowski, *The Warsaw Uprising of 1944*, Cambridge, 1974, p. 274.
3. V.I. Lenin, *Selected Works*, Vol. 4, p. 292.
4. Lenin, Vol.4, p. 292n. For a discussion of the Lenin-Luxemburg debate on the national question T. Cliff, *International Struggle and the Marxist Tradition, Selected Writings*, Vol.1, London, 2001, p. 90.
5. See A. Read and D. Fisher, *The Deadly Embrace. Hitler, Stalin and the Nazi-Soviet Pact 1939–1941*, London, 1988, p. 14 and B. Newman, *The Story of Poland*, London no date, p. 44.
6. N. Ascherson, *The Struggles for Poland*, London 1987, p. 84.
7. W. Borodziej, *The Warsaw Uprising of 1944*, Madison, 2007, p. 20.
8. Quoted in A. Rossi, *The Russo-German Alliance*, London, 1950, p. 8.
9. Read and Fisher, *The Deadly Embrace*, p. 24 and Rossi, *Russo-German Alliance*, pp. 40 and 63.
10. See Read and Fisher, p. 442.
11. A. Rossi, *The Russo-German Alliance*, London 1950, p. 37.
12. See Read and Fisher, *The Deadly Embrace*, p. 328.
13. Rossi, p. 54.
14. N. Davies, *Rising '44. The Battle for Warsaw*, London, 2004, p. 30.
15. Read and Fisher, p. 334.
16. In his reply to Ribbentrop's telegram congratulating him on 60th birthday. Rossi, p. 60n.
17. Davies, p. 30.
18. Borodziej, p. 14.
19. Rossi, p. 71.
20. G. Sanford, *Katyn and the Soviet Massacre of 1940*, London, 2005, p. 12 and Davies, p. 151.
21. Sanford, p. 12.
22. See Borodziej, p. 23, and J. Rose, Introduction to M. Edelman, *The Ghetto Fights*, London, 1990, pp. 27–8.

23. As reported by Goebbels. See Davies, p. 85.
24. G. Godden, *Murder of a Nation. German Destruction of Polish Culture*, London, 1943, pp. 3–7 and Borodziej, p. 15.
25. Quoted in Read and Fisher, p. 388.
26. Ascherson, pp. 93–4.
27. See Sanford.
28. See the various estimates in Sanford, p. 28. See also T. Bor-Komorowski, *The Secret Army*, London, 1950, pp. 46 and 67.
29. M.J. Chodakiewicz, *Between Nazis and Soviets*, Maryland, 2004, p. 265.
30. Bor-Komorowski, p. 46 and Davies, p. 91.
31. J. Gumkowski and K. Lesyczynski, *Poland under Nazi Occupation*, Warsaw, 1961, pp. 215–6.
32. J. Karski, *Story of a Secret State*, London, 1945, p. 108.
33. Karski, p. 314.
34. Borodziej, p. 18 and Davies, p. 180.
35. Ciechanowski, p. 69. Ciechanowski shows the dominance of Pilsudski supporters in the army where '65% of all divisional and brigade commanders had served during the First World War in Pilsudski's Legions'. Ciechanowski, p. 72.
36. Ciechanowski, p. 71.
37. Davies, p. 171.
38. Bor-Komorowski, p. 25. Most estimates suggest a lower figure in the range of 200,000 with auxiliaries in addition.
39. Bor-Komorowski, p. 153.
40. Ascherson, p. 102.
41. Ciechanowski, p. 2.
42. Quoted in Karski, p. 102.
43. Ascherson, p. 102 and Borodziej, p. 21.
44. Karski, p. 196 and Borodziej, p. 20.
45. W.R.C. Lukas, 'The Big Three and the Warsaw Uprising', in *Military Affairs*, Vol. 45, No. 1, October 1975, p. 129 mentions 300, while Bor-Komorowski (p. 121) claims 168 in 1941. See also Godden, pp. 60–61.
46. Quoted in W.J. Rose, *The Rise of Polish Democracy*, London, 1944, p. 76.
47. Bor-Komorowski, p. 103.
48. Borodziej, p. 19.
49. Karski, p. 72.
50. Ascherson, p. 109.
51. See Rose; and M. Gilbert, *The Righteous: The Unsung Heroes of the Holocaust*, London, 2002, pp. 119–39.
52. Gilbert, p. 119.
53. Gilbert, p. 123.
54. H. Langbein, *Against All Hope*, London, 1994, p. 145.
55. Hanson, p. 60.
56. Hanson, p. 46. See also Borodziej, p. 21.
57. See Ciechanowski, p. 290.
58. Bor-Komorowski, p. 49.
59. *Ibid.*
60. See Bor-Komorowski, pp. 111–3 and Ciechanowski, pp. 90–3 for a detailed discussion.
61. Borodziej, p. 25.

62. Ascherson, p. 102 and Ciechanowski, p. 7.
63. Lukas, p. 130.
64. Karski, p. 315.
65. Bor-Komorowski, pp. 73 and 155.
66. Ascherson, p. 102 and Ciechanowski, p. 115. See also Davies, p. 209.
67. Borodziej, pp. 33–4.
68. Ciechanowski, p. 79.
69. See Ciechanowski, p. 150.
70. See Bor-Komorowski, p. 170 and Ciechanowski, pp. 102–3.
71. See Ciechanowski, pp. 98–9.
72. Ascherson, p. 105.
73. Quoted in Hanson, p. 60.
74. Bor-Komorowski, p. 43.
75. Bor-Komorowski, p. 201.
76. Ciechanowski, p. 277.
77. Ciechanowski, p. 218.
78. Ciechanowski, pp. 127–8.
79. Quoted in Ciechanowski, p. 166.
80. Quoted in Ciechanowski, p. 187. Bor has an alternative translation on p. 177.
81. Quoted in Ciechanowski, p. 180.
82. See Borodziej, pp. 48–50, and Bor-Komorowski, p. 187–8.
83. Bor-Komorowski, p. 188.
84. Bor-Komorowski, p. 202.
85. Ciechanowski, pp. 180–1.
86. Ciechanowski, p. 213 and Borodziej, p. 61.
87. Quoted in Borodziej, p. 61.
88. Quoted in W. Churchill, *The Second World War*, Vol. 6, London, 1954, p. 116.
89. Davies, p. 165.
90. Ciechanowski, p. 239.
91. G. Kolko, *The Politics of War*, New York, 1968, p. 116.
92. Bor-Komorowski, p. 204.
93. Bor-Komorowski, p. 182.
94. Davies, p. 236, Bor-Komorowski, p. 205.
95. See Davies, p. 226, Churchill, Vol. 6, p. 116 and Borodziej, p. 74.
96. Borodziej, p. 76 and Davies, p. 245.
97. Quoted in Hanson, p. 76.
98. Quoted in Hanson, p. 77.
99. Hanson, p. 77.
100. Ascherson, p. 129.
101. Borodziej, p. 77.
102. Davies, p. 288.
103. Bor-Komorowski, pp. 209, 252.
104. Bor-Komorowski, p. 225.
105. Hanson, p. 132. See also Davies, p. 288.
106. Churchill, Vol. 6, p. 115.
107. Quoted in Churchill, Vol. 6, pp. 115–6.
108. For details see Davies, p. 256.
109. Quoted in Borodziej, p. 80.

110. I. Geiss and W. Jacobmeyer (eds), *Deutsche Politik in Polen 1939–1945*, Opladen, 1980, p. 191.
111. Quoted in Churchill, Vol. 6, p. 117.
112. Quoted in Churchill, Vol. 6, p. 118.
113. Davies, p. 268.
114. Quoted in Churchill, Vol. 6, p. 119.
115. Lukas, p. 130, and Davies, p. 346.
116. See Davies, pp. 307–13.
117. Churchill, Vol. 6, p. 127.
118. Lukas, p. 131.
119. Davies, p. 437.
120. Churchill, Vol. 6, p. 127.
121. I. Deutscher, *Stalin*, London, 1966, p. 510.
122. Quoted in Bor-Komorowski, p. 376.

CHAPTER 5

1. G. Kurt Piehler, foreword to V.O. Lumans, *Latvia in World War I*, no place, 2006, p. ix.
2. Quoted in I. Feldmanis, 'Latvia under the Occupation of National Socialist Germany 1941–45' in A. Caune *et al., The Hidden and Forbidden History of Latvia under Soviet and Nazi Occupations 1940–1991. Selected Research of the Commission of the Historians of Latvia*, Riga, 2007, p. 85.
3. My emphasis. Quoted in R. Griffin (ed.) *Fascism*, Oxford, 1995, p. 218.
4. A. Zunda, 'Resistance against Nazi German Occupation in Latvia: Positions in Historical Literature' in Caune, p. 161.
5. Quoted in G.P. Bassler, *Alfred Valdmanis and the Politics of Survival*, Toronto, 2000, p. 115.
6. Quoted in Bassler, p. 146.
7. Bassler, p. 105.
8. D. Bleiere *et al., History of Latvia: the 20th Century*, no place, 2006, p. 297.
9. Feldmanis, p. 85.
10. Feldmanis, p. 78.
11. Miervaldis Birze quoted in M. Vestermanis, 'The Holocaust in Latvia: 'A Historiographic Survey' in *Symposium of the Commission of the Historians of Latvia*, Vol. 2, p. 47.
12. *European Court of Human Rights*, Case of Kononov v. Latvia. Application no. 36376/04. Judgment of 17 May 2010, Section 152.
13. Bassler, pp. 17–18.
14. G. Swain, 'The Disillusioning of the Revolution's Praetorian Guard: The Latvian Riflemen, Summer-Autumn 1918' in *Europe-Asia Studies*, Vol. 51, No. 4 (June 1999), pp. 669.
15. Bassler, p. 15.
16. See Lumans, p. 18.
17. M.M. Laserson, 'The Recognition of Latvia', in *The American Journal of International Law*, Vol. 37, No. 2, April 1943, p. 237.
18. Bassler, p. 20.
19. G. Swain, *Between Stalin and Hitler*, Abingdon, 2004, p. 6.
20. Exhibit in the Museum of the Occupation of Latvia, Riga.

21. V. Lacis, the Minister of the Interior, quoted in A. Plakans (ed.), *Experiencing Totalitarianism: The invasion and occupation of Latvia by the USSR and Nazi Germany, 1939–1991: A Documentary History*, Bloomington, Indiana, 2007, p. 41.
22. Plakans, p. 32; V. Nollendorfs *et al., The Three Occupations of Latvia 1940–1991*, Riga, 2005, p. 14, Swain, *Between Stalin and Hitler*, p. 44. See also Bleiere, pp. 245–6.
23. Plakans, p. 59.
24. Swain, *Between Stalin and Hitler*, p. 20.
25. Swain, *Between Stalin and Hitler*, p. 32.
26. Swain, *Between Stalin and Hitler*, p. 33.
27. Bleiere, p. 251; Swain, *Between Stalin and Hitler*, p. 18.
28. Swain, *Between Stalin and Hitler*, p. 17.
29. Plakans, p. 61.
30. A. Senn, 'The Sovietization of the Baltic States' in *Annals of the American Academy of Political and Social Science*, May 1958, p. 123.
31. Swain, *Between Stalin and Hitler*, p. 3.
32. Bleiere, p. 258.
33. Swain cites 14,194 – Swain, *Between Stalin and Hitler*, p. 39, while Nollendorfs suggests 15,500 in Nollendorfs, p. 23.
34. Or 'year of terror'. T. Puisans (ed.), *Unpunished Crimes: Latvia under Three Occupations*, Stockholm, 2003, p. 31. See also Bleiere, p. 260; Nollendorfs, p. 27.
35. A. Podolsky, 'Problems of Collaboration and Rescuing Jews on Latvian and Ukrainian Territories During Nazi Occupation: An Attempt at Comparative Analysis' in *The Holocaust Research in Latvia*. Materials of an International Conference, 12–13 June 2003, Riga and 24 October 2003, Riga and the Holocaust Studies in Latvia in 2002–03. (*Symposium of the Commission of the Historians of Latvia*, Vol. 12), p. 90.
36. S. Dimanta and I. Zalite, 'Structural Analysis of the Deportations of the 1940s' in Puisans, p. 105–6.
37. Bleiere, p. 260.
38. Bleiere, p. 259. This amounted to 2 per cent of all Latvia's Jews as against 0.8 per cent of the general population. Dimanta and Zalite, p. 101.
39. M. Dean, *Collaboration in the Holocaust*, Houndmills, 2000, p. 7.
40. Bleiere, p. 260.
41. Bleiere, p. 261; Swain, *Between Stalin and Hitler*, p. 50.
42. Bleiere, pp. 266–7.
43. Dean, p. 13.
44. A. Stranga, 'The Holocaust in Occupied Latvia, 1941–1945' in Caune, p. 168.
45. Dean, p. 163–4.
46. Stranga, pp. 164, 166.
47. D. Erglis, 'A Few Episodes of the Holocaust in Krustpils', in Caune, p. 187.
48. R. Viksne, 'Members of the Arajs Commando in Soviet court Files: Social Position, Education, Reasons for Volunteering, Penalty' in Caune, p. 189.
49. Stranga, p. 166.
50. Viksne, p. 200.
51. Viksne, p. 201.
52. Swain, *Between Stalin and Hitler*, p. 53.
53. Bleiere, p. 284. See also Podolsky.

54. Instructions to the Ostland Reichskommissar about the goals of his work in the Baltic States and Belarus, 8 May 1941 in Plakans, p. 93. See also A. Dallin, *German Rule in Russia, 1941–1945*, London, 1981, pp. 47, 182–4; Bleiere, p. 269.
55. Feldmanis, p. 120.
56. Bleiere, pp. 284–6. Plakans suggests the figure was 12,000. Plakans, p. 91.
57. Swain, *Between Stalin and Hitler*, p. 74. See also Plakans, p. 119.
58. Swain, *Between Stalin and Hitler*, p. 108.
59. Quoted in F. Gordon, 'A Tragedy of False Premises' in Puisans, p. 113.
60. A. Aizsilnieks, 'The Exploitation of Latvia's Economy' in Puisans, p. 120.
61. Aizsilnieks, in Puisans, p. 121 and Plakans, p. 98.
62. Swain, *Between Stalin and Hitler*, p. 91.
63. Quoted in Swain, *Between Stalin and Hitler*, p. 91.
64. Comment of an anonymous Estonian quoted in T.P. Mulligan, *The Politics of Illusion and Empire, German Occupation Police in the Soviet Union, 1942–1943*, New York, 1988, pp. 55 and 79.
65. Aizsilnieks, in Puisans, p. 125.
66. It is interesting to note that the Lithuanian Self-Administration successfully blocked the formation of a similar legion there. Feldmanis, p. 88.
67. I. Feldmanis, 'Waffen-SS Units of Latvians and Other Non-Germanic Peoples in World War I: Methods of Formation, Ideology and Goals', in Caune, p. 126.
68. Bassler, p. 151.
69. Bleiere, p. 272.
70. Mulligan, p. 80 and Bleiere, p. 286.
71. Bassler, p. 151.
72. J. Mezaks, 'Latvia throughout History' in Puisans, p. 32.
73. Feldmanis, 'Waffen-SS Units', p. 128.
74. Bleiere, p. 297; J. Riekstins, 'The June 1941 Deportation in Latvia', in Caune, p. 84.
75. Zunda, p. 153.
76. Bassler, p. 170.
77. A. Bilmanis, *A History of Latvia*, Princeton, 1951, p. 369.
78. Bleiere, p. 298.
79. Bleiere, p. 295.
80. Plakans, pp. 134–6.
81. Bilmanis, p. 369.
82. Zunda, p. 151.
83. Swain, *Between Stalin and Hitler*, p. 133.
84. Swain, *Between Stalin and Hitler*, pp. 81, 110.
85. Swain, *Between Stalin and Hitler*, pp. 123, 133.
86. Lumans, p. 356.
87. Zunda, pp. 149 and 151.
88. Swain, *Between Stalin and Hitler*, p. 139–40.
89. Bleiere, pp. 328–9.
90. Swain, *Between Stalin and Hitler*, pp. 144–5.
91. Bilmanis, p. 372.
92. A. Dundurs, 'Latvia under the Communists' in *The Furrow*, March 1951, p. 165.
93. H. Strods, 'Latvia's National Partisan War 1944–1956' in Puisans, pp. 207, 211.

94. Bassler, p. 183.
95. Quoted in Bassler, p. 186.
96. Quoted in Bassler, p. 182.

CHAPTER 6

1. J.S. Sirinelli (ed.) *La France de 1914 à nos jours*, Paris, 1993, p. 172.
2. Sirinelli, p. 128.
3. Sirinelli, p. 133, F. Knight, *The French Resistance*, Southampton, 1975, p. 13.
4. Quoted in Sirinelli, pp. 137–8.
5. C. de Gaulle, *The Complete War Memoirs*, New York, 1998, p. 32.
6. F. Broche, G. Caitucoli, J-F Muracciole, *La France au Combat*, no place or date, p. 36.
7. Details from M. Serraut's speech to the French Senate, 19 March 1940, quoted in Knight, p. 36.
8. Broche *et al.*, p. 113 and C. Tillon, *Les FTP*, Paris 1962, p. 17.
9. Y. Durand, *La France dans la deuxième guerre mondiale, 1939–1945*, Paris, 1989, p. 13.
10. O. Paul, *Farewell France*, London, 1941, p. 35.
11. De Gaulle, p. 65.
12. De Gaulle, p. 55.
13. T. Draper, *The Six Weeks' War*, London, 1946, p. 244.
14. De Gaulle, p. 73.
15. W. Churchill, *The Second World War*, Vol. 2, London, 1949, p. 183.
16. Ybarnegaray, quoted in Churchill, Vol. 2, p. 187.
17. Gabriel Péri, quoted in *The Times*, 5 October 1938.
18. Quoted in A. Rossi, *La physiologie du Parti Communiste Français*, Paris, 1948, p. 15. See also pp. 395–6.
19. Broche *et al.*, p. 113.
20. Broche *et al.*, p. 34.
21. Broche *et al.*, p. 44, see also de Gaulle, p. 85.
22. Broche *et al.*, p. 53.
23. De Gaulle, p. 82.
24. De Gaulle, p. 106.
25. See A. Prost, *La Résistance, une histoire sociale*, Paris, 1997, p. 43.
26. Knight, p. 230.
27. I. Birchall, *Bailing out the System*, London, 1986, p. 32. For a gripping account of six individual resisters see H. Frenay, *Volontaires de la nuit*, Paris, 1975.
28. Muraccioli, p. 101.
29. De Gaulle, p. 497.
30. Broche *et al.*, p. 101.
31. Quoted in H. Michel and B. Mirkine-Guetzévitch (eds), *Les Idées politiques et sociales de la Résistance. Documents clandestins: 1940–44*, Paris, 1954, p. 83.
32. Quoted in Michel and Mirkine-Guetzévitch, p. 73.
33. Quoted in Michel and Mirkine-Guetzévitch, p. 52.
34. Members of Action Française, for example. See H. Noguères, *La vie quotidienne des resistants de l'armistice a la Liberation, 1940–1945*, Paris, 1984, p. 72.
35. Noguères, p. 64.

36. Michel and Mirkine-Guetzévitch, p. 52.
37. Quoted in Michel and Mirkine-Guetzévitch, p. 153.
38. Quoted in Michel and Mirkine-Guetzévitch, p. 156.
39. Michel and Mirkine-Guetzévitch, p. 157.
40. Quoted in Michel and Mirkine-Guetzévitch, p. 198.
41. De Gaulle, p. 483.
42. Quoted in Michel and Mirkine-Guetzévitch, p. 195.
43. L. Moulin, *Jean Moulin*, Paris, 1999, pp. 165–6.
44. De Gaulle, p. 307.
45. De Gaulle, p. 306.
46. De Gaulle, p. 390.
47. Moulin, p. 317.
48. Quoted in Moulin, p. 311.
49. Quoted in Noguères, p. 207.
50. Noguères, p. 217.
51. Sirinelli, p. 212 and Broche *et al.*, pp. 188–9.
52. Moulin, p. 323.
53. Broche *et al.*, pp. 181–2.
54. A.L. Funk, *The Politics of Torch*, Kansas, 1974, pp. 173–4, 212.
55. Funk, p. 23.
56. Quoted in Funk, p. 251.
57. Funk, p. 10.
58. De Gaulle, p. 363.
59. The breadth of the resistance was illustrated by the fact that the assassin was a Royalist, though his precise motives have never been fully elucidated.
60. Funk, p. 232.
61. Funk, p. 130.
62. Details in Knight, p. 102.
63. Durand, pp. 123–4.
64. See for example de Gaulle's letter to the CNR on 10 May 1943, reprinted in Moulin, p. 338 and Moulin himself, p. 282.
65. G. Bidault, *Resistance*, London, 1967, p. 37.
66. Broche *et al.*, p. 564.
67. Frenay, p. 254.
68. Broche *et al.*, pp. 478–9.
69. Broche *et al.*, p. 478, de Gaulle, p. 703.
70. M. Chaubin (ed.) *Resistance et Libération de la Corse*, no date or place of publication, p. 70. In addition there were 637 Italians and 72 French soldiers killed.
71. *Le Patriote*, 10 September 1943.
72. De Gaulle, p. 468.
73. Broche *et al.*, p. 575.
74. Tillon, pp. 313–4.
75. Quoted in Tillon, p. 318.
76. Broche *et al.*, pp. 571–3.
77. Tillon, p. 322.
78. Tillon, p. 348.
79. Tillon, p. 352.
80. Tillon, p. 374.
81. De Gaulle, p. 644.

82. De Gaulle, p. 648.
83. De Gaulle, p. 647.
84. De Gaulle, p. 661.
85. See I. Birchall, *Workers Against the Monolith*, London 1974.
86. S. Hessel, *Indignez Vous!*, no place, 2011, pp. 9–11.

CHAPTER 7

1. H. Dalton, *Memoirs, 1931–1945*, London, 1957, p. 265.
2. Quoted in M. Parker, *The Battle of Britain*, London, 2000, p. 78.
3. E. Bevin, *The Job to be Done*, Surrey, 1942, p. 7.
4. *Britain Under Fire*, London, no date, no page.
5. Quoted in T. Harrisson, *Living Through the Blitz*, Harmondsworth, 1978, p. 162.
6. Harrisson, p. 162.
7. V. Brittain, *England's Hour*, London, 1981, p. 38.
8. Harold Nicholson paraphrasing the views of Clement Attlee, the Labour Party leader. Quoted in Harrisson, p. 162.
9. Quoted in Parker, p. 278.
10. Churchill on 18 June 1940, quoted in I. Montagu, *The Traitor Class*, London, 1940, p. 7.
11. Extract from press statements made by Churchill, January 1927 (Churchill Papers, CHAR 9/82B).
12. *The Times*, 9 May 1936.
13. Quoted in I. Birchall, *Bailing out the System*, London, 1986, p. 10.
14. *The Times* 26 September 1921.
15. Quoted in M. MacAlpin, *Mr Churchill's Socialists*, London, 1941, p. 82.
16. *The Times* 26 November 1938.
17. See for example his parliamentary speech quoted in *The Times*, 13 November 1936.
18. W. Churchill on 13 May 1940 in *The Times*, 14 May 1940. The well-known part of the speech is in italics added by the author.
19. Quoted in Brittain, p. 53. The well-known part of the speech is in italics added by the author.
20. Brittain, p. 54. The well-known part of the speech is in italics added by the author.
21. *The Times*, 28 October 1940.
22. Quoted in A. Calder, *The People's War*, London, 1971, p. 114.
23. See D. Edgerton, *Warfare State: Britain, 1920–1970*, Cambridge, 2006, p. 32.
24. Edgerton, p. 22.
25. The figures are for 1938. F. McDonough, 'Why Appeasement?' in *Britain 1918–1951*, Oxford 1994, p. 72. See also G.C. Peden, 'The Burden of Imperial Defence and the Continental Commitment Reconsidered', in *The Historical Journal*, Vol. 27, No. 2 (1984), p. 410.
26. B. Farrell, 'Yes, Prime Minister: Barbarossa, Whipcord, and the Basis of British Grand Strategy, Autumn 1941', *The Journal of Military History*, Vol. 57, No. 4 (Oct. 1993), p. 624.
27. L. Woodward, *British Foreign Policy in the Second World War*, Vol. 2, London, 1971, p. 43.
28. Woodward, *British Foreign Policy in the Second World War*, Vol. 1, London, 1970, p. 453.

29. Woodward, Vol. 2, p. 548.
30. Directive to British representatives attending a Moscow conference in Woodward, Vol. 2, pp. 36–7.
31. Quoted in Woodward, Vol. 2, p. 358.
32. Quoted in M. Hastings, *Bomber Command*, London, 1979, p. 43.
33. Quoted in Hastings, p. 116.
34. Hastings, p. 134.
35. Hastings, p. 123.
36. Hastings, p. 180.
37. See for example, M. Middlebrook, *The Battle of Hamburg*, Harmondsworth, 1980, p. 25.
38. My emphasis. Quoted in Hastings, p. 330.
39. The figures are much disputed. McKee thinks 70,000 probably perished (A. McKee, *Devil's Tinderbox*, New York, 1982, p. 322). Weidauer gives figures from 35,000 to 250,000 but argues the latter is a gross exaggeration. (W. Weidauer, *Inferno Dresden*, Berlin, 1990, pp. 105–15). See also F. Taylor, *Dresden*, London, 2004, p. 357.
40. Taylor, *Dresden*, p. 373.
41. Quoted in McKee, p. 270.
42. *Ibid.*
43. Hastings, p. 226.
44. Quoted in Hastings, p. 233.
45. Hastings, p. 178.
46. Figures calculated from R. Goralski, *World War II Almanac,* London, 1981, pp. 425–8.
47. M. Rader, *No Compromise. The Conflict Between Two Worlds*, London, 1939, p. 317.
48. Brittain, p. 225.
49. Mass Observation, FR89, April 1940.
50. FR2067, 'The Mood of Britain, 1938 and 1944', March 1944 , p. 3.
51. See R. Croucher, *The Engineers' War*, London, 1982, p. iv.
52. FR600, 'Preliminary report on morale in Glasgow', March 1941, p. 17.
53. M. Barsley, *Ritzkrieg*, London, 1940, p. 8.
54. FR600, p. 4.
55. FR2067, p. 7.
56. Calder, pp. 218, 264.
57. Mass Observation, FR1401, September 1942.
58. Bevin, p. 2.
59. Quoted in J. Attfield and S. Williams (eds), *1939. The Communist Party and War*, London, 1984, pp. 25–6.
60. Attfield and Williams, pp. 25–6.
61. J. Mahon, *Harry Pollitt*, London, 1976, p. 269.
62. Calder, p. 459.
63. Calder, p. 292.
64. Croucher, p. 170.
65. FR2067, p. 3 – The mood of Britain 1938–44....
66. Calder, p. 371.
67. Brittain, pp. 152–3, Calder, p. 21.
68. Calder, p. 220.
69. *Daily Worker*, 3 November 1943, quoted in S. Bernstein and A. Richardson, *War and the International*, no place, 1986, p. 79.

70. FR600, p. 40.
71. Croucher, p. 164.
72. Calder, p. 299.
73. For details see Bernstein and Richardson.
74. Bernstein and Richardson, p. 79.
75. M. Davis, *Comrade or Brother?*, London, 1993, p. 187.
76. Croucher, p. 190.
77. See Croucher, p. 375.
78. J. Bierman and C. Smith, *Alamein*, London, 2002, pp. 15, 30.
79. Bierman and Smith, p. 184.
80. R. Kisch, *The Days of the Good Soldiers*, London, 1985, p. 9.
81. Kisch, p. 45.
82. Kisch, p. 40.
83. Kisch, p. 15.
84. Kisch, pp. 49–50.
85. Kisch, p. 53.
86. Kisch, p. 51.
87. Kisch, p. 54.
88. D.N. Pritt MP, reporting on the actions of the C-in-C in the Commons, *The Times*, 26 April 1944.
89. *The Times*, 6 July 1944.
90. Kisch, p. 111.
91. *The Times*, 22 November 1945.
92. During the war Eden made a specific commitment on Indonesia to the Dutch. See Woodward, Vol. 2, p. 179.
93. *The Times*, 12 November 1945.
94. *The Times*, 17 November 1945.
95. *The Times*, 20 December 1945.
96. *The Times*, 25 January 1946.
97. Kisch, p. 141.
98. See Kisch, pp. 153–9.
99. John Keegan, 'Towards a Theory of Combat Motivation' in P. Addison and A. Calder (eds), *Time to Kill. The Soldier's Experience of War in the West*, London, 1997, p. 8.
100. C. and E. Townsend (eds), *War Wives*, London 1990, pp. 128–9.
101. Calder, p. 608.
102. Calder, p. 613.
103. *Ibid*.
104. Kisch, p. 7.
105. FR1647, March 1943, p. 7.
106. Calder, p. 609.
107. *The Times*, 19 February 1943.
108. *The Times*, 5 June 1945.
109. My emphasis. *The Times*, 25 June 1945.

CHAPTER 8

1. N.A. Wynn, *The African American Experience During World War II*, Lanham, Maryland, 2010, p. 12.
2. G. Kolko, *The Politics of War*, New York, 1990, p. 19.

3. R. Overy, *Why the Allies Won*, London, 1995, p. 254.

4. Though it did rule areas such as the Philippines and Puerto Rico, for example.

5. F.D. Roosevelt, Speech of 29 December 1940 in www.americanrhetoric. com/speeches/PDFFiles/FDR%20-%20Arsenal%20of%20Democracy.pdf. Accessed 23 June 2008.

6. F.D. Roosevelt, 'The Four Freedoms' Speech of 6 January 1941 in www. americanrhetoric.com/speeches/PDFFiles/FDR%20-%20Four%20Freedoms. pdf.

7. S. Ambrose, *Rise to Globalism*, Harmondsworth, 1993, p. xi.

8. S. Terkel, *Race: How Blacks and Whites Think and Feel about the American Obsession*, New York, 1992.

9. Quoted in P. Smith, *Democracy on Trial*, New York, 1995, p. 96.

10. Smith, p. 15.

11. P. Irons, *Justice at War*, Berkeley, 1983, p. 12.

12. The Johnson-Reed Act quoted in M.A. Jones, *American Immigration*, Chicago, 1960, p. 277.

13. De Witt's report, quoted in Smith, p. 124.

14. Irons, p. 54.

15. Irons, p. 284.

16. Irons, p. 281.

17. Colonel Bendetsen, one of DeWitt's subordinates, quoted in Irons, p. 58.

18. Smith, p. 432.

19. J. Dower, *War without Mercy*, e-book, 1993, p. 82, and oral testimony – Wing Luke Museum, Seattle.

20. Irons, pp. 70, 348.

21. Smith, p. 263.

22. Smith, p. 313.

23. Smith, p. 296.

24. S. Terkel, *'The Good War': An Oral History of World War Two*, New York, 1984, p. 59.

25. N. Ferguson, 'Prisoner Taking and Prisoner Killing in the Age of Total War: Towards a Political Economy of Military Defeat', in *War in History*, 2004, 11 (2), p. 181.

26. Terkel, *'The Good War'*, p. 59.

27. Terkel, *'The Good War'*, pp. 60–1.

28. R. Schaffer, *Wings of Judgment*, Oxford, 1985, p. 83.

29. General David M. Schlatter, deputy chief of air staff in the Eighth Air Force, quoted in Schaffer, p. 96.

30. Colonel Harry F. Cunningham quoted in Schaffer, p. 147.

31. Schaffer, p. 132.

32. Quoted in Schaffer, p. 217.

33. G. Alperovitz, 'Hiroshima: Historians Reassess' in *Foreign Policy*, No. 99, 1995, pp. 15–34.

34. 31 May 1945 meeting of the Interim Committee and its Scientific Advisory panel. B.J. Bernstein, 'Truman and the A-Bomb: Targeting Noncombatants, Using the Bomb, and His Defending the "Decision"', *Journal of Military History*, Vol. 62, No. 3, July 1998, p. 559.

35. Bernstein, p. 562.

36. J. Hersey, *Hiroshima*, Harmondsworth 1946, pp. 40–41.

37. M. Hachiya, *Hiroshima Doctor*, London, 1958, pp. 24–5.

38. L. London, *Whitehall and the Jews, 1933–1948*, Cambridge, 2000, p. 59.
39. London, p. 131.
40. Quoted in D.S. Wyman, *The Abandonment of the Jews: America and the Holocaust*, Massachusetts, 1984.
41. London, p. 2.
42. R. Beir, *Roosevelt and the Holocaust*, Fort Lee, New Jersey, 2006, p. 237. Wyman's estimate is 200,000, p. 285.
43. Beir, p. 226.
44. Wyman, p. 24.
45. Beir, p. 260.
46. Beir, p. 156.
47. Wyman, p. 127.
48. Wyman, p. 123.
49. Wyman, p. 304.
50. Quoted in Wyman, p. 292.
51. Wyman, p. 301.
52. See for example a useful summary in Beir, pp. 248–54, and J.H. Kitchens, 'The Bombing of Auschwitz Re-examined', in *The Journal of Military History*, Vol. 58 No. 2 (April 1994), pp. 233–66.
53. Beir, p. 263.
54. J. Barfod, *The Holocaust Failed in Denmark*, Copenhagen, 1985, p. 30.
55. See E. Levine, *Darkness over Denmark*, New York, 2000, p. 74.
56. Barfod, pp. 15–24. See also M. Goodman, 'Resistance in German-occupied Denmark', in R. Rohrlich (ed.), *Resisting the Holocaust*, Oxford, 1998, pp. 213–37.
57. Rohrlich, p. 8.
58. Jorgen Kieler quoted in Levine, p. 102.
59. Levine, for example, estimated that over ten percent of the Danish Brigade were Jewish. Levine, p. 128.
60. M. Cohen, 'Culture and Remembrance', in Rohrlich, p. 20. Although fewer than 1 per cent of the French population, Jews formed up to 20 per cent of the Maquis. Rohrlich, p. 3.
61. Rohrlich, p. 2.
62. E. Tzur, 'From Moral Rejection to Armed Resistance', in Rohrlich, p. 40.
63. A. Foxman, quoted in E. Sterling, 'The Ultimate Sacrifice', in Rohrlich, p. 59.
64. Rohrlich, p. 59.
65. C.L.R. James, *et al.*, *Fighting Racism in World War II*, New York, 1980, p. 15.
66. Quoted in Beir, p. 147.
67. James *et al.*, p. 351.
68. A.R. Buchanan, *Black Americans in World War II*, Santa Barbara, California, 1977, p. 63.
69. Buchanan, p. 64.
70. D. Kryder, *Divided Arsenal*, Cambridge, 2000, p. 168.
71. Wynn, p. 31.
72. Buchanan, p. 84.
73. Wynn, p. 7.
74. Buchanan, p. 67.
75. James *et al.*, p. 17.
76. *The Pittsburgh Courier*, 7 February 1942.
77. Dempsey Travis, quoted in Terkel, *'The Good War'*, p. 149.

78. Terkel, 'The Good War', p. 153.
79. Dempsey Travis, quoted in Terkel, 'The Good War', p. 149.
80. Crisis, quoted in Buchanan, p. 114.
81. James et al., p. 28.
82. James et al., p. 44.
83. See H. Cayton, 'White Man's War' in Pittsburgh Courier, 28 February 1942.
84. James et al., p. 181. Wynn describes another survey: 'Of 1008 blacks interviewed in New York, 42% felt that it was more important to make democracy work at home than to defeat Germany and Japan when questioned by a black interviewer. This figure dropped to 34% when interviewer was white.' (Wynn, p. 100).
85. Wynn, p. 102.
86. 'Victory at Home, Victory Abroad Sweeps Nation', Pittsburgh Courier, 21 March 1942.
87. F. Bolden, 'U.S. Generously Supplies Propaganda Material for Axis Enemies', Pittsburgh Courier, 28 March 1942.
88. 'Lynching vs Morale – A Soldier Writes a Letter', Pittsburgh Courier, 14 November 1942.
89. R. Boyer and H. Marais, Labor's Untold Story, New York, 1955, p. 331.
90. Kryder, p. 103.
91. Buchanan, p. 18.
92. Kryder, p. 56n.
93. James et al., p. 21.
94. Quoted in James et al., pp. 101–2.
95. Quoted in Kryder, p. 58.
96. Buchanan, p. 23.
97. Mark Ethridge quoted in Wynn, p. 49. See also James et al., p. 191 and Pittsburgh Courier, 4 and 18 July 1942.
98. James et al., p. 193. After a year, and with mid-term elections out of the way. Kryder, pp. 92–3.
99. Wynn, p. 18.
100. Kryder, p. 111.
101. Wynn, p. 61.
102. Wynn, p. 59.
103. Kryder, p. 108.
104. H. Cayton, 'America's Munich', Pittsburgh Courier, 14 March 1942.
105. 'Detroit Rioters Quelled', Pittsburgh Courier, 7 March 1942.
106. James et al., p. 235.
107. James et al., p. 273, and Wynn, p. 69. See also R. Hofstadter and M. Wallace, American Violence. A Documentary History, New York, 1970, pp. 253–58.
108. Examples include the shipyards at Mobile, Alabama. See Buchanan, p. 56 and Wynn p. 50, the Detroit Packard strike. See Buchanan, 1977, p. 41, the US Rubber Company, Hudson Naval Ordinance, and so on.
109. James et al., p. 137.
110. Wynn, p. 52.
111. James et al., p. 263.
112. 'Ghetto Document Exposed', Pittsburgh Courier, 9 October 1943.
113. 'Racism: Cause and Cure', Pittsburgh Courier, 10 July 1943.
114. For details of Harlem see Wynn, pp. 69–70 and Buchanan, pp. 53–6.
115. See '1942 in Retrospect', Pittsburgh Courier, 2 January 1943.

116. Kryder, p. 142.
117. Kryder, p. 173.
118. 'Soldiers Organize Council at Fort Bragg', *Pittsburgh Courier*, 25 April 1942.
119. Kryder, p. 71.
120. Kryder, pp. 168–207.
121. Quoted in Kryder, p. 176.
122. Quoted in Kryder, p. 180.
123. Kryder, p. 190.
124. Kryder, p. 193.
125. Kryder, p. 194.
126. Buchanan, p. 76.
127. Wynn, p. 135.
128. James *et al.*, p. 17.

CHAPTER 9

1. P. Hoffmann, 'The Second World War, German Society, and Internal Resistance to Hitler', in D. Clay Large (ed.), *Contending with Hitler*, Cambridge, 1991, p. 122.
2. Halder quoted by Churchill, *The Second World War*, Vol. 1, 1948, p. 281.
3. N. Henderson, *Failure of a Mission*, London, 1940, p. 57.
4. Henderson, p. 148.
5. My emphasis. Henderson, p. 192.
6. Henderson, p. 247.
7. According to Peter Hoffmann this was implicit in British policy from the start. See P. Hoffmann, 'The War, German Society and Internal Resistance', in M. Laffan (ed.), *The Burden of German History, 1919–1945*, London, 1989, p. 200, although Churchill writes the concept was formulated by Roosevelt in 1943, and the PM heard it 'with some feeling of surprise ...', W. Churchill, *The Second World War*, Vol. 4, 1950, p. 615.
8. Quoted in D. Gluckstein, *The Nazis, Capitalism and the Working Class*, London, 1996, p. 219.
9. Quoted in A. Beevor, *Berlin, The Downfall 1945*, London 2003, p. 29.
10. Quoted in G. MacDonogh, *After the Reich*, London, 2007, p. 99.
11. H. Graml, 'Resistance Thinking on Foreign Policy', in H. Graml *et al.*, *The German Resistance to Hitler*, London, 1970, p. 18.
12. Graml, in Graml, pp. 1–2.
13. Graml, in Graml, p. 14.
14. H. Mommsen, 'Social Views and Constitutional Plans of the Resistance', in Graml, p, 75.
15. Restoration was the constitutional proposal of Oster, Schulenburg and Heinz. See Mommsen, in Graml, p. 106.
16. Quoted by Mommsen, in Graml, p. 108.
17. H. Mommsen, 'The Political Legacy of the German Resistance: A Historiographical Critique', in D. Clay Large, p. 157.
18. Quoted by Mommsen in Graml, p. 120.
19. Quoted in E. Gerstenmaier, 'The Kreisau Circle', in H. Royce, E. Zimmermann and H-A. Jacobsen, *Germans Against Hitler*, Bonn, 1960, p. 33.
20. *Young Guard*, quoted in Gluckstein, p. 212.
21. Quoted in Gluckstein, p. 213.

22. *Break the Chains*, SPD declaration of 18 June 1933, quoted in Gluckstein, p. 213.

23. Gluckstein, p. 88.

24. Gluckstein, p. 56.

25. For a full discussion of this see Gluckstein, pp. 97–126.

26. Otto Wels, quoted in Gluckstein, p. 121.

27. G. Gross, *Der Gewerkschaftliche Widerstandskampf der Deutschen Arbeiterklasse Während der Faschistischen Vertrauensräte Wahlen, 1934*, Berlin, 1962, p. 52.

28. Quoted in Gluckstein, p. 123.

29. Gluckstein, p. 211.

30. See for example, Gluckstein, p. 217.

31. L. Crome, *Unbroken. Resistance and Survival in the Concentration Camps*, London, 1988, pp. 75–9.

32. Report from Central Germany in December 1937 in *Berichte der Sozialdemokratischen Partei Deutschlands*, p. 1669.

33. D. Peukert, 'Working Class Resistance: Problems and Options' in Clay Large, p. 41.

34. MacDonogh, pp. 261–2 and *The Oxford Companion*, p. 485.

35. E.D. Weitz, *Creating German Communism, 1890–1990*, Princeton, 1997, p. 280. One source gives the figure of up to 100,000 dead. (L. Niethammer, U. Borsdorf, P. Brandt *et al.*, *Arbeiterinitiative 1945*, Wuppertal, 1976, p. 34).

36. Niethammer, p. 105.

37. See G. Aly, *Hitler's Beneficiaries*, London, 2006, pp. 298–9.

38. JCS 1067, the key US directive on occupation operations, quoted in H. Koehler, *Deutschland auf dem Weg zu sich selbst*, Stuttgart, 2002, p. 440.

39. This is discussed at length in MacDonogh. See also E. Mandel, *The Meaning of the Second World War*, London, 1986, p. 163.

40. Quoted in MacDonogh, p. 26.

41. US and French troops also carried out rapes. See MacDonogh, pp. 26, 50–57, 79, 98–103, 114–15.

42. See Kolko, p. 326.

43. Kolko, p. 327.

44. Quoted in Kolko, p. 504.

45. Quoted in Kolko, p. 505.

46. MacDonogh, pp. 69–70.

47. See Niethammer, p. 109.

48. Niethammer, p. 206–7, 257.

49. Niethammer, p. 237.

50. For a full discussion of this phenomenon see Niethammer.

51. Quoted in Gluckstein, p. 221.

52. Niethammer, p. 180.

53. Niethammer, p. 179.

54. Niethammer, p. 43.

55. Quoted in Niethammer, p. 642.

56. See Niethammer, p. 182.

57. Quoted in Niethammer, p. 642.

58. Leaflet issued in Leipzig, quoted in Niethammer, p. 236.

59. Niethammer, p. 242.

60. Niethammer, pp. 263–6.

61. Niethammer, p. 340.
62. Niethammer pp. 425–6.
63. S. Terkel, 'The Good War': An Oral History of World War Two, New York, 1984, p. 381.
64. Quoted in Niethammer, p. 648.
65. MacDonogh p. 349.
66. Brown Book. War and Nazi Criminals in West Germany, no date, GDR, p. 12.
67. J. Herz, 'Denazification and Related Policies', in J. Herz (ed.), From Dictatorship to Democracy, Connecticut, 1982, p. 25, and MacDonogh, p. 356.
68. Herz, p. 29.
69. O. v Mengersen, The Impact of the Holocaust. Sinti and Roma in Germany: Past and Present, Heidelberg, 2010, pp. 6–7.
70. The equivalent figures of the US and France zones were just over a third and just over a half respectively. M. Fulbrook, Germany, 1918–1990. The Divided Nation, London, 1991, p. 147.
71. Brown Book, p. 12.
72. Herz, in Herz, p. 20.
73. Fulbrook, p. 148.
74. Fulbrook, p. 147.
75. M. Fichter, 'Non-State Organizations – Problems of Redemocratization', in Herz, p. 62.

CHAPTER 10

1. K. von Schuschnigg, Austrian Requiem, London, 1947, p. 160.
2. Die Rote Fahne, 10 February 1934.
3. J. Hindels, Österreichs Gewerkschaften in Widerstand, 1934–1945, Vienna, 1976, p. 30.
4. Hindels, p. 113–4.
5. O. Molden, quoted in Hindels, p. 211.
6. See S. Bolbecher et al., Erzählte Geschichte. Berichte von Widerstandskämpfern und Verfolgten, Vol. 1, Vienna, no date, p. 164.
7. Schuschnigg, p. 23.
8. Report of the meeting quoted in Hindels, p. 191. Ironically, many left-wing political prisoners were eventually freed as Hitler demanded from Schuschnigg that all political prisoners were freed. However, while all Nazi prisoners remained free, those of the left were watched closely and arrested by the Gestapo shortly afterwards.
9. See testimony of H. Pepper and F. Danimann, in Bolbecher, pp. 167–70.
10. See the argument of W. Neugebauer, Der österreichische Widerstand, 1938–1945, Vienna, 2008, p. 46.
11. See T. Kirk, 'Nazi Austria: The Limits of Dissent', in T. Kirk and A. McElligott, Opposing Fascism. Community, Authority and Resistance in Europe, Cambridge, 1999, p. 135, and Neugebauer, p. 50.
12. Neugebauer, p. 67.
13. Kirk, in Kirk and McElligott, p. 139.
14. See Neugebauer, p. 46.
15. Neugebauer, p. 114.

16. Quoted in Bolbecher *et al.*, p. 13.
17. O. Rathkolb, quoted in J. Miller, *One, by One, by One. Facing the Holocaust*, New York, 1990, p. 69.
18. W. Garscha, 'Entnazifizierung und gerichtlich Ahndung von NS-Verbrechen' in E. Talos (ed.), *NS Herrschaft in Österreich*, Vienna, 2002, p. 852. Tribunals registered 536,000 of whom 98,000 were 'illegals.' (i.e. banned under Austrofascism), p. 853.
19. Neugebauer, p. 236.
20. Quoted in B. Bailer-Galanda, 'Die Opfer des Nationalsozialismus und die so genannte Wiedergutmachung', in Talos, p. 885.
21. Galanda in Talos, p. 886.
22. *Ibid.*
23. See Bolbecher *et al.*, pp. 310, 312–14, 317, 319, 325.
24. Neugebauer, pp. 238–9.
25. Garscha, in Talos, p. 861.
26. Details in Miller, pp. 73–7.
27. Bolbecher *et al.*, p. 326.
28. Bolbecher *et al.*, p. 347.

CHAPTER 11

1. L. Longo, *Sulla via dell'insurrezione nazionale*, Rome, 1971, p. 14.
2. Though they were largely absent at the fascist party's foundation in 1919, on the eve of Mussolini's ascent to power in 1922 its congress was no longer dominated by 'workers, craftsmen, petty bourgeois but members of the middle and upper classes, of the aristocracy, industrialists, landowners ... '. De Felice quoted in J. Baglieri, 'Italian Fascism and the Crisis of Liberal Hegemony: 1901–1922', in S. Larsen, *et al.* (eds), *Who Were the Fascists*, Bergen, 1980, p. 330.
3. T. Behan, *The Italian Resistance*, London, 2009, p. 9.
4. T. Abse, 'Italian Workers and Italian Fascism', in R. Bessel (ed.), *Fascist Italy and Nazi Germany*, Cambridge, 1996, p. 49.
5. P. Morgan, 'Popular attitudes and resistance to Fascism in Italy', in T. Kirk and A. McElligott, *Opposing Fascism*, Cambridge, 1999, p. 167; Behan, p. 11.
6. Behan, p. 11.
7. Morgan, in Kirk and McElligott, p. 173.
8. P. Spriano, *Storia del Partito comunista italiano*, Vol. 4, Turin, 1976, pp. 9–11.
9. Behan, p. 20.
10. Quoted in Spriano, pp. 71–2.
11. Spriano, pp. 6, 46 and 73, and Behan, p. 79.
12. Behan, p. 77.
13. Spriano, p. 4 quotes official reports from different parts of Italy expressing public hostility to Italian involvement.
14. Behan, p. 78.
15. See Longo, p. 18.
16. January 1943 leaflet of unknown origin quoted in Spriano, p. 170.
17. R. Battaglia, *The Story of the Italian Resistance*, London, no date, p. 31.
18. Tim Mason has an interesting discussion about the details of this strike and the possible distortions in the account made due to the political needs of the

Italian CP. See T. Mason, *Nazism, Fascism and the Working Class*, Cambridge, 1995, pp. 274–94.

19. Spriano, p. 180.
20. Battaglia, p. 32.
21. Comments of Mussolini reported in Spriano, p. 212.
22. Quoted in Behan, p. 43.
23. Quoted in Spriano, p. 181 and Behan, p. 43.
24. E. Agarossi, *A Nation Collapses*, Cambridge, 2000, p. 52.
25. Behan, p. 43.
26. Quoted in I.C.B. Dear and M.R.D. Foot, *The Oxford Companion to the Second World War*, p. 588.
27. D. Mack Smith, *Mussolini*, London, 1983, p. 63.
28. D. Guerin, *Fascism and Big Business*, New York, 1973, p. 117.
29. I.S. Munro, *Through Fascism to World Power*, London, 1933, p. 147.
30. Quoted in Spriano, p. 253.
31. Agarossi, p. 36.
32. Agarossi, p. 14.
33. W. Churchill, *The Second World War*, Vol. 5, 1951, p. 167.
34. Behan, p. 216.
35. Quoted in Spriano, p. 275.
36. Quoted in Spriano, p. 272.
37. Quoted in C. Pavone, *Una guerra civile, Saggio storico sulla moralità nella Resistenza*, Turin, 1991, p. 9 and Spriano, p. 259.
38. Spriano, p. 300.
39. My emphasis. Churchill, Vol. 5, p. 89, Churchill to Roosevelt 5 August 43.
40. Pavone, p. 8. Behan points out that the ruling group realised some concessions were necessary and so 'democracy began to seep through the cracks', but the changes were minimal. Behan, p. 28.
41. Quoted in Spriano, p. 142.
42. Spriano, p. 346–9 and Pavone, p. 10.
43. 'Memorandum on the urgent need to organise national defence against the occupation and threat of a coup by the Germans', 30 August 1943, quoted in Longo, p. 33.
44. L. Valiani, *Tutte le strade conducono a Roma*, Bologna, 1983, pp. 32–3.
45. Quoted in Spriano, p. 303.
46. See R. Lamb, *War in Italy, 1943–1945*, London, 1993, p. 17.
47. For full details see Agarossi.
48. Quoted in Pavone p. 6.
49. Quoted in Agarossi, p. 97.
50. See Agarossi, p. 118, and Behan, p. 29.
51. Battaglia, p. 54. It is notable that the prisoners were offered freedom if they joined Mussolini's puppet regime of Salò, but only 1.3 per cent accepted. Behan, p. 54.
52. Pavone, p. 48.
53. G. Aly, *Hitler's Beneficiaries*, London, 2006, p. 52.
54. Aly, p. 154.
55. L. Ginzburg, *Scritti*, Einaudi, Torino, 1964, quoted in G. Candeloro and V. Lo Curto, *Mille anni*, Florence, 1992, p. 535. See also Pavone, p. 174.
56. Quoted in Pavone, p. 22.

57. Dante Livio Bianco of the Justice and Liberty Partisans in Piedmont, quoted in Pavone, p. 251.
58. Quoted in Pavone, p. 23.
59. Noel Charles, in L. Mercuri (ed.) *Documenti sull'Italia nella Seconda Guerra Mondiale*, 1943–5, p. 134.
60. Valiani, p. 118.
61. *La Nostra Lotta*, January 1944, No. 2, quoted in Longo, pp. 102.
62. *La Nostra Lotta*, in Longo, p. 106.
63. *La Nostra Lotta*, in Longo, p. 111.
64. *La Nostra Lotta*, in Longo, p. 113.
65. *Ibid.*
66. For a full account see Behan, pp. 190–207.
67. Valiani, p. 79.
68. Diary of Fausto Lucchelli, quoted in Guderzo, pp. 168–172.
69. G. Guderzo, *L'altra guerra*, Bologna, 2002, p. 158.
70. Behan, p. 1.
71. Battaglia suggests a smaller number of between 150,000 and 200,000, Battaglia, p. 257.
72. Quoted in Mercuri, pp. 138–9, 143 and149.
73. L. Lewis, *Echoes of Resistance. British Involvement with the Italian Partisans*, Tunbridge Wells, 1985, p. 25.
74. Quoted in Pavone, p. 97.
75. Pavone, p. 131.
76. Quoted in Pavone, p. 136.
77. Communist spokesman in Turin, quoted in Pavone, p. 136.
78. Quoted in Battaglia, pp. 184–5.
79. Behan, p. 176.
80. Details in Battaglia, p. 172n and Lewis, p. 25.
81. See Guderzo, p. xiv.
82. Quoted in Guderzo, p. 405.
83. Guderzo, p. 409.
84. See Lewis, p. 28.
85. Behan, pp. 183–4.
86. Lamb, p. 220.
87. McCaffery, quoted in Lamb, p. 217. See also Behan, p. 187.
88. Report of Sargent to Anthony Eden, quoted in B. Davidson, *Scenes from the Anti-Nazi War*, New York, 1980, p. 236.
89. Valiani, p. 212.
90. Battaglia, p. 78.
91. Document of 11 June 1944, in Mercuri, p. 18.
92. Quoted in Pavone, p. 190.
93. See Pavone, pp. 177–8.
94. Valiani, p. 156.
95. See Lamb, p. 57 and Behan, Chapter 11.
96. Guderzo, p. 15 and Pavone, p. 482.
97. Valiani, p. 128.
98. Valiani, p. 129.
99. Pavone, p. 476.
100. Longo, p. 129.
101. Quoted in Pavone, p. 484.

102. See Battaglia, p. 221 and Lamb, p. 227–8.
103. Longo, p. 25.
104. Lamb, p. 228.
105. Behan, p. 211.
106. *Atti de Comando generale del C.V.L.*, dated 2 December 1944 in Longo, p. 271, English translation in Davidson, p. 238.
107. See also discussion in Davidson, p. 240 and Lamb, p. 227.
108. See for example, Battaglia p. 88.
109. Guderzo, p. 120.
110. Quoted in Behan, p. 95.
111. Spriano, p. 334 and Pavone p. 365.
112. Davidson, p. 215.
113. D. Sassoon, *The Strategy of the Italian Communist Party*, London, 1981, p. 28.
114. Valiani, p. 241. Lewis gives different figures: PCI – 38 per cent, Autonomous (non-political) Brigades – 30 per cent, Christian Democrat and Action Party – 12–13 per cent each, with 17 per cent whose loyalties were not recorded. Lewis, p. 24. See also Behan, p. 49.
115. Sassoon, p. 4.
116. Quoted in Battaglia, p. 186.
117. P. Broué, 'The Italian Communist Party, the War and the Revolution', in *Through Fascism, War and Revolution: Trotskyism and Left Communism in Italy, Revolutionary History*, Vol. 5, spring 1995, p. 113.
118. Broué, p. 114.
119. Quoted in Pavone, p. 175. In November 1943 the PCI declared: 'Badoglio and his generals cannot lead the fight. Only the forces led by the Committee for National Liberation can do that.' *La Nostra Lotta*, November 1943, in Longo, p. 59.
120. Quoted in Sassoon, p. 22.
121. Broué, p. 114.
122. See Sassoon, p. 17.
123. 'Hail the government of national unity', *Il Combattente*, May 1944, in Longo, p. 180.
124. *Il Combattente*, December 1943, quoted in Longo, p. 74.
125. Pavone, p. 364.
126. Pavone, p. 365.
127. Quoted in A. Peregalli, 'The Left Wing Opposition in Italy During the period of the Resistance', in *Revolutionary History*, p. 125.
128. Quoted in Behan, p. 50.
129. See Behan, pp. 47–9.
130. Valiani, p. 173.
131. Peregali, p. 136.
132. Peregali, pp. 127–8.
133. Peregali, p. 130 and Behan, p. 197.
134. Quoted in Pavone, p. 403.
135. Quoted in Pavone, p. 406.
136. *L'Unità*, March 1944, Longo, p. 173.
137. *La Nostra Lotta*, September 1944, Longo p. 234.
138. *La Nostra Lotta*, August 1944, Longo, pp. 226–7.
139. Quoted in Behan, p. 215.

140. Quoted in Longo, p. 226.
141. See for example Longo, pp. 203, 213 and 214.
142. Quoted in Battaglia, pp. 260–1.
143. Battaglia, pp. 265–6.
144. Battaglia, p. 267.
145. Battaglia, p. 269.
146. Davidson, p. 271.
147. Davidson, pp. 271–2.
148. Davidson, p. 273.
149. Davidson, p. 274.
150. Davidson, p. 275.

CHAPTER 12

1. A. Read and D. Fisher, *The Proudest Day*, London, 1997, p. 45.
2. *Hansard*, 11 March 1942.
3. This was approximately 350 million.
4. P. French, *Liberty or Death*, London, 1977, p. 183.
5. C. Bates, *Subalterns and Raj*, Abingdon, 2007, p. 157, J. Newsinger, *The Blood Never Dried*, London, 2006, p. 157.
6. N. Mansergh (ed.), *The Transfer of Power, 1942–7*, Vol. 4, London, 1973, p. 362.
7. Mansergh, Vol. 4, p. 272.
8. Read and Fisher, p. 45.
9. Read and Fisher, p. 64.
10. Read and Fisher, pp. 66–7.
11. At the outbreak there were 60,000 British and 160,000 Indian troops. By the end there were 2.5 million in total and the financial burden was almost five times greater than in 1939. This figure is for 1943–4. 'War Cabinet, WM (42) 105th Conclusions, Minute 2' in N. Mansergh (ed.), *The Transfer of Power, 1942–7*, Vol. 2, London, 1971, p. 590.
12. See 'War Cab Paper WP (42) 328, Sterling balances' in Mansergh, Vol. 2, p. 521.
13. War Cabinet WM (42) 105th Conclusions, Minutes 1 and 2 in Mansergh, Vol. 2, p. 590.
14. Newsinger, p. 157.
15. Quoted in 'Government of India, Home Dept, to Secretary of State, 1 May 42', in Mansergh, Vol. 2, p. 4.
16. See 'Marquess of Linlithgow to Mr Amery, 11 July 1942', in Mansergh, Vol. 2, p. 363.
17. *Dictionary of National Biography*, quoted in French, p. 131.
18. Mansergh, Vol. 4, p. 36.
19. See Mansergh, Vol. 4, pp. 77, 305.
20. Mansergh, Vol. 4, p. 674.
21. Mansergh, Vol. 4, p. 558.
22. Mansergh, Vol. 4, p. 157.
23. Mansergh, Vol. 4, pp. 673–674.
24. Mansergh, Vol. 4, pp. 1033–4.
25. S. Sarkar, *Modern India, 1885–1947*, Houndmills, 1989, p. 406.
26. Mansergh, Vol. 4, p. 376.

27. French, p. 188.
28. Mansergh, p. 486.
29. Newsinger, p. 158.
30. Mansergh, Vol. 4, p. 701.
31. Mansergh, Vol. 4, p. 355.
32. Quoted in French, p. 188.
33. Quoted in G.P. Pradhan, *India's Freedom Struggle: An Epic of Sacrifice and Suffering*, Delhi, 1990, p. 157.
34. Quoted in Sarkar, p. 377.
35. Jimmy Thomas in 1924, quoted in T. Cliff and D. Gluckstein, *The Labour Party: A Marxist History*, London, 1996, p. 96.
36. French, p. 170 and Newsinger, pp. 144–7.
37. See S. Gopal, *Jawaharlal Nehru. A Biography*, Delhi, 1989, pp. 121–4, 126.
38. Quoted in R.C. Majumdar, *History of the Freedom Movement in India*, Vol. 3, Calcutta, 1963, p. 597.
39. Sarkar, p. 376.
40. Mansergh, Vol. 2, p. 759.
41. See War Cabinet paper W.P (42) 395, in Mansergh, Vol. 2, p. 920. Later on British policies became even too much for Mudaliar and he advocated a compromise with Congress.
42. Mansergh, Vol. 4, p. 287.
43. Quoted in P.N. Chopra (ed.), *Historic Judgement on Quit India Movement. Justice Wickenden's Report*, Delhi, 1989, p. 231.
44. Quoted in Majumdar, p. 619.
45. Majumdar, p. 621.
46. Read and Fisher, p. 315.
47. Mansergh, Vol. 2, pp. 158–162.
48. Mansergh, Vol. 2, pp. 622–3.
49. Mansergh, Vol. 2, p. 624.
50. Read and Fisher, p. 166.
51. Chopra, *Historic Judgement*, p. 136 and G. Pandey (ed.), *The Indian Nation in 1942*, Calcutta, 1988, p. 6.
52. French, p. 155.
53. Mansergh, Vol. 2, p. 1002 and G. Pandey, 'The Revolt of August 1942 in Eastern UP and Bihar', in Pandey, p. 156.
54. P.N. Chopra (ed.), *Quit India Movement. Vol. 2. Role of Big Business*, New Delhi, 1991, p. 65.
55. Sarkar, pp. 394–5.
56. French, p. 159.
57. French, p. 159, and Read and Fisher, p. 330.
58. Sarkar, p. 395.
59. See G. Omvedt, 'The Satara Prati Sarkar' in Pandey, pp. 224–57, and Pradhan, p. 175.
60. H. Sanyal, 'The Quit India movement in Medinipur District', in Pandey, p. 46.
61. Sanyal, in Pandey, pp. 59–60.
62. Sanyal, in Pandey, pp. 59, 133.
63. Sanyal, in Pandey, pp. 133–4.
64. Sanyal in Pandey, p. 135–8. Quoted in Chopra, *Historic Judgement*, p. 65.
65. Majumdar, p. 676.

66. P.N. Chopra (ed.), *Quit India Movement. British Secret Documents*, Delhi, 1986, p. 162.
67. J. Narayan, *Selected Works*, Vol. 3, New Delhi, 2003, p. 115.
68. Narayan, p. 131.
69. Narayan, p. 142.
70. Narayan, p. 120.
71. Narayan, p. 204.
72. Narayan, p. 115.
73. 'The ABC of Dislocation', quoted in Chopra, *British Secret Documents*, p. 360.
74. Chopra, *Role of Big Business*, p. iv.
75. Chopra, *British Secret Documents*, pp. 80–1.
76. Chopra, *Role of Big Business*, p. 62.
77. Bates, p. 160.
78. Quoted in Pandey, in Pandey, pp. 139–40.
79. Mansergh, Vol. 2, p. 853.
80. Read and Fisher, p. 329 and Majumdar, p. 650.
81. Sarkar, pp. 395–6.
82. Majumdar, p. 660 and Newsinger, p. 155.
83. Majumdar, 650.
84. Chopra, *British Secret Documents*, p. 188.
85. Chopra, *British Secret Documents*, p. 42.
86. The latter figures are according to Nehru. Cited in Chopra, *Historic Judgement*, p. 19.
87. Majumdar, p. 658 and Sarkar, pp. 395–6.
88. Read and Fisher, p. 278.
89. Majumdar, p. 601.
90. Majumdar, p. 666.
91. T.S. Sareen (ed.), *Indian National Army. A Documentary Study*, New Delhi, 2004, Vol. 4, p. 32.
92. Quoted in K.K. Ghosh, *The Indian National Army. Second Front of the Indian Independence Movement*, Meerut, 1969, p. 137.
93. Sareen, pp. 308–9, 137.
94. Pradhan, p. 184.
95. M. Gupta and A.K. Gupta, *Defying Death. Struggles against Imperialism and Feudalism*, New Delhi, 2001, p. 187.
96. Sareen, p. 38.
97. Sareen, pp. 37–8.
98. Quoted in Read and Fisher, p. 363.
99. Quoted in N. Tarling, *A Sudden Rampage. The Japanese Occupation of Southeast Asia*, London, 2001, p. 89.
100. Quoted in Tarling, p. 123.
101. Read and Fisher, p. 59.
102. Figure for 1941. Ghosh, p. 61.
103. Quoted in Ghosh, p. 65.
104. Ghosh, p. 59.
105. Sarkar, p. 411.
106. Quoted in Ghosh, p. 72.
107. Sareen, p. 199.
108. Ghosh, p. 34.

109. Sareen, p. 214.
110. Memoirs of Lt General Kawabe, in Sareen, p. 311.
111. R. Dayal (ed.), *We Fought Together for Freedom. Chapters from the Indian National Movement*, Delhi, 1995, pp. 198–9.
112. Quoted in Ghosh, p. 140.
113. Sareen, p. 323.
114. Read and Fisher, p. 344.
115. Quoted in Dayal, p. 203.
116. P. Heehs, 'India's Divided Loyalties' in *History Today*, July 1995, p. 22.
117. French, p. 207 and Read and Fisher, p. 345.
118. Quoted in Sarkar, p. 404.
119. Sarkar, p. 411.

CHAPTER 13

1. M.C Ricklefs, *A History of Modern Indonesia*, London, 1981, p. 117.
2. Ricklefs, p. 145 and T. Friend, *The Blue-Eyed Enemy. Japan against the West in Java and Luzon, 1942–1945*, Princeton, 1988, p. 14.
3. Ricklefs, p. 147.
4. B. Dahm, *Sukarno and the Struggle for Indonesian Independence*, Ithaca, 1966, pp. 29–30 and three-millionths of 1 per cent went to university. Ricklefs, p. 152.
5. T. Friend, *The Blue-Eyed Enemy. Japan against the West in Java and Luzon, 1942–1945*, Princeton, 1988, p. 15.
6. Dahm, p. 91.
7. R. Cribb and C. Brown, *Modern Indonesia. A History Since 1945*, London, 1995, p. 1.
8. Ricklefs, p. 163.
9. For details see H. Benda, 'The Communist Rebellions of 1926–1927 in Indonesia', in *The Pacific Historical Review*, Vol. 24, No. 2 (May 1955), pp. 139–52 and Ricklefs, p. 170.
10. Quoted in Dahm, p. 149.
11. Dahm, p. 116.
12. Dahm, p. 215.
13. M.H. Thamrin quoted in N. Tarling, *A Sudden Rampage. The Japanese Occupation of Southeast Asia, 1941–1945*, London, 2001, p. 176.
14. Admiral Maeda, quoted in Dahm, p. 219.
15. Quoted in Tarling, p. 129.
16. Quoted in Dahm, p. 225.
17. Quoted in Dahm, p. 249–50.
18. Quoted in S. Sato, *War, Nationalism and Peasants*, New York, 1994, p. 11.
19. Quoted in Sato, p. 13.
20. M. Nakamura, 'General Imamura and the Early Period of Japanese Occupation', in *Indonesia*, Vol. 10 (October 1970), p. 7.
21. Tarling, pp. 175–7.
22. B. Anderson, *Java in a Time of Revolution*, London, 1972, p. 12.
23. Sato, pp. 84,144.
24. Cribb and Brown, p. 14.
25. Anderson, p. 12.
26. Sato, p. 76.

27. Friend, p. 163–4.
28. Sato, p. 165.
29. Sato, p. 157–8.
30. This is the estimate of Friend, p. 163–4, though Sato figures are between 15 and 20 per cent. Sato, p. 160.
31. Friend, p. 189.
32. 'Principles Governing the Administration of Occupied Southern Regions' of 20 November 1941, quoted in Sato, p. 52. See also Nakamura, p. 5.
33. Sato, p. 39.
34. Sato, p. 54.
35. Dahm, p. 244.
36. Sato, p. 71.
37. Friend, pp. 165–6.
38. Dahm, p. 315.
39. The role of this is discussed in Nakamura, p. 3.
40. Dahm, p. 218.
41. Quoted in Tarling, p. 187.
42. Dahm, p. 305.
43. Friend, p. 105.
44. Nakamura, p. 17.
45. Dahm, p. 221 and Tarling, p. 178.
46. Friend, p. 107.
47. Ricklefs, p. 191.
48. Anderson, p. 39.
49. Tarling, p. 179.
50. Sjarifuddin's life was spared after pleas from Sukarno and Hatta. Anderson, p. 38.
51. Anderson, pp. 40–4.
52. Ricklefs, p. 191.
53. See Sukarno quote above, in Dahm, p. 149.
54. B. Siong, 'Captain Huyer and the massive Japanese arms transfer in East Java in October 1945', in Bijdragen tot de Taal-, Land- en Volkenkunde, No. 159 (2003), No. 2/3, downloaded from www.kitlv-journals.nl. Accessed 12 January 2010, p. 295.
55. Sato, p. 64.
56. Anderson, p. 85.
57. Friend, p. 120.
58. Anderson, p. 67.
59. Calculated from a sample by Friend, p. 234.
60. Friend, p. 232. See also Ricklefs, p. 235.
61. Anderson, p. 74.
62. Anderson, p. 82, Dahm, p. 314.
63. Anderson, p. 91.
64. Quoted in Anderson, p. 113.
65. Anderson, p. 191.
66. Cribb and Brown, p. 19.
67. Anderson, p. 194.
68. J. Suryomenggolo, 'Workers' Control in Java, Indonesia, 1945–1946', in I. Ness and D. Azzellini (eds), Ours to Master and to Own, Chicago, 2011, p. 221.

69. Anderson, p. 270.
70. G.M. Kahin, *Nationalism and Revolution in Indonesia*, Ithaca, 1970, p. 173.
71. Quoted in Kahin, p. 174.
72. Anderson, p. 308.
73. Anderson, p. 310.
74. Anderson, p. 118.
75. Suryomenggolo, p. 215.
76. Anderson, p. 146.
77. Anderson, p. 126.
78. See A. Lucas, 'Social Revolution in Pemalang, Central Java, 1945', in *Indonesia*, Vol. 24 (October 1977), pp. 87–122.
79. Lucas, p. 114.
80. Lucas, pp. 101–2.
81. Lucas, p. 110.
82. Lucas, pp. 111–5.
83. Ricklefs, p. 206.
84. Anderson, p. 342.
85. Lucas, p. 120.
86. Ricklefs, p. 194.
87. Ricklefs, p. 196, Friend, p. 175 and Dahm, p. 302; R.G. Mangkupradja, H. Wanasita Evans and R. McVey, 'The Peta and My Relations with the Japanese: A Correction of Sukarno's Autobiography', in *Indonesia*, Vol. 5, (April 1968), p. 124, Anderson, p. 36.
88. Siong, 'Captain Huyer', p. 202 and Anderson, p. 100.
89. Anderson, p. 102.
90. There was shooting in Semarang, but this was because the Japanese had mistaken British-led Gurkhas to be Indonesians. Siong, 'Captain Huyer', p. 292.
91. Anderson, p. 106.
92. H.B. Siong, 'The Secret of Major Kido; The Battle of Semarang, 15–19 October 1945', in *Bijdragen tot de Taal-, Land- en Volkenkunde*, No. 152 (1996), No. 3, downloaded from www.kitlv-journals.nl. Accessed 12 January 2010, p. 406.
93. Anderson, p. 148.
94. Quoted in Anderson, p. 135.
95. See R. McMillan, *The British Occupation of Indonesia, 1945–1946*, Abingdon, 2005, p. 10, Anderson, pp. 135–6.
96. Siong, 'The Secret of Major Kido', p. 393.
97. Siong, 'The Secret of Major Kido', p. 413.
98. McMillan, p. 30.
99. Quoted in McMillan, p. 77.
100. *Ibid*.
101. Quoted in McMillan, p. 79.
102. Quoted in McMillan, p. 24.
103. Friend, p. 223.
104. McMillan, p. 14.
105. Friend, p. 226.
106. McMillan, p. 37.
107. Siong, 'Captain Huyer', p. 294.
108. Quoted in Anderson, p. 160.

109. McMillan, p. 44, Anderson, p. 161.
110. Quoted in Anderson, p. 183.
111. Quoted in Anderson, p. 164.
112. Quoted in Anderson, p. 163.
113. Friend, p. 228.
114. McMillan, p. 71.
115. Quoted in McMillan, p. 148.
116. McMillan, p. 73. See also Anderson, pp. 135–6.
117. McMillan, p. 20.
118. Quoted in McMillan, pp. 87–8.
119. Quoted in McMillan, p. 125.

CHAPTER 14

1. According to Leon Blum, quoted in A-G. Marsot, 'The Crucial Year: Indochina 1946', *Journal of Contemporary History*, Vol. 19, No. 2 (April 1984), p. 351.
2. P. Franchini, *Les mensonges de la guerre d'indochine*, no place, 2005, p. 158.
3. D. Marr, *Vietnam 1945. The Quest for Power*, Berkeley, 1995, p. 548; K. Ruane, *War and revolution in Vietnam*, London, 1998, p. 16.
4. Notes from the Provisional French Government to the US, 20 January 1945, in G. Porter (ed.), *Vietnam: The Definitive Documentation of Human Decisions*, Vol. 1, London, 1979, p. 19.
5. Quotation from a nineteenth-century prospectus. The last two words were in English in the original. Quoted in P-R. Feray, *Le Viet-Nam au XXe siecle*, Paris, 1979, p. 41.
6. Feray, p. 50.
7. The latter was 90 per cent of the population. Figures are for 1931, Feray, p. 84.
8. The figure is for 1937. Feray, p. 65.
9. P. Xanh, *Ho Chi Minh, the Nation and the Times, 1911–1946*, Hanoi, 2008, p. 45.
10. S. Tonnesson, *The Vietnamese Revolution of 1945*, London, 1991, p. 119.
11. The figure is for 1940. Feray, p. 84.
12. Le Manh Hung, *The Impact of World WarII on the Economy of Vietnam, 1939–45*, Singapore, 2004, pp. 248–9.
13. J. Neale, *The American War*, London, 2005, pp. 8 and 11. P. Ripert, *La guerre d'Indochine*, no place, 2004, p. 58 states that 50 per cent of land in Cochinchina was owned by 2.5 per cent of the population.
14. Tonnesson, p. 46.
15. *Ibid.*
16. Le Manh Hung, p. 255.
17. Marr, p. 96.
18. Marr, p. 97.
19. Le Manh Hung, p. 256 and Marr, p. 98.
20. Quoted in Le Manh Hung, p. 253.
21. Ho Chi Minh, *Selected Writings*, Hanoi, 1977, p. 62. Although one million, or 10 per cent of the affected population, seems more plausible. According to Marr, p. 104.
22. Le Manh Hung, p. 204. In most cases Tokyo's coup of 9 March 1945 met minimal resistance from the French.Spector, p. 32; Marr, pp. 56–8.

23. Le Manh Hung, p. 254.
24. My emphasis. Ho Chi Minh, p. 41.
25. Ho Chi Minh, p. 42.
26. Tonnesson, pp. 101–2.
27. Marr, p. 191.
28. Marr, p. 162.
29. Phan Chu Trinh and Ho Chi Minh, quoted in Xanh, pp. 166–7.
30. Ho Chi Minh, p. 45.
31. Feray, pp. 193, 196 and Marr, p. 238.
32. N. Van, *Revolutionaries They Could Not Break. The Fight for the Fourth International in Indochina, 1930–1945*, London, 1995, p. 307.
33. Quoted in Xanh, p. 165.
34. Xanh, p. 166.
35. This was set up in December 1944. Ho Chi Minh, p. 47.
36. Marr, pp. 169–70.
37. Marr, p. 170.
38. Neale, p. 16.
39. Quoted in D. Horowitz (ed.), *Containment and Revolution*, London, 1967, p. 220.
40. Feray, p. 193.
41. Xanh, p. 105; Tonnesson, p. 117.
42. R. Spector, 'Allied Intelligence and Indochina, 1943–1945', *The Pacific Historical Review*, Vol. 51, No. 1 (February 1982), p. 37.
43. Porter, pp. 19–20.
44. J. Valette, *Indochine, 1940–1945. Français contre Japonais*, Paris, 1993, pp. 481–4.
45. Quoted in A.W. Cameron (ed.), *Viet-Nam Crisis. A Documentary History. Vol. 1*, New York, 1971, pp. 10–11.
46. See Tonnesson, pp. 62–3.
47. Ruane, p. 10.
48. Quoted in Cameron, p. 36.
49. Spector, p. 35.
50. Spector, p. 37.
51. Spector, p. 40.
52. Spector, p. 41.
53. Spector, p. 42.
54. Report on OSS 'Deer Mission' by Major Allison K. Thomas, 17 September 1945, in Porter, pp. 75–6.
55. Instructions of the Standing Committee of the Central Committee of the ICP, 12 March 1945, in Porter, p. 21.
56. Marr, p. 233.
57. Tonnesson, pp. 349–50.
58. Marr, p. 2.
59. Marr, p. 143.
60. Tonnesson, pp. 118–9.
61. Marr, pp. 207–8.
62. Porter, p. 47. Resolutions of the Viet Minh Conference to establish a 'Free Zone', 4 June 1945, pp. 47–9, and Marr, pp. 353–4.
63. A General Uprising Order by Vo Nguyen giap, representative the Provisional Executive Committee of the Free Zone, 12 August 1945, pp. 56–7 and Marr, p. 366.

64. Marr, p. 191.
65. R. Morrock, 'Revolution and Intervention in Vietnam', in Horowitz, pp. 218–9.
66. Quoted in Van, p. 19.
67. *Tranh dau*, 19 May 1939, quoted in Van, p. 56.
68. Tonnesson, p. 336.
69. Marr, pp. 386–8.
70. Marr, pp. 389–94.
71. Marr, p. 402.
72. Quoted in Tonnesson, p. 336.
73. Van, p. 325.
74. Marr, p. 455.
75. Marr, p. 456–7.
76. Marr, p. 464.
77. Marr, p. 455. Tonnesson, p. 354.
78. Van, p. 328.
79. Van, p. 339.
80. Van, p. 338.
81. Van, p. 160.
82. Marr, pp. 460–1.
83. Feray, p. 193.
84. Cameron, p. 52.
85. Cameron, p. 54.
86. See for example Marr, p. 465.
87. Quoted in Van, p. 162.
88. Quoted in Spector, p. 47.
89. General Sir William Slim, Commander-in-Chief of Allied Land Forces South-east Asia to General Gracey on 28 August 1945, quoted in J. Springhall '"Kicking out the Vietminh": How Britain Allowed France to Reoccupy South Indochina, 1945–46', in *Journal of Contemporary History*, Vol. 40, No. 1, January 2005, p. 119.
90. C. de Gaulle, *The Complete War Memoirs*, New York, 1998, p. 928.
91. Marr, p. 543–4.
92. Springhall, p. 115.
93. Mounbatten on 24 September 1945, quoted in Springhall, p. 121.
94. Marr, p. 541.
95. *The Times*, 25 September 1945.
96. Springhall, p. 122.
97. Marr, p. 541.
98. Quoted in Springhall, p. 123.
99. Quoted in Springhall, p. 125.
100. Springhall, p. 125.
101. Porter, p. 69.
102. Marr, p. 369.

CONCLUSION

1. J. Keegan, *The Second World War*, London, 1990, p. 5.
2. H. Strachan, *The First World War*, London, 2003, pp. 43–4.
3. D. Mitchell, *1919, Red Mirage*, London, 1970, p. 16.

4. C. von Clausewitz, *On War*, Harmondsworth, 1968, p. 386.
5. Quoted in T. Cliff, *Trotsky*, London, 1993, Vol. 4, p. 369.
6. Keegan, pp. 484–5.
7. *European Resistance Movements 1939–1945. Presentations at the First International Conference on the History of the Resistance Movements*, London, 1960, p. 8.
8. R. Overy, *Why the Allies Won*, London, 1995, p. 312.
9. S. Hessel, *Engagez-vous!*, no place, 2011, pp. 13–14.

Index

CPSIA information can be obtained
at www.ICGtesting.com
Printed in the USA
FSHW010019131221
86849FS

9 780745 328027